Collection Development and Management for 21st Century Library Collections

AN INTRODUCTION

VICKI L. GREGORY

Neal-Schuman Publishers, Inc.
New York   London

16 15   6 5 4 3

Published by Neal-Schuman Publishers, Inc.
100 William St., Suite 2004
New York, NY 10038

Printed and bound in the United States of America.

The paper used in this publication meets the minimum requirements of American National Standard for Information Sciences—Permanence of Paper for Printed Library Materials, ANSI Z39.48-1992.

Library of Congress Cataloging-in-Publication Data

Gregory, Vicki L., 1950-
    Collection development and management for 21st century library collections : an introduction / Vicki L. Gregory.
        p. cm.
    Includes bibliographical references and index.
    ISBN 978-1-55570-651-7 (alk. paper)
    1. Collection management (Libraries)   2. Collection management (Libraries)—United States.   3. Collection development (Libraries)   4. Collection development (Libraries)—United States.   I. Title.

Z687.G68 2011
025.2'1—dc22
                                                                2011009274

Dedicated to my husband, William Stanley Gregory,
who has on occasion retrieved a manuscript from
the trash can with loving encouragement to finish it.

Contents

List of Figures

CD-ROM Contents

The companion CD-ROM found on the inside back cover contains two major resources.

The first is a set of 21 collection development and management policies from each of the major types of libraries. Policies from small, medium, and large libraries are represented. The policies are reproduced in PDF format.

The second resource is an Excel spreadsheet listing 360 major publishers, distributors, and wholesalers. This directory comprises the major companies from whom libraries buy books, periodicals, and audiovisual materials of all kinds. Each company's website and a brief description of their products or services can be found here.

The author and the publishers express their gratitude to each library who kindly granted permission for their policies to be reproduced here. A listing of those libraries by library type appears below.

Academic Libraries

Berry College Memorial Library, Mount Berry, GA
Boise State University, Albertsons Library, Boise, ID
Canisius College, Buffalo, NY
Central Piedmont Community College, Charlotte, NC
Dartmouth College Library, Hanover, NH
Florida Atlantic University Libraries, Boca Raton, FL
Kenyon College, Library and Information Services, Gambier, OH
St. Mary's University, Louis J. Blume Library, San Antonio, TX
Portland Community College, Portland, OR

Public Libraries

Campbell County Public Library System, Gillette and Wright, WY
Morton Grove Public Library, Morton Grove, IL
Newark Public Library, Newark, NJ
Pasadena Public Library, Pasadena, CA
Pikes Peak Library District, Colorado Springs, CO

School Libraries

Liberty County School System, Hinesville, GA
Stockbridge High School Library, Stockbridge, MI
University Laboratory High School Library, Urbana, IL
Whitefish High School Library, Whitefish, MT

Special Libraries

Northeastern Seminary, Rochester, NY
University of Kansas Medical Center, Dykes Library, Kansas City, KS
University of Maryland, Health Sciences and Human Services Library,
    Baltimore, MD

Preface

Collection Development and Management for 21st Century Library Collections: An Introduction describes how librarians select, acquire, and maintain resources in all formats.

Unlike previous textbooks in this area, the approach used here is not strictly based on formats per se, but rather on the processes that librarians need to use in evaluating, gathering, maintaining, and preserving materials. In other words, there are no separate chapters dedicated to books, serials, or electronic resources; instead, each conceptual chapter covers multiple formats. As has always been the case, but especially as witnessed over the last 35 years spanning my professional career, the formats of the materials collected and used by libraries change, but the overall processes used to select and evaluate them tend to remain the same. In the pages that follow, I describe the synergy and drive behind planning, developing, licensing, acquiring, and managing collections that are both physical and virtual, used in-house and remotely, and constantly changing.

Although collection development, the acquisitions process, and collection maintenance issues are universal concerns for all types of libraries, in different library settings, differences in emphasis on the various elements of collection development and maintenance processes become quickly apparent. Ethics, intellectual freedom, copyright, and licensing impact all areas of collection development and management like never before. Therefore, while it is important to take an overarching view of these processes, differences engendered by type of library will be brought out where appropriate.

The primary audience for this book will naturally be students in graduate programs of library and information science. However, librarians changing professional assignments into collection development and maintenance or those needing to catch up on, for example, electronic materials should also find this work useful.

In many schools of library and information science, collection development is included within a broader picture of collection management or maintenance and often folded into those courses. Many classes will actually emphasize, in such cases, not collection development itself but collection management, sometimes with but a week or a single instructional unit given over to acquisitions. Thus, it is important to make clear distinctions among these three major elements:

- **Collection management** may be best defined as the process of information gathering, communication, coordination, policy formulation, evaluation, and planning that results in decisions about the acquisition, retention, and provision of access to information sources in support of the intellectual needs of a given library community.
- **Collection development** is thus the subpart of collection management that has primarily to do with decisions that will ultimately result in the acquisition of materials.
- **Acquisition** is the process of actually securing materials for the library's collection, whether by purchase, as gifts, or through loan or exchange programs.

Organization

Collection Development and Management for 21st Century Library Collections: An Introduction begins with a comprehensive overview of the field, moves into individual chapters covering each step of the collection life cycle, and ends with a chapter looking at the future.

Chapter 1 takes a look at how new elements are influencing library collections today: open access, Web 2.0, the "Long Tail," and globalization. Each of these elements affects how and what the library owns, leases, or uses.

Chapter 2 looks at needs assessment from a collection development standpoint and at marketing the collection. A needs assessment is similar to market research but in this case with a library emphasis. Marketing plans are discussed and examples of marketing activities are drawn from different types of libraries.

Chapter 3 concerns the purpose and component parts of a good collection development policy, and Chapter 4 covers the selection of library resources with an overview of sources for reviews, selection criteria, and variables in the process among different types of libraries.

Chapter 5 concerns all aspects of the acquisition of print, electronic, and audiovisual resources along with a discussion of gifts to libraries and exchange programs in which some libraries participate. Exchange programs can be local, national, or international.

Chapter 6 discusses the budget and fiscal management of collection development and acquisitions departments. A short introduction to bookkeeping is included with most of the terminology that a new acquisitions librarian will need to know.

Chapter 7 is about the evaluation and assessment plus the weeding of a collection. Differences in procedures among different types of libraries are discussed.

Chapter 8 looks at cooperative collection development and how resource sharing facilitates a good cooperative collection development program.

Chapter 9 examines the legal issues that concern collection development librarians, such as copyright and licensing of electronic resources. This chapter is not intended to make lawyers out of librarians, but will introduce you to a number of these important concepts in order to better inform you as to how to recognize those issues and how best to proceed when you are confronted with them. In addition, legal obligations related to issues of diversity and the Americans with Disabilities Act are also discussed here. Because Chapter 4 covers some diversity issues as well, this chapter focuses on the issues not discussed there along with issues of special needs users.

Chapter 10 concerns ethics and intellectual freedom as they affect acquisitions and collection development librarians, particularly because these librarians may be wined and dined by vendors. Intellectual freedom is one of the core values of librarianship and, since it is often tied to censorship, can also be viewed as a professional ethics area.

Chapter 11 addresses preservation of both print and electronic materials. This is an area of great concern as electronic materials can be quite ephemeral unless libraries or other organizations specifically target them for preservation.

Chapter 12 is a look into the future of collection development and collection development librarians as viewed by several authors. One predicted difference from their current role concerns more active involvement in the creation and maintenance of locally produced digital materials. Another has to do with quality assurance of materials that users find on the web, particularly when searching in the library or on its website. Naive users may view these materials as being just as much a part of the collection as the carefully selected materials on the library shelves.

The text ends with a selective bibliography of further readings for each part of the collection management life cycle.

This book's companion CD-ROM contains examples of collection development policies as instituted at various university, college, community college, public, school, and special libraries. These policies illustrate the differing approaches taken by the various types of libraries represented and were selected as indicative of how the factors and considerations described in the text can be successfully melded into a policy.

As with all areas of library work, continuing education, involvement with professional associations, and reading the newly published library literature will be important to maintain your professional skills if you intend to become a collections librarian. I hope you will keep reading, keep learning, and keep building better collections that meet the needs of your users.

Acknowledgments

I wish to thank my graduate assistants Bridgette Woodley and Arlen Benson for their help with bibliographic searches and with the library vendor listing. Thanks also to Amy Knauer at Neal-Schuman for all her assistance in the final editing and production of this book. Others have helped along the way, and I thank them as well. You know who you are!

1

The Impact of New Technologies on Collection Development and Management

Overview

Welcome to one of the most interesting subjects in library and information science: collection development and management. The selection and management of library resources is truly at the heart of the library profession, along with its back-office twin towers—cataloging and classification. While the critically important collection sciences of cataloging and classification must regrettably be left to another day, this textbook concentrates on what may be as much the art as the science involved in the development and control of the collection itself. Selecting, acquiring, assessing, weeding, and preserving a collection are the main focus here, with its organization and use secondary matters.

This initial chapter looks at some of the newer technologies and current issues that are influencing library services generally and their effect on collection development and maintenance. These issues will be expanded upon as they are explored in later chapters dealing with various specific aspects of collection development and maintenance.

The process of selecting materials and adequately maintaining the currency and relevance of any library's collection, in whatever format, has always required a high level of tolerance for continuous change, whether evolutionary or sudden. This is true not only in terms of deciding what newly available materials should be acquired; it requires, as well, a clear-headed recognition of the need for constant evaluation and reevaluation of the items already in hand. Over the decades, to meet the challenges of the selection and evaluation processes as libraries became more widespread and thus more available to the general population and not the exclusive provinces of academics, clerics, and prosperous private collectors, fairly standardized processes for collecting print materials and most types of audiovisual materials came to be developed. Some of these processes date back to the late 19th and into the 20th centuries, since which time they have been refined and disseminated by library schools and handed down by experienced librarians to their successors.

But these standard processes necessarily have had to evolve as conditions, user needs, and potentially available resources changed. Over time, the problems have considerably altered in nature and scope. Today, libraries cannot fail to include significant electronic resources in their collections and take steps to make those resources available, through the purchasing and maintaining of the hardware and software necessary to allow for their effective use. With libraries today also being called upon to provide the means for users to access collections remotely from their homes or offices, and to make available and participate in various online social networks (i.e., going where their users are), the focus of collection development and indeed even the concept of what constitutes a library collection is changing.

Automated and electronic records were initially the more or less exclusive domain of library technical services divisions, first cataloging and then circulation. Electronic records have become one of the standard services, and in many cases a central focus, of the typical library reference department. Today, acquisitions departments regularly use the services of electronic vendors and services such as OCLC, and user demand for all types of electronic resources and records has brought collection development into the electronic age.

The fast-growing user preference for electronic resources has severely impacted the collection development budgets of most libraries. Because the new electronic library resources usually do not completely supplant existing materials, purchasing them does not eliminate the cost of buying print formats. They therefore represent still another format that must be collected if the library is to keep up with the times and meet the demands of its patrons. Unfortunately, more than subject matter expertise is needed to select these materials and avoid unnecessary duplication; the selector must also possess sufficient technical expertise (or have access to those with technical expertise) to evaluate knowledgably both the hardware and software resources that may be needed to access any new product and to analyze how well the product performs. In the case of social networking of access to a library's collection, there are also considerations of security for the library's network and computer stations.

The fast-developing phenomena of open access, the so-called information commons, web 2.0/social networking, and the "Long Tail" (see below) are, along with globalization generally, all impacting the way librarians and information specialists must view the collection development process and collection issues for their libraries. Instead of making these issues subjects for a last chapter as a sort of nod to the future, they deserve introduction and discussion right from the beginning as they have a wide and pervasive impact. Thus they are also properly discussed throughout this text and its chapters as appropriate.

The Long Tail

In his seminal 2006 book, *The Long Tail*, Chris Anderson, then editor in chief of *Wired* magazine, assesses the future of consumer buying, suggesting that industries and businesses will continue to serve more and more consumers needing a greater number of things, but that satisfying the needs of readers, music lovers, and such through public entities such as traditional libraries is soon to be a thing of the past. Choice and wide availability are becoming increasingly central touchstones of 21st century life, to list as mundane but revealing examples cable television service with 200–300 channels and movie multiplexes with 16 or more screens. Anderson thus concentrates on and emphasizes the increasing importance of the niche market (p. 5). To some degree, libraries have always been this way, especially large research libraries holding major collections of works on obscure and narrow subjects. If Anderson is correct in his thesis that the niches are beginning to crowd out the rooms, then libraries, especially public ones, will feel increasing pressure to have more books, serials, and materials in electronic formats. Anderson further asserts, "Many of our assumptions about popular taste are actually artifacts of poor supply-and-demand matching—a market response to inefficient distribution" (p. 16). By apparently obviating many of these inefficiencies, the dissemination of materials over the web can, Anderson argues, potentially provide the consumer an almost unlimited array of goods, which any conventional business or organization that is limited by inventory space could never hope to provide. It is as simple as the difference between buying a book through Amazon.com and searching bookstores for an out-of-print book or academic title.

The point of all this from a library acquisitions perspective is that, traditionally, readers or researchers may have been satisfied with what was locally available, partly because they had no other viable choice and partly because they may have been less than fully aware of all the choices available. The web has now expanded awareness of resources and opened up so many other means of acquiring materials that what is demanded of local libraries is expanding, sometimes exponentially.

> The average Borders carries around 100,000 titles. Yet about a quarter of Amazon's book sales come from **outside** its top 100,000 titles. Consider the implication: If the Amazon statistics are any guide, the

market for books that are not even sold in the average bookstore is already a third the size of the existing market—and what's more, it's growing quickly. If these growth trends continue, the potential book market may actually be half again as big as it appears to be, if only we can get over the economics of scarcity. (Anderson, 2006: 22)

Other booksellers are experiencing this same trend:

In 2005, Barnes & Noble sold 20 percent more unique titles than it sold in 2004, something its CEO, Steve Riggs, attributes to three forces: (1) the efficiencies of print-on-demand, which keeps more books in print; (2) the increase in the number of smaller and independent publishers; and (3) self-publishing. (Anderson, 2006: 77)

That which affects mass-market booksellers must also naturally be reflected in the changing demands on the local public library. If Amazon.com can supply the unusual books they want, library patrons ask, why not the local public library? (In Chapter 2 the various ways to assess the needs of users are discussed in detail.) Like retail businesses, libraries have inventory, warehouse, and shelf space issues, in contrast to many of the web businesses providing information with which the library is now competing. The implication for libraries that concentrate their acquisition and collecting efforts on materials with broad appeal is that they may need to begin to focus on developing broader collections of unique titles to meet the narrower demand for more different works.

The web and other electronic sources are also creating new, nontraditional uses of the public library by adults and children. Children especially are increasingly familiar with computers and their use in acquiring online information and products. Users' familiarity with the increasingly large array of electronic resources may quickly change libraries' needs, from holding multiple copies of best sellers and hits to acquiring resources somewhere out on the Long Tail. Of course, there is a question whether libraries can or should aspire to be more like online retailers that enjoy virtually no limitations of space.

Although Anderson's depiction of the Long Tail is one-tailed, library selection is probably best viewed as a normal curve, which is two-tailed (see Figure 1.1). If viewed in terms of subject areas and issues as librarians generally do when they make selections, there is a "long tail" of material on each side of a subject. The majority of the titles that libraries buy and bookstores sell are in the range of plus or minus one standard deviation, or 68 percent of the titles published on an average subject or issue. Research libraries may already buy in the range of plus or minus two standard deviations, or roughly 95 percent. However, with the experience of the web and online bookstores it appears that the true demand for titles now stretches much farther than the 68 percent range. If the Long Tail thesis is to be reflected in developing a

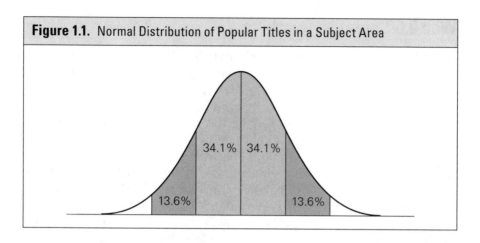

Figure 1.1. Normal Distribution of Popular Titles in a Subject Area

balanced library collection, selectors should consider a wider range of titles than they have in the past.

Are libraries already Long Tail organizations? Many librarians would like to think so; however:

> The Long Tail is more than simply a couple thousand niche-titles tucked away in the stacks. The Long Tail includes 80 percent of the books printed *every year*. What percentage of these books does *your* library buy? According to Bowker, 172,000 new titles and editions were published in the U.S. in 2005; 206,000 new titles were published in the U.K. Still think you have a grip on the Long Tail? Not likely, unless of course your library rivals the Library of Congress. (Casey and Savastinuk, 2007: 64)

One of the ways that libraries have always sought to better serve their constituencies is through selection of the best materials from the ever-widening array of print and other, now often primarily electronic resources. Anderson (2006: 108) uses the word *filters* to describe the way users may use technological solutions to discover the best materials on a particular subject. However, librarians have to learn to use their evaluation skills rather than sometimes simplistic absolute decision rules to put together a collection of the best materials whether in print or electronic form. Instead of relying totally on software solutions, the user can have the benefits of a human filter through consulting a librarian.

Basically, the two major implications of the Long Tail future are that (1) everything possible must be available and (2) the user will need help cutting through the maze to find the best resources. Sounds like serious work for an acquisitions librarian.

Web 2.0/Social Networking

Web 2.0 can play a part here as wikis and blogs become more prevalent as major sources of information on a variety of subjects. If Web 2.0 is anything, it is all about participating and sharing in the production of resources. "While the old Web was about Web sites, clicks, and 'eyeballs,' the new Web is about communities, participation and peering. (Peering is a new form of horizontal organization that rivals hierarchical forms in creating products and services and, in a few cases, physical things [Tapscott and Williams, 2006: 23].) As users and computing power multiply, and easy-to-use tools proliferate, the Internet is evolving into a global, living, networked computer that anyone can program" (Tapscott and Williams, 2006: 19).

Social networking through the web with sites such as Twitter, Myspace, Facebook, Second Life, YouTube, and Flickr is becoming a widespread if not dominant form of communication among computer users, and most popular phenomena prognosticators forecast that this type of collaborating will continue and grow exponentially. Libraries are themselves social institutions, in the sense that information flows through them to readers and patrons, so librarians need to be involved with the social networking movement. To do otherwise is to risk becoming irrelevant to users, somewhat like failing to speak the patron's language.

> We belong where our users can be found—and they are increasingly found online, interacting in completely new ways. A librarian who connects with a local teenager on MySpace.com, helping her find the information that she needs to get into the college of her choice, is an invaluable community resource. (Farkas, 2007: xix)

This different mode of interacting will also inevitably change the range and nature of resources needed for the librarian and user to be satisfied with the outcome of the user's interface with the library (these interactions are sometimes referred to in the literature as transactions). All librarians need to be prepared to work with users and information from blogs, wikis, Twitter, and other social networking sites. ABC News (2004) named bloggers People of the Year for 2004, demonstrating their importance in early 21st century culture. It was noted earlier that same year, "Political bloggers' activity during the election year and their representation at the Democratic National Convention [Boston] made them more visible to both the mainstream media and average Internet user" (Farkas, 2007: 11).

Wikis are a major new tool for collaboration among professional librarians, authors, and others conducting project work, because wikis allow authors in different fields to access, read, comment on, and even edit a work while it is in progress. Librarians must consider that wikis constitute a serious potential threat to the continued publication of certain kinds of long-standing reference works. Younger library clientele increasingly access Wikipedia much more often than a standard print encyclopedia. "It [Wikipedia] has become one of the most visited sites on the Web. It represents the future of publishing, and every company that produces information—from publishers to data providers—should be scared" (Tapscott, 2009: 71). The reliability and credibility problems with Wikipedia, as they tend to be solved over time, may make Tapscott's broad assertion closer and closer to the truth. Thomas Friedman (2006: 124) stated, "It is not an accident that IBM today has a senior staffer who polices Wikipedia's references to IBM and makes sure everything that goes in there is correct. More young people will learn about IBM from Wikipedia in coming years than from IBM itself" (p. 124).

Podcasts are another emerging means of communication and information gathering. The ability of scholars, activists, teachers, and so on to put voice-based material on their websites for others to hear also leads library users to have higher expectations of the materials offered by their local libraries. Of course, some libraries are already using podcasting for training and orientation purposes. Podcast technology could also be useful to a collection development librarian to obtain discussion of new materials from specific interest groups within the library's community or organization.

> No matter what type of library you work in, your patrons will be using some type of social software, whether they IM [instant message], blog, or listen to podcasts. It's important to be aware of the tools your patrons use to see if you can provide services using the same tools. (Farkas, 2007: 8)

Another form of Web 2.0 technology is user-based tagging. This sort of tagging is relatively new and consists of the attachment of descriptive keywords or metadata to digital objects by users for the purpose of future retrieval. In other words, user-based tagging allows users to get directly involved in the bibliographic access process by assigning keywords that make sense to them. Since standardized subject heading lists often lag behind the newest trends and technologies (waiting to see if a fad becomes established or fades away), the user can immediately tag the resource with an up-to-date terminology, and if it proves indeed faddish and fades from the scene, it can later be easily changed if and as the subject name changes.

This tool, though not always described as such, is used by several of the Web 2.0 networks that deal with the organization of data. Good current examples are Flickr and Delicious.

As the number of tags increases, a kind of grassroots organization often develops that is referred to as a folksonomy, or a nonhierarchical ontology that is created as a natural result of user-based tagging, for the technically inclined.

> Folksonomies are an illustration of the collective intelligence at work. A collective intelligence is achieved when a critical mass of participation is reached within a website or networked system, allowing the participants to act as a filter for what is valuable. A folksonomy is created from the aggregate of user-created tags within a website and therefore provides an inclusive organization scheme reflective of the collective intelligence of the community. (Courtney, 2007: 94)

Social networking is not confined to the web. Text messaging or texting is a phenomenon that has taken over the lives of many teens and young adults. This technology has created what have been called "smart mobs" (Rheingold, 2002). Anyone who walks around on a university campus, in a grocery store, an amusement park, or virtually anywhere else knows that people are demanding and using instant and ubiquitous communication devices. Cell phones, PDAs, beepers, or BlackBerries are in almost constant use, keeping their users easily connected to friends and family and never alone. Mobile communication is undoubtedly a fact of modern life that will increasingly affect the way that people expect to access information through a library's collection. For instance, most current-generation mobile devices feature easy access to the web, suggesting a demand for library reference help that goes beyond traditional telephone service and other interactive library services, therefore requiring the resources to make these services possible.

The Information Commons, Open Access Serials, and Open Source Software

Social networking and Web 2.0 technologies naturally lead into a discussion of the information commons and open access. The concept of an information commons is a response to the firm grip (some would say stranglehold) of the copyright regime on most intellectual property. Particularly for scientists and academics who expect to see their ideas widely disseminated, copyright regulations have tended to place those works in a straitjacket devised by the publishers, and not the authors, of the resources that copyright law was originally intended to protect.

The philosophy behind the information commons and Creative Commons licensing (Lessig, 2001) is to advance innovation, stimulate creativity, and promote the sharing of information resources, allowing the author to determine what can and cannot be done with his or her materials.

Open source software, although arguably not fully in the public domain in the sense of a work to which copyright has expired, is by definition available for little or no cost and distributed essentially without restrictions on subsequent use. Open source software such as DSpace or Greenstone is often used to support digital repositories that may house open access serials or other resources.

Many examples of information commons exist in the scholarly publication environment. The Scholarly Publishing and Academic Resources Coalition (SPARC) is one of the most prominent. SPARC was formed as a constructive response to perceived market dysfunctions in the scholarly communication system. SPARC has been influential in helping to provide alternatives to high-priced journals and digital aggregated databases and is generally credited with raising the consciousness of scholars about alternatives to traditional publication formats and new publishing initiatives (Association of Research Libraries, 2009).

SPARC is but one example of such initiatives. Many universities are developing institutional repositories where their scholars can upload their work and related materials into the repository for widespread distribution or publication across the web.

Open access is the current buzzword for serials publications. To users, open access promises the nirvana of free availability of serial literature on the web. But most publishers take a different and somewhat dimmer, if not darker, view. Usually their definition of open access means that authors can put their own version of a manuscript up on their website, but the pdf version or other edited version of the manuscript belongs to the publishers who may then charge for copies. Open access is still in its infancy, but it seems doubtful that charge per use will ultimately prevail; thus we can expect to find more and more open access journals of scholarly publications that are free to the user, at least the user who can access the appropriate portal.

Globalization

Globalization is more than a buzzword—it is becoming central to many aspects of modern life. But this is nothing new for libraries, which have always cooperated, nationally and internationally, even from the earliest days of the development of national postal systems in the 18th century. Interlibrary loan has been a traditional hallmark of the best inclinations of the profession to do the utmost to provide materials to those who need them. Often this was even at the expense of local users; as late as the 1970s, when a library in a distant country borrowed material from a U.S. library, the U.S. librarian would routinely make its return due in about six months because it would not be unusual for the item to move by cargo ship. It might easily take a month or more to reach the destination library, with the same problem involved in shipping it back to the United States.

Such problems seem almost antique today as the world in so many ways has grown smaller and "flatter" (according to Thomas L. Friedman) with all the types of transactions that can and do take place quickly. While overnight package delivery systems and inexpensive facsimile transmission of documents were revolutionary in their own ways, it is the World Wide Web that has become the premier means of communication that brings us all so much closer together.

The web has greatly contributed to the increasing globalization and flattening of today's world. *Globalization* was the word originally chosen to describe the changing relationships between governments and big business, but its meaning has expanded to include individuals as well.

> I am convinced that the flattening of the world, if it continues, will be seen in time as one of those fundamental shifts or inflection points, like Gutenberg's invention of the printing press, the rise of the nation-state, or the Industrial Revolution—each of which, in its day, . . . produced changes in the role of individuals, the role and form of governments, the ways business was done and wars were fought, the role of women, the forms religion and art took, and the way science and research were conducted, not to mention the political labels that we as a civilization have assigned to ourselves and to our enemies. (Friedman, 2006: 49)

It cannot be overemphasized that the World Wide Web is just that—worldwide. A resource put up on the web from Tampa, Florida, is as likely to be used in India as it is in nearby St. Petersburg, or for that matter in not so nearby St. Petersburg, Russia. While there is certainly a danger that ubiquity can be confused with authoritativeness, leading to the common expectation that everything worth reading is on the web, careful librarians are right to be professionally skeptical that all that glitters is on the web, and must, in particular through their selection, choice, and collection of materials, ensure that their library's users come to know that dependence on the web can be a risky proposition. And it should not be the source of serious discouragement that readers come to librarians only if they cannot find what they are looking for on the web. But information on the web helps shape opinions and knowledge about the world in general.

Arguably, we are, in many ways, becoming what we put up on the web. But just as every book was not necessarily freely accessible to all segments of the public in a traditional library context, whether for reasons of preservation, age of reader, or something else, so placing an entire collection on the web can be problematic. Thus, holdings available electronically at a distance should not be treated as the comprehensive measure of a library collection. For instance, global access presents problems with intellectual property laws, which vary significantly from country to country, both in substance and degree of enforcement. Differences in free speech principles can also be significant and can create problems. Even leaving aside exceptional cases such as North Korea, which tries to cut itself off from the web, or the People's Republic of China, which conditions much internal commercial activity and its trade relations on compliance with governmental restrictions on web content and site access, numerous countries impose fairly draconian laws to prevent publication of some kinds of materials—for example, Germany prohibits the use of the swastika and other Nazi symbols and materials. So while a person in California can legally put up a swastika on his website in the United States, that same site would be illegal in Germany. In Poland, two people were arrested on June 26, 2006, for putting up a website, which resides on a server in the United Kingdom, dealing with extremist views, especially Nazism. Even in the United Kingdom itself, criticism of governmental figures can much more easily subject one to legal liability than in the United States.

It also must be remembered that in other countries copyright laws may differ from those in the United States. It would, for instance, except in very limited situations, be permissible in the United States to scan and put a work created in 1916 on the web; however, if the copyright is also registered in Great Britain, the work would probably not be in the public domain as the copyright length in Britain is 25 years longer than the maximum protection offered under the U.S. Copyright Act. This situation is discussed more fully in Chapter 9.

Vocabulary

Be sure to be able to define the following terms and concepts from this chapter:

blog	Creative Commons	Facebook	Flickr
folksonomy	globalization	Library 2.0	Long Tail
Myspace	open access	podcast	repository
Second Life	SPARC	tagging	Web 2.0
wiki	Wikipedia	YouTube	

Discussion Questions

1. Do you see evidence of the Long Tail phenomenon in your own choice of books, music, and movies? Describe.
2. In your own words, what is an online social network?
3. How may the use of social networks, blogs, and similar software change what a user needs from a library?

References

ABC News. 2004. "Internet Phenomenon Provides Unique Insights into Peoples' Thoughts." People of the Year; Bloggers, December 30. http://abcnews.go.com/WNT/person ofweek/story?id=372266&page=1.

Anderson, Chris. 2006. *The "Long Tail": Why the Future of Business Is Selling Less of More.* New York: Hyperion.

Association of Research Libraries. 2009. "What Is SPARC?" Association of Research Libraries. Accessed May 11. http://www.arl.org/sparc/about/index.shtml.

Casey, Michael E., and Laura C. Savastinuk. 2007. *Library 2.0: A Guide to Participatory Library Service.* Medford, NJ: Information Today.

Courtney, Nancy, ed. 2007. *Library 2.0 and Beyond: Innovative Technologies and Tomorrow's User.* Westport, CT: Libraries Unlimited.

Farkas, Meredith G. 2007. *Social Software in Libraries: Building Collaboration, Communication, and Community Online.* Medford, NJ: Information Today.

Friedman, Thomas L. 2006. *The World Is Flat: A Brief History of the Twenty-First Century.* Updated and expanded ed. New York: Farrar, Straus and Giroux.

Lessig, Lawrence. 2001. *The Future of Ideas: The Fate of the Commons in a Connected World.* New York: Random House.

Rheingold, Howard. 2002. *Smart Mobs: The Next Social Revolution.* Cambridge, MA: Basic Books.

Tapscott, Don. 2009. *Grown Up Digital: How the Net Generation Is Changing Your World.* New York: McGraw Hill.

Tapscott, Don, and Anthony D. Williams. 2006. *Wikinomics: How Mass Collaboration Changes Everything.* New York: Penguin Group.

Selected Readings

Abram, Stephen. 2005. "Web 2.0—Huh?! Library 2.0, Librarian 2.0." *Information Outlook* (December 1): 44–46.

Aharony, Noa. 2009. "Web 2.0 Use by Librarians." *Library and Information Science Research* 31 (January): 29–37.

Breeding, Marshall. 2006. "Web 2.0? Let's Get to Web 1.0 First." *Computers in Libraries* (May 1): 30–33.

Buczynski, James A. 2008. "Looking for Collection 2.0." *Journal of Electronic Resources Librarianship* 20, no. 2: 90–100.

Burkhanna, Kenneth J., Jamie Seeholzer, and Joseph Salem Jr. 2009. "No Natives Here: A Focus Group Study of Student Perceptions of Web 2.0 and the Academic Library." *Journal of Academic Librarianship* 35 (November): 523–532.

Burkhardt, Andy. 2010. "Social Media: A Guide for College and University Libraries." *College and Research Library News* 71 (January): 10–12.

Gillespie, Tarleton. 2007. *Wired Shut: Copyright and the Shape of Digital Culture.* Cambridge, MA: MIT Press.

Lin, Andrew. 2009. *The Wikipedia Revolution: How a Bunch of Nobodies Created the World's Greatest Encyclopedia.* New York: Hyperion.

Miller, Paul. 2005. "Web 2.0: Building the New Library." *Ariadne* 45 (October 30). http://www.ariadne.ac.uk/issue45/miller/intro.html.

Mossberger, Karen, Caroline J. Tolbert, and Ramona S. McNeal. 2008. *Digital Citizenship: The Internet, Society, and Participation.* Cambridge, MA: MIT Press.

O'Sullivan, Dan. 2009. *Wikipedia: A New Community of Practice?* Farnham, UK: Ashgate.

Scoble, Robert, and Shel Israel. 2006. *Naked Conversations: How Blogs Are Changing the Way Businesses Talk with Customers.* Hoboken, NJ: John Wiley.

2

Assessing User Needs and Marketing the Collection to Those Users

Overview

The mission and goals of any library revolve around meeting the informational, educational, or recreational needs of its clientele. How do librarians know the needs of their users or potential users? The answer to this question is one of the major keys to successful collection development. In this chapter you will be introduced to needs assessment and how to do one for your library. The focus is on using a needs assessment for collection development purposes, but you will also find that libraries do needs assessments for services, building arrangements, and other administrative and service-oriented purposes. The other side of the coin is that once you have what people need, how do you let them know what the library has to offer?

Biblarz, Bosch, and Sugnet (2001: vii) define a needs assessment as a "process of using one or more techniques to collect and analyze data regarding library users or potential users. Specifically, the data collected will be directly or indirectly related to the needs, in the broadest sense, of users, or customers, for information in all formats. Interpretation of the data will influence the management of collections."

Knowledge of the service community, whether a geographical area or an organization, is the keystone of effective collection development. The more the collection development staff knows about the work roles, general interests, education, information and communication behavior, values, and related characteristics of potential library users, the more likely it is that the collection will be able to provide the necessary information when it is needed.

A library generally has a strong base of patrons who use it on a regular basis and others who come to it sporadically. However, there is generally an even larger number of nonusers in any community or organization that the library serves. A needs assessment study can be aimed at any or all of these constituencies.

Community analysis as a part of a needs assessment has to be done on a regular basis:

> There are many similarities between "needs assessment projects" and marketing studies, and they frequently employ the same data-collecting methods. Both focus on gaining insights about the people ("target populations") being studied. Often their goals are similar in that they want to improve the usefulness/value of a service or "product." Additionally, both can produce data valuable for other projects. . . . Libraries of all types need to market themselves, especially in today's environment, and one builds useful/effective collections, in part, through a solid understanding of the service population. (Evans and Saponaro, 2005: 20–21)

Librarians may think they know their users, but the demographics of any community will change over time. Those changing demographics increase the number of nonusers if librarians do not recognize the need to change or expand their services and collections. For example, materials and services in different languages may be needed. Spanish materials are commonly requested, but other immigrant groups may need or desire materials in Slavic or other Eastern European or Asian languages. Remember to examine your potential users' other activities as this information can provide valuable insight on hobbies and other interests to which the library can cater. Advertising relevant materials to civic groups or others that meet within your service area can bring in additional users.

The essential nature of information needs assessment is obvious when you consider the service role—libraries and information centers will continue to be supported by their parent organizations only to the extent that they provide information services that users perceive as useful. Although there are certainly other reasons, collection development is generally the main reason for conducting a needs assessment. One should be careful to focus a user needs analysis survey on a few major areas of concern, or even one concern. Research literature and common sense tell us that items on a survey that may seem peripheral or unrelated to the survey's purpose cause respondents to be suspicious of the survey or the motives of the investigator, which often leads to nonparticipation or, worse yet, deliberately misleading responses.

Conducting a community analysis or needs assessment need not be a daunting task. The traditional journalist's approach to writing a news story by asking who, what, when, where, and how constitutes an appropriate and easy-to-apply methodology for building a philosophically grounded collection needs assessment. With this approach, you, as the librarian, need to consider collecting the following types of information to use in your analysis of the results of your needs assessment study (Gregory, 2006: 15–17).

Who and What Will Be Studied?

Historical Data

Historical data can provide clues as to which areas of the collection might be weeded or no longer need new materials. Circulation records, for example, can be data-mined for a wealth of information about the current collection. Interlibrary loan records may provide information about kinds of materials that may be required to meet new needs.

Geographic Data

Geographic data can help in the determination of service points, which in turn influences the number of copies of various titles that the library needs to acquire. How far away do your users live from the library? How do they get to the library—walk, drive, public transportation? Knowledge of all of these factors can guide the collection development librarian in terms of numbers of copies and document delivery questions.

Legal Basis and Authority

The librarian must know if there are any legal restrictions on what the library may buy with monies allocated for collection development.

Political Information

Political information about the community or organization is also vital. Who is really influencing fiscal decisions? What are the policies concerning allocation of collection development funds? The answers may not influence which titles are acquired, but they will influence the way in which funds are secured and allocated. You may think that this is something that you learn the first day on the job, so why study it? In my experience, many of the so-called rules and regulations that may be passed along to you are really customs, not rules. Occasionally it is good to question such assumptions and determine what you really can and cannot do.

Demographic Data

Demographic data are fundamental in formulating a collection development program. Basic changes in the composition of the community or user population are inevitable, but only by monitoring the user community can such changes be anticipated. Over time there are population shifts and changes in the age, racial, and ethnic composition of the potential user base. It will be useful to include educational backgrounds and economic status as well.

Economic Information

Economic information about your community of users may also play a part in determining which materials may be useful to the business community. If industries and businesses are shutting down, a significant number of users may be looking for information about jobs and retraining.

Social and Educational Organizations

Social and economic organizations reflect community values. Educational and other organizations may bring special needs to the library.

Cultural and Recreational Organizations

Cultural and recreational organizations may provide useful clues to specialized interest areas in the community. Are reading groups prominent in your area? Can the library facilitate the operation of such groups by providing multiple copies of likely selections and reading club guides to these works? Are there hobby groups in your community to which you could provide meeting space and materials of interest?

Other Community Organizations

Other community organizations such as other libraries, bookstores, video outlets, newspapers, and so on may also affect demands made upon the library collection.

Where Are Data Collected?

Published Sources

First, see what information is already collected in print or online, and then design an assessment (interview, community forum, survey, etc.) instrument to collect information that is not readily available.

Key Informants

After reviewing existing printed sources, a good next step is to interview people who ought to know about the information needs and interests of the user base. In public libraries, these key informants might be public officials, business leaders, clergy, and so on. In academic libraries, you might interview deans, the chair of the faculty senate, faculty who are known to be heavy library users, and so on. In school media centers, the principal, key faculty leaders, and the head of the PTA would be likely key informants. This method is used as an initial or screening stage for a more extensive study.

Community Forum

A community forum is like a town meeting. This approach avoids selection bias by the researcher, as all members of the potential user community are invited to participate. The key to success for this approach is extensive publicity in all available media. The researcher needs to prepare starter questions but should also make room for spontaneous questions (some of which may be planted to avoid dead air). It often helps to have a moderator who is not on the library staff and thus is not subject to emotional involvement. Public libraries often use consultants to moderate such meetings.

Focus Groups

Instead of or in addition to a community forum, the library or its consultant may want to organize small focus groups of library users or nonusers to explore particular concerns in more depth than can be obtained in a community forum. With a smaller group of participants, issues can be explored in great depth. Successful focus groups need an experienced facilitator and a recorder to capture information for later study.

Social Indicators

Social indicators include data about age, education, income, and so on. Much of this information can be found in existing sources such as census reports, reports from regional planning agencies, and so forth. Social scientists have developed a method that makes use of social indicators to determine the needs of various segments of the community. By selecting factors that researchers think are highly correlated with special groups or segments of the population, surveyors may be able to extrapolate the information needs of the community.

Survey

Surveys can consist of personal interviews or mailed questionnaires (particularly important if the library wants to hear from nonusers) or a site-based survey (or a combination of all three).

Surveys should always be kept as simple and easy as possible while still obtaining the needed information:

- A survey should be as simple as possible, both for those taking it and for those analyzing it.

- Limit response possibilities to a range from five to ten.
- Offer an even number of choices to avoid the middle-of-the-road choice whenever possible.
- Use simple sentences: do not include two concepts or situations in the same question.
- Use language your users or potential users will understand; avoid jargon whenever possible.
- Avoid complexity and ambiguity: users should feel comfortable answering the questions.
- The survey should be easy to return: provide preaddressed, stamped envelopes where necessary; self-mailers have been known to increase return rates. If done in the library, provide a large, very visible box for returns. (University of Arizona, 2009)

Always be sure to make the survey meaningful for respondents. If they understand the reasoning behind the survey, they are more likely to spend the time to fill it out thoughtfully.

- The purpose of the survey should be clear before starting to write.
- How the data will be used should be understood before beginning.
- How many responses are expected?
- Will Excel or a statistical program such as SPSS be required to analyze the results?
- Does someone on the team have the skills to analyze the data? (University of Arizona, 2009)

When Should the Data Be Collected?

Research shows that there are several ways to design the timing of a good study.

- Pick a typical or normal time.
- Pick a time of heavy usage based on past performance.
- Pick some combination of the two.

The intention is to collect information from users that will help in your collection development decisions. In an academic library, November and December may be the peak time for term papers for undergraduates and thus a high-traffic time for the library. Students will need numerous types of materials and their met and unmet needs can be of great use to collection development staff.

How Are the Data Interpreted?

In general, data interpretation should follow the steps below.

- Summarize data and describe findings in a draft or preliminary report.

- Graph or chart your data to make it easier to sell your recommendations.
- Get reactions and comments on the draft report and prepare a set of conclusions and recommendations.
- Prepare final report with priorities assigned to recommendations.
- Library units should examine the report for implications regarding their work.

After this is done, do not do what so many libraries do—that is, simply file it away. Give careful consideration to the data and its implications for the library collection and services. Consider: Do the present objectives of the library coincide with your new knowledge of its community of users?

Tips for a Good Study

Generally, using more than one method greatly enhances the findings. The researcher may, for example, consult with key informants about a draft questionnaire and revise it as a result. Key informants are a good source for determining what needs to be asked in interviews or questionnaires. Also, consulting all existing sources will allow you to construct a shorter survey or interview instrument if you are supplementing your knowledge of the community, not trying to capture everything in the instrument. A good rule of thumb is to ask people only what you cannot find out from existing sources. (Note: You may want to ask for some demographic or personal information for cross-tabulation purposes, but you should already have a demographic picture of your community from existing information sources.)

Remember that there are examples of excellent needs assessment reports and projects on the web. The Logan Heights Branch (2009) of the San Diego Public Library posted its needs assessment on the web (http://www.sandi-ego.gov/public-library/pdf/logan_needs.pdf). Although this assessment includes much more than the collection, an analysis of the collection is embedded in the report. This is just one example of a well-planned needs assessment.

The University of Arizona (2009) has posted a needs assessment tutorial online that may be helpful before you get started. Working through the material on their site will help you better understand the logistics of doing a needs assessment (http://digital.library.arizona.edu/nadm/tutorial/).

Marketing Your Collection

Now that you have completed a needs assessment for your library, the next step is to get the word out about what you have added or what you already have that fits the needs that you have identified. For public libraries, marketing and community outreach are among the most important activities in which librarians need to participate. Likewise, school media centers must necessarily market themselves to faculty, parents, and students. Special libraries have always been forced to market themselves to their users or organizations to demonstrate their worth. In contrast, only academic libraries have tended to shrink from marketing activities, which are all too often viewed as insufficiently academically oriented.

The *Encyclopedia of Business and Finance* defines the term *marketing*:

> The term *market* is the root word for the word *marketing*. *Market* refers to the location where exchanges between buyers and sellers occur. *Marketing* pertains to the interactive process that requires developing, pricing, placing, and promoting goods, ideas, or services in order to facilitate exchanges between customers and sellers to satisfy the needs and wants of consumers. Thus, at the very center of the marketing process is satisfying the needs and wants of customers. (Marion, 2001)

Marketing of the library, its collections, and its services has not always been a focal point for librarians, but today can be accomplished much more easily than in the past through webpages, newsletters, inexpensive giveaways, exhibits, educational outreach, press releases, and public service announcements as well as displays and library publications.

Librarians do not often think of marketing as a part of their job. They do not see themselves as selling anything, naturally enough. But note the last sentence in the definition above: satisfying the needs and wants of library users is very much a part of library work. Librarians have materials that they want users to see and use, so how is that different from selling?

Many business selling techniques can be adapted for use in libraries. Take the "up-sell," which involves bringing to users' attention something similar to what they have already found that may also be of interest.

Bookstores often make a point of actually putting a book in the hand of a customer who has inquired about a title—not pointing or telling the customer where something is located. Librarians have known for a long time that going with users to the location of the materials that they need is appreciated, but the stress of time and numbers of users may tempt the librarian to remain a pointer. This tendency needs to be resisted.

There is also the "hand-sell," where particular items are targeted by bookstore employees to push. Special displays can bring these items to the customer's attention. Placing items near the cash register is also an example of this kind of marketing activity. These techniques are easily transferred to a library setting.

Successful marketing requires a plan. That plan needs to contain the specifics for the marketing mix, the resources you will need including costs, the expected results of the plan, and controls that allow you to monitor the costs and results as the plan unfolds. Also, it is a good idea to include how you will evaluate the marketing effort to measure how well you did. A good evaluation includes more than anecdotal evidence. Your marketing plan should include measurable outcomes.

Public Libraries

Since their beginnings in the mid-19th century, public libraries have practiced marketing techniques to bring their collections and services to the attention of their clientele. Marketing strategies can also be seen in their planning processes. Public libraries tend to do more needs assessment in order to more closely match their users' needs with the materials that they purchase. As publicly funded institutions, their budget is more closely tied to satisfying the public than for many other types of libraries. An important element in user satisfaction is getting the word out about what is happening at the library and new resources.

Public library collections can be seen as somewhat similar to the offerings available in large bookstores. Most public libraries stress new materials and are constantly weeding out materials that are not circulating at some predetermined level owing to space and mission considerations. Bringing new materials to the attention of users is a crucial part of a public librarian's job. Marketing in a public library thus involves or could involve many of the techniques discussed above.

As an example of an innovative marketing technique, Florida's Orange County Public Library System came up with the idea of using their online catalog to market their collections and events to the million or so residents in the Orange County area. For example, a library event with Carl Hiaasen as featured speaker was advertised through the catalog with a MARC record being specially made for the event. The catalog record contained all of Hiaasen's works in a 505 field. Thus, a search on his name or on any of his books brought up the event record. The event record not only helped get the word out about the event, but also served to bring all of his titles to the attention of users (Bost and Conklin, 2006).

Getting an audience for an event or users for materials depends heavily on informing people about what is happening in the library.

Academic Libraries

Amy Fry (2009: 33) states, "I realize now that, in a way, everybody's got to sell something; indeed marketing is an important element in my work in the academic library field."

Also, in reference to academic libraries, Singh (2009: 25) writes:

> The library in an academic institution is considered as an invaluable resource for gaining knowledge for students, faculty and staff.

However, it is not difficult for an academic library to become complacent because it has no natural information competitors on campus to stimulate *marketing* initiatives. One of the possible reasons for the complacency on the part of libraries could be the uncomfortable attitudes of librarians toward "marketing" terminologies.

Further, academic librarians and staff often view negatively any of the library's precious funds being spent on marketing activities. Gossip can quickly make the rounds about how much money is being "wasted" on marketing that could be spent more appropriately for items in the library collection, when, in fact, marketing activities are necessary to make sure that users and potential users know about the resources and services available at the library or through its website.

With specific reference to academic libraries although it is applicable to any type of library, Burkhardt (2010: 11) recommends using one or more types of new social media (Facebook, Twitter, etc.) to provide information about new additions to the library's collection, possibly with links to text or video. Librarians who do bibliographic instruction and those training students and faculty also need to market what is available through the social media used by the library. Different venues may be appropriate depending on the materials in the collection that are being discussed. Marketing the collection is all about communicating with potential users.

Academic libraries may also do outreach to local schools. St. Cloud State University (SCSU) in Minnesota participated in History Day, a nationwide program that brings students in the 6th through 12th grades into libraries, historical societies, and archives to give students a fun way to learn about history.

> This event was "outreach in action" to the community. People who attended had no connection to SCSU, yet discovered resources available to them as community members. The community participants were shown that the academic library has other uses that go beyond the university. (Steman and Motin, 2010: 29)

Similarly, a library marketing project at the University of British Columbia attempted to educate academics about the potential of the library as the heart and soul of the university rather than just a place to come when a research paper is assigned (Empey and Black, 2006). The librarians' efforts included tabletop displays at university events about the library and their services, posters, giveaways, and exhibits in a display case at the library entrance. They also took advantage of university publications, including the student newspaper, as another way to spread the message about the library.

In terms of "to market or not to market," complacency is not an option.

The risks of being reticent about marketing are too great: a poor image, false perceptions, lack of support and advocacy, and missed opportunities in the big institutional picture. Marketing can and does serve many purposes. Not only can it be instrumental in raising the profile of the academic library, but marketing also serves to educate and inform users about the important research function the library provides. Librarians are only too aware that most individuals do not understand the complexities of library resources and services and that too many students do not recognize the link between using the library and academic success. (Empey and Black, 2006: 31)

It is not such a stretch from needs assessment to marketing the collection. The result of performing a needs assessment is a better understanding of what users want. Simply buying materials may not be enough, however. The library needs to market its new resources. Matthews (2009) urges librarians to move beyond surveys, forms, and other data-gathering methods to actually market the library's collection and services as a product.

Fagan (2009) has found that virtual libraries are not being used or visited as often as the physical library. Her article in *Computers in Libraries* addresses how libraries need to market their virtual libraries, with tips on how to go about it.

Special Libraries

Most special libraries exist to serve the needs of a particular organization or discipline. The continued existence of these libraries depends on their ability to publicize their collections and services because they also need to be able to demonstrate a good return on investment. Companies with libraries want to know that the library is valuable to their business and profits, more so than getting information elsewhere or doing without. Since many special librarians are solo librarians, it is easy for them to forget about marketing when there are reference questions, acquisitions, and other activities to perform daily. Many special librarians may complain that they have no time to market their library. However, taking the time to market your library effectively is extremely important to its viability, and not just its visibility.

Special libraries are part of the culture of their parent organization and thus need to demonstrate the shared values and goals of that organization. This culture should carry over to the library's marketing efforts.

A favorite technique with many special librarians is to hold an open house to bring users and potential users into the library. Offer attendees refreshments such as wine and cheese, fruit, cookies, or just coffee and tea. Use this opportunity to show off new databases or other materials or services. If you have nothing new to show off, have an open house during National Library

Week or when new staff members are hired. You may want to hold an open house semiannually to get new employees acquainted with the library and the services you provide. Getting people into the library is the first step toward making them users of your services.

Special librarians seem to be the ones who are most involved in marketing activities of some kind or other. Even small things such as taking requested materials to individuals and taking the time to encourage them to become more acquainted with library services can pay off down the line. Successful marketing in special libraries is a main key to survival.

School Library Media Centers

Media specialists have many constituencies with whom to communicate what they have to offer—students, teachers and staff, administrators, parents, community members, and even legislators. Establishing good relations with each constituency can help the library flourish. Without knowledge of the library and its collection and services, these groups will not support the school library media center as they should. Different tactics are called for, but all are important if the library is to continue to improve.

Because the American Association of School Librarians (AASL) recognizes the importance of marketing the school library, they held a contest for the best marketing video in 2010 and featured that video on the AASL website. The contest rules called for the videos to show how school libraries make the community thrive.

There are many ways to get your message across, which can be found in the references and suggested readings for this chapter. Start with the more local of your constituent groups and use them to help you reach beyond the school.

Conclusion

Knowing what your community wants and needs and then telling them about your collection and services is important for all types of libraries. Libraries cannot play the central role that they should be playing unless potential users know about the library and feel welcome there. After determining what the community wants through a needs assessment, the next most important step is getting people into the library to make them loyal users.

Vocabulary

Be sure that you know the meaning of the following words or concepts.

community analysis	community forum	community outreach
focus group	key informant	market analysis
marketing	marketing plan	

Activities

Scenarios

Choose one of the scenarios below for your needs assessment. This activity is best done in small groups.

Prepare a plan for a needs assessment project that includes gathering appropriate demographic data from published sources, interviews with key informants, and either a field survey or an activities survey. Provide dummy data and analyze your results. Be sure to include the information required to answer the following questions:

- What sources will you use to find the demographic and social data needed? How will it be used in the final report?
- How will you identify key informants? How will you structure the interviews?
- How will you identify the respondent sample for the field survey or activities survey?
- What questions will be asked? Format the questions in the same manner as you would distribute them.
- Provide dummy data to analyze. You are not expected to actually administer the survey. Simply make up plausible data.
- How will you compile information from responses? Use the dummy data to illustrate your compilation methods. It is also appropriate to include dummy data for the interviews of key informants.
- How and to whom will you communicate the results of the survey?
- What actions should be taken based on the results of the needs assessment? Again, base your response on the dummy data you provided.

Scenario A

The staff of a public library in a small town realizes that the town's population base is changing. Previously, Spanish materials were the only type other than English that the library felt the need to collect. Due to some new industry in the town, a new group of immigrants has moved in. Their native languages appear to be of Slavic origin, and the librarians are not sure which Slavic languages they speak. These immigrants also seem to speak English very well, so the librarians are not sure if they need materials in their native languages or not. How do you proceed to assess their needs?

Scenario B

You have just been hired as a school media specialist for a private middle school (or elementary or high school). It has been three years since the school has hired a professional librarian. The collection has suffered from neglect. Your initial examination finds that many of the materials need to be discarded, plus some areas of the curriculum do not seem to be addressed at all. How do you proceed to assess the needs of the teachers and students?

Scenario C

A large cancer hospital has decided to introduce a library for patient information that will be open to anyone in the community. The budget is somewhat limited for the first two years with a promise for more generous funding in the future. How do you proceed to establish the initial most desperate needs of the community and to devise a plan for the collection as more funding becomes available?

Marketing Campaign

In groups of four to five students, based on type of library, design a brochure or write a press release to market a new or updated area in the collection (e.g., art books of local artists) or a new format of materials (e.g., e-books or a new digital library). Identify the constituency for the marketing campaign, and also how the product (brochure or press release) will be distributed.

Discussion Questions

1. Because of rough economic times, there have been rumors that most school media positions will be eliminated. (Or put yourself in a special library within a company where there are rumors about the library being closed.) Describe how you would try to stop such a decision. Your answer can include what you would do as well as how your state library association could help you get your message across.
2. Although your library seems to be in good shape with the city and county, other public libraries in your state are experiencing deep cuts to their book budgets. What can you do to help ensure that your library does not experience similar budget cuts?
3. After completing a needs assessment and discovering that students want more databases with full-text articles, your academic library has recently licensed a number of expensive article databases that are not being used as much as you expected based on the needs assessment. How can you generate more interest in these new materials?

References

Biblarz, Dora, Stephen Bosch, and Chris Sugnet, eds. 2001. *Guide to Library User Needs Assessment for Integrated Information Resource Management and Collection Development*. Lanham, MD: Scarecrow Press.

Bost, Wendi, and Jamie Conklin. 2006. "Creating a One-Stop Shop: Using the Catalog to Market Collections and Services." *Florida Libraries* 49 (Fall): 5–7.

Burkhardt, Andy. 2010. "Social Media: A Guide for College and University Libraries." *College and Research Library News* 71 (January): 10–12.

Empey, Heather, and Nancy E. Black. 2006. "Marketing the Academic Library: Building on the '@Your Library' Framework." *College and Undergraduate Libraries* 12, no. 1: 19–33.

Evans, G. Edward, and Margaret Zarnosky Saponaro. 2005. *Developing Library and Information Center Collections.* 5th ed. Westport, CT: Libraries Unlimited.

Fagan, Jody Condit. 2009. "Marketing the Virtual Library." *Computers in Libraries* 29 (July/August): 25–30.

Fry, Amy. 2009. "Lessons of Good Customer Service." *Library Journal* 134 (September 1): 33–34.

Gregory, Vicki L. 2006. *Selecting and Managing Electronic Resources.* Rev. ed. New York: Neal-Schuman.

Logan Heights Branch Library [San Diego, CA]. 2009. "Community Library Needs Assessment Components." City of San Diego. Accessed March 31. http://www.sandiego.gov/public-library/pdf/logan_needs.pdf.

Marion, Allison McClintic, ed. 2001. "Marketing." In *Encyclopedia of Business and Finance.* Gale Cengage. eNotes.com, 2006. http://www.enotes.com/business-finance-encyclopedia/marketing.

Matthews, Brian. 2009. *Marketing Today's Academic Library: A Bold New Approach to Communicating with Students.* Chicago: American Library Association.

Singh, Rajesh. 2009. "Does Your Library Have an Attitude Problem Towards 'Marketing'? Revealing Inter-relationships between Marketing Attitudes and Behavior." *Journal of Academic Librarianship* 35 (January): 25–32.

Steman, Thomas, and Susan Motin. 2010. "History Day: Another Outreach Opportunity for Academic Libraries." *College and Research Libraries News* 71 (January): 26–29.

University of Arizona. 2009. "Needs Assessment Tutorial." University of Arizona. http://digital.library.arizona.edu/nadm/tutorial/.

Selected Readings

Angelis, Jane, and Joan M. Wood. 1999. "A New Look at Community Connections: Public Relations for Public Libraries." *Illinois Libraries* 81 (Winter): 23–24.

Bishop, Kay. 2007. *The Collection Program in Schools: Concepts, Practices, and Information Sources.* 4th ed. Westport, CT: Libraries Unlimited.

Blake, Julie C., and Susan P. Schleper. 2004. "From Data to Decisions: Using Surveys and Statistics to Make Collection Management Decisions." *Library Collections, Acquisitions, and Technical Services* 28: 460–464.

Doucett, Elizabeth. 2008. *Creating Your Library Brand: Communicating Your Relevance and Value to Your Patrons.* Chicago: American Library Association.

Duff, Wendy M., and Catherine A. Johnson. 2001. "A Virtual Expression of Need: An Analysis of E-mail Reference Questions." *American Archivist* 64 (Spring/Summer): 43–60.

Empey, Heather, and Nancy E. Black. 2006. "Marketing the Academic Library: Building on the '@Your Library' Framework." *College and Undergraduate Libraries* 12, no. 1: 19–33.

Farmer, Lesley S. J. 2001. "Collection Development in Partnership with Youth: Uncovering Best Practices." *Collection Management* 26, no. 2: 67–78.

Flowers, Helen F. 1998. *Public Relations for School Library Media Programs: 500 Ways to Influence People and Win Friends for Your School Library Media Center.* New York: Neal-Schuman.

Fry, Amy. 2009. "Lessons of Good Customer Service." *Library Journal* 134 (September 1): 33–34.

Hahn, K. L., and L. A. Faulkner. 2002. "Evaluative Usage-Based Metrics for the Selection of E-journals." *College and Research Libraries* 63 (September): 215–227.

Ismail, Lizah. 2009. "What They Are Telling Us: Library Use and Needs of Traditional and Non-traditional Students in a Graduate Social Work Program." *Journal of Academic Librarianship* 35 (November): 555–564.

Karp, Rashelle S., ed. 2002. *Powerful Public Relations: A How-to Guide for Libraries.* Chicago: American Library Association.

Kohl, Susan. 2000. *Getting Attention: Leading Edge Lessons for Publicity and Marketing.* Boston: Butterworth-Heinemann.

Koontz, Christie, and Dean Jue. 2004. "Unlock Your Demographics." *Library Journal* 129 (March 1): 32–33.

Malenfant, Kara J. 2010. "Leading Change in the System of Scholarly Communication: A Case Study of Engaging Liaison Librarians for Outreach to Faculty." *College and Research Libraries* 71 (January): 63–76.

Matthews, Brian, and Jon Bodnar. 2008. *SPEC KIT 306.* Association of Research Libraries, September.

Steinmacher, Michael. 2000. "Underlying Principles of Library Public Relations." *Kentucky Libraries* 64 (Winter): 12–15.

Thorsen, Jeanne. 1998. "Community Studies: Raising the Roof and Other Recommendations." *Acquisitions Librarian* 10, no. 20: 5–13.

Westbrook, Lynn, and Steven A. Tucker. 2002. "Understanding Faculty Information Needs." *Reference and User Studies Quarterly* 42 (Winter): 144–148.

3

Collection Development Policies

Overview

In this chapter we look at the rationale behind developing and maintaining a current collection development policy. Each part of the policy will be examined from the perspective of both writing it and using it in the library for collection development and management purposes. Not all libraries have a written collection development policy, so some of you may find yourselves needing to help compose a collection development policy in your first professional position.

Collection development policies serve as blueprints for the operations of a library as a whole, for it is through these policies that the library carries out its central tasks of acquiring, organizing, and managing library materials. These policies also typically set up the general framework for establishing the library's collection goals, in terms of both new acquisitions and the maintenance of existing items. Policies are usually developed by libraries with two audiences in mind—the library's staff members and the broader community of patrons and other users. Collection development policies certainly vary greatly as a result. In most libraries, what we find today consists of a combination of descriptions of practices, guidelines for decision making, and provisions intended to protect against unwarranted pressures to acquire, not to aquire, or to discard certain types of materials or particular items.

Collection development policies help to ensure consistency in procedures and are also important in achieving appropriate balance in a library's collection. Consistency is needed because selectors, in using and revising the policies, are necessarily forced to confront the overall goals and objectives of the library and to reflect these goals and objectives in the collection they are building, whether that collection is owned and housed locally in hard copy form or in an electronic format or is simply accessed through the web. Of course, proper collection balance does not mean that all areas must receive

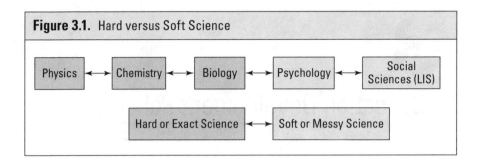

Figure 3.1. Hard versus Soft Science

equal coverage, but rather that the collection reflects the proper balance necessary to meet the needs of the particular library's users.

Although we talk of collection development policy as a blueprint, it is not as exact as a hard science (see Figure 3.1), which is why we need professional librarians to design and implement collection development decisions.

As it is a time-consuming task, Gardner (1981: 222–224) provides extensive reasons why it is worth the time of the librarians to write a collection development policy, including the following:

- Forcing the staff to think through library goals and commit themselves to these goals, helping them to identify long- and short-range needs of users and to establish priorities for allocating funds
- Helping ensure that the library will commit itself to all parts of the community, both present and future
- Helping set standards for the selection and weeding of materials
- Informing users, administrators, and other libraries of the collection's scope, facilitating coordination of collection development among institutions
- Helping to minimize selectors' personal bias and to highlight imbalances in selection criteria
- Serving as an in-service training tool for new staff
- Helping ensure continuity, especially in larger collections, providing a pattern and framework to ease transition from one librarian to the next
- Providing a means of staff self-evaluation, or evaluation by outsiders
- Helping demonstrate that the library is running a businesslike operation
- Providing information to assist in budget allocations
- Contributing to operational efficiency in terms of routine decisions, which helps junior staff
- Serving as a tool to handle complaints with regard to inclusions or exclusions

In addition to print materials, there has been a rapid infusion of all types of electronic resources (including electronic journals, databases, image collections, maps, encyclopedias, stock market reports, and other business and financial information). These electronic resources have, as might be expected, often strained the rules and guidelines typically found in current collection development policies. For instance, what constitutes the library's collection? Is it simply the items that are purchased and housed locally or does it include licensed materials housed on a server at the vendor's site? Does (or should) the library collection be considered to include materials that are freely available on the Internet? These and other similar basic philosophical issues must be resolved before a collection development policy can successfully incorporate electronic resources.

Purpose of Collection Development Policies

A written collection development policy is important for a number of reasons, and the absence of such a policy tends to lead to a feeling that the collection is being developed on an ad hoc basis.

> Libraries without collection development policies are like businesses without business plans. Without a plan, an owner and his employees lack a clear understanding of what the business is doing now and what it will do in the future, and potential investors have little information about the business's prospects. The owner has no benchmarks against which to measure progress. Daily decisions are made without context. Even a library with written policy statements suffers if those statements are not reviewed, revised, and updated regularly. Selections, deselections, and priority setting throughout the library occur in isolation and without coordination if the library has no recorded rationale for decisions. (Johnson, 2009: 72–73)

Collection development policies typically serve a number of purposes, which include informing and directing library processes in acquiring and making resources available to users, and which serve as a protection for the library against challenges to its procedures and resources. These purposes—informing, directing, and protecting—can be accomplished in many ways through a traditional collection development policy.

A good collection development policy will provide the staff and users with information as follows:

- Describe the library's user community, defining the institutional mission of the library, and identifying its users' likely needs
- Provide selection criteria and guidelines for the use of those charged with selecting library materials
- Identify those selection tools and processes that are most appropriate for the particular library

- Define the process for identifying materials for weeding, cancellation, storage, and replacement of materials
- Facilitate consistency and communication among the collection development librarians
- Establish who is responsible for various aspects of the collection development process and management activities
- Create a plan for the future of the collection and the budgeting of resultant library expenditures
- Serve as a training document for new collection development librarians and those charged with management of the library as a whole
- Provide guidelines for dealing with gift materials
- Provide guidelines for dealing with complaints about materials or services thought by patrons or administrators to be inappropriate
- Provide a framework and context for decisions concerning library access, space allocations, budgeting, and fundraising priorities
- Support cooperative collection development activities by documenting what the library has done in the past and what the library is currently doing with collecting levels by discipline
- Identify both the strengths and the relative weaknesses of the library's current collections
- Aid in preparing grant proposals and planning development initiatives through its supporting documentation
- Serve as a communication vehicle with the library's staff, administration, and various constituencies

A good collection development policy will carry out its protecting purposes by containing provisions in such areas as the following:

- Protecting intellectual freedom
- Informing the library's governing or funding body concerning the library's current direction
- Providing a clear and carefully described rationale for the library's collection goals and practices
- Making clear the principles by which decisions are made to protect the library against charges of bias and irresponsible behavior
- Protecting the library from pressures to acquire or provide access to inappropriate or irrelevant resources
- Acting as an informational tool for use within the library's user and patron community and for its community at large
- Providing some protection to the library, when budgets decrease or materials costs increase, against complaints by the user community

A collection development policy that encompasses electronic resources must also include the policy for handling the following issues with electronic resources:

- Cancellation or retention of print resources when the electronic version of the resource becomes available
- Provision of or limitations on remote access to electronic resources owned or licensed by the library
- Justification of new costs, which could include the costs of hardware and supplies in addition to the cost of the material
- Location of resources and the cost of maintaining appropriate Internet or other network links
- Possible duplication of certain e-journals or databases, based on purchasing bundles available from different electronic information aggregators
- Negotiation of the terms of licenses for use of the material, including provisions addressing these new types of legal considerations in the collection development policy itself
- Consideration of the special preservation and long-term access issues that electronic resources present
- Satisfaction by the library of the technical requirements for access to the resource, including such matters as determining the formats and computer platforms supported by the materials
- Cancellation problems, which include whether the library loses all rights to materials previously licensed once cancellation occurs
- Performance questions, such as whether the electronic product really performs its intended job better (i.e., does it make information more easily or accurately available than its print counterpart?)
- Training of staff and users in the use of new electronic resources
- Access and organizational issues concerning whether to catalog Internet-available items or electronic bundles of resources
- Cooperative collection development issues, such as the ability to provide copies on interlibrary loan

The flood of electronic materials that are coming into the library have caused many libraries to reexamine their collection development policies and update them to reflect the addition of concerns specific to the electronic format.

Basic Elements of a Collection Development Policy

This section presents the major components of any collection development policy along with a brief explanation of the kinds of information that belong in each section. For additional information and examples, you may wish to consult Frank W. Hoffmann and Richard J. Wood's (2005) book, *Library Collection Development Policies: Academic, Public, and Special Libraries.* Hoffmann and Wood have pulled together examples from a number of different library policies for every element of a collection development policy. Also note that many libraries now put their entire policy on their website. An

Internet search will allow you to find examples of numerous policies from a wide variety of libraries.

Title Page/Cover

This page identifies the type of document and the library to which it belongs. Be sure that the title page is adequately descriptive and contains the date when it was written and approved.

Signature Page

The signature page, which may be included in the title page, contains signatures of the librarian and supervisors plus at least the chair of the library board in a public library setting. The college or university academic vice president or provost are the likely signers for an academic library. This page provides legitimacy to the overall document. Although many of the uses of a collection development policy are internal, challenges may occur in any type of library, thus making it extremely important that everyone in the hierarchy acknowledge the policy by signing off on the document. Any individuals in the chain of command who may receive complaints directly about the library should be cognizant of the policy and its contents.

Table of Contents

As with any document, a table of contents allows users to quickly find what they need. Wood and Hoffman (1996: 34) list a number of features that all good tables of contents should include:

- Headings should correspond, word for word, with those contained in the text.
- Subheadings should be included, if possible, with a uniform cutoff point (regarding what is to be included) established throughout the text.
- Page numbers should be included in the text and cited for each content heading.
- Appendixes, tables, and other sidebar-type information should be noted at their proper sequence within the text.

Often when staff members need to consult a collection development policy, the matter is urgent. It is important that all staff members be able to quickly find whichever part of the policy is needed.

Statement of Purpose

State the purpose of the library collection development policy. "The library's purpose statement often focuses on the communication function: internally, with users, staff, and administrators, and externally, with other libraries and institutions. Communication embraces a wide variety of vital operations, including training, budgeting, cooperative acquisitions, and shared services" (Hoffman and Wood, 2005: 5).

If this is a policy for a college library, it may state that the library's purpose is to support the curriculum and faculty research, or it may take a broader view that in addition to the materials designed to support the academic program the library also strives to provide light or recreational reading for students and faculty.

A public library policy may state its purpose as serving the needs of local citizens and providing information to the public and city, town, or county government as to the principles on which materials are added to the collection.

Background Statement

For a background statement, describe the library's user community as defined by demographic materials and any insights gained through a needs assignment. Also define the institutional mission of the library and identify its users' likely needs.

Usually background statements include some or all of the following:

- Geographical data as well as a demographic description of the community as a whole, which may include information about social services required by segments of the potential user population
- Special features of the area and organization that play a role in the services and collections that may be particularly needed by this library or library system
- The location of the library facilities and any special services offered in different locations
- A description of any cooperative agreements with other libraries that are available to users (such as borrowing privileges)

Responsibility for Collection Development and Management

All policies need to clearly address the issue of responsibility for the collection. This section should state the responsibilities of the collection development librarians and director. Usually the major day-to-day work is delegated to the collection development librarians, but oversight is generally the responsibility of the director.

Academic libraries will usually cover the responsibility of the library to work with faculty members in each discipline to develop those areas of the collection. In smaller academic libraries the faculty may play an active role in development. Generally the larger the library, the more likely that faculty will work with a member of the collection development team only for special purchases or new specialty areas, such as the support of a new academic program or degree. If the size of the library dictates a large number of people participating in the selection process, a chart or diagram may be included to help the reader visualize the structure.

In the case of school media centers, a district supervisor or the school principal may have ultimate responsibility for the collection, with the media specialist delegated to do day-to-day selection.

Mission, Goals, and Objectives Statements

Although some libraries use the library's mission, goals, and objectives statements in their collection development policies, it is more effective to develop a mission, goals, and objectives specifically for the policy. In the latter case, the mission, goals, and objectives of the collection should be clearly tied to those of the library. Some libraries now put a vision statement first, thus having a vision, a mission, goals, and objectives.

This portion of the policy can be problematic. "In many instances, libraries don't utilize mission, goal, and objectives statements in tandem; this despite the fact that these three concepts are interrelated and vital to the overall way some libraries interpret these concepts" (Hoffman and Wood, 2005: 20). A close reading of this section in many collection development policies that can be found on the web shows that libraries often confuse these concepts in their policies. This is obviously a long-standing problem.

> To develop effective policy-making strategies, the proper use of mission, goals and objectives must be understood. Often in a collection development policy, I find objectives that read more like goals, goals that read more like a mission, and no real objectives as all. Goals are broad statements of intentions, and objectives are narrower statements that show *how* these intentions are to be carried out. Objectives are measurable and tell you what actions must be completed or moved forward in a particular goal. (Futas, 1995: 9; emphasis in original)

Although the mission statement may at times seem vacuous and read a little like an endorsement of the national flag, motherhood, and apple pie, the goals and objectives should nevertheless be written in such a way as to provide a framework for judging the success of the library's collection development work.

Identification of Target Audiences

A public library usually has a number of user constituencies or target audiences: children, young adults, adults seeking leisure reading, adults researching local history, genealogy, or other subjects, and businesspeople. The library may also have a large senior citizen user group that, in addition to the materials listed above, may need large-print resources and equipment to enlarge materials not available in that format. The library may likewise have a large disabled population with a number of different special needs. The language and background diversity of users will also need to be reflected in the collection.

Academic libraries have a primary clientele of faculty, staff, and students. However, many academic libraries also have a role in the community; for example, advanced high school students may be allowed to use the library. In some cases, colleges and universities cultivate such high school students in the hope of drawing them to attend that university. School media centers serve teachers and students primarily, but they, too, may have other constituents. Special libraries usually have a more narrowly defined user base as they are often not open to the public or only in a limited manner. Their clientele is generally the organization to which they belong.

Budgeting and Funding

This section addresses how the library is funded and what effect that has on the spending of collection development dollars. In academic libraries, in addition to general funds for reference and undergraduate materials, funds may also be allocated to each college and even down to the department level. Usually, there is a cutoff time when the funds revert to the collection development librarians in order for them to have time to expend the funds before the end of the fiscal year.

In a large public library, the different departments may be allocated a specific sum of money for collection development, or collection development may be centralized so that a group of selectors purchases for the library or system of libraries. Some libraries have a committee of selectors who review suggestions for purchases. These selection committees may review or preview serials and audiovisual and electronic resources as a group before ordering them for the collection.

School media specialists will receive a budget for collection development and usually will confer with teachers about the kinds of resources needed to match the curriculum. In the higher grades, the teachers may be organized by department, with department chairs working with the media specialist in the selection of materials for that area.

Special librarians may be solo librarians or one of several. Collection development decisions are usually somewhat easier in a special library because of the focus of the collection in one area. Librarians may often be working with researchers using the library and therefore will be very cognizant of user needs. In larger medical or law libraries, the processes may more resemble those of academic libraries.

Selection or Evaluation Criteria

The selection criteria are often seen as the core of the policy. They can explain why one item is chosen over another—an accountability factor, so to speak. As all libraries feel that they do not receive enough funds to fully meet all user needs, a number of different criteria need to be considered when purchasing library materials.

General Criteria

1. User needs and wants: Data gathered from a needs assessment, interlibrary loan requests, reference questions, and so on, can be used to determine the needs of users.
2. Holdings of other libraries: For sources that are not needed often, it may be possible to rely on nearby libraries.
3. Gaps in the collections: Missing volumes of serials or missing titles of famous authors can be revealed and worked into an acquisition plan.

Specific Criteria

1. Recency: How old are your titles on average? For example, are Western genre titles not circulating because they aren't wanted or because they have already been read?
2. Reputation of author or publisher, and so on. Standard items must be bought to keep the users happy. For example, a new Danielle Steele novel cannot be ignored by public libraries.

Analysis of Subject Fields

This section discusses the evaluation of the collection by classification number or breakdown by general subject area. This analysis should focus on the current strength and the desired strength of the collection. There are a number of ways to format and analyze the collection by subject area. The RLG Conspectus and the Western Library Network (now OCLC Western) Conspectus Model are the most prominent in the library literature. If your library is small, you can use a smaller scale than the full Conspectus or simply rank items using stars (*, **, ***, ****) or some similar way to indicate differences in collecting and desired collecting strength (for examples, see Figures 3.2, 3.3, and 3.4).

The Conspectus Model allows libraries to compare the current and desired strengths of a collection by subject area, using codes as follows:

CL: current collection strength
AC: acquisition commitment
GL: collection goal or desired strength of collection
PC: preservation commitment

Figure 3.2. Conspectus-Like Example Using Dewey Decimal Classification (Large Academic Library): Sea (Naval) Forces and Warfare

Call #	Subject	CL	AC	GL	PC	Comments
359	Sea (naval) forces and warfare	1	0	4	0	New Naval ROTC program requires more resources in all areas below. Also new professor in history with research emphasis in naval warfare. Also check for age of titles. May need to weed as well as buy new materials.
359.1–.2	Naval life and resources	1	0	3	0	
359.3	Organization and personnel of naval forces	2	0	3	0	
359.4–.7	Naval operations, training, administration, installations	2	0	4	0	Needs weeding and updating.
359.8	Naval equipment and supplies	1	0	4	0	
359.9	Specialized combat forces; engineering and related services	1	0	3	0	

Note: CL = Current Collection Strength; AC = Acquisition Commitment; GL = Collection Goal; PC = Preservation Commitment.

Figure 3.3. Conspectus-Like Example Using the Dewey Decimal System (Small to Medium-Size Public Library): Public Administration and Military Science

Call #	Subject	CL	AC	GL	PC	Comments
351	Administration of central governments	1	0	1	0	Major interests are 353.
352	Administration of local governments	2	0	2	0	Needs weeding and updating
353	Administration of United States federal and state governments	3	0	3	0	U.S. and Florida are used most heavily.
354	Administration of specific central governments; international administration	1	0	2	0	High school students have a new assignment dealing with the United Nations.
355	Military science	3	0	3	0	See note on 358.
356	Foot forces and warfare	1	0	1	0	Needs weeding.
357	Mounted forces and warfare	1	0	1	0	Needs weeding.
358	Air and other specialized forces and warfare; engineering and related services	2	0	3	0	Presence of a large Air Force base causes a large circulation of this area.
359	Sea (naval) force and warfare	2	0	2	0	Needs weeding as materials are more than 10 years old.

Note: CL = Current Collection Strength; AC = Acquisition Commitment; GL = Collection Goal; PC = Preservation Commitment.

Figure 3.4. Conspectus-Like Example for a Library Using Library of Congress Classification: Books (General. Writing. Paleography)

Call #	Subject	CL	AC	GL	PC	Comments
Z4–8	History of books and bookmaking	3	3	4	0	Growing need in the fine arts bookmaking program.
Z40–104.5	Writing	2	0	3	0	Growing need in the fine arts bookmaking program.
Z105–115.4	Paleography, manuscripts	2	2	3	0	Medieval studies needs more materials to support a new graduate degree.
Z116	Book industries and trade	2	0	2	0	Needs weeding.
Z116.A5–265	Printing	3	0	3	0	Need more materials on early printing.
Z266–276	Bookbinding, book decoration	2	2	3	0	Growing need in the fine arts bookmaking program.
Z278–549	Book selling and publishing	2	0	3	0	Need more materials on electronic publishing.
Z551-656	Copyright	2	0	4	0	Materials needed on copyright and electronic materials.
Z657–659	Freedom of the press, censorship	3	0	4	0	Journalism is coming up for reaccreditation and needs more resources to be successful.

Note: CL = Current Collection Strength; AC = Acquisition Commitment; GL = Collection Goal; PC = Preservation Commitment.

Indicators are used to describe the level at which the library attempts to build the particular subject collection:

0   Out of Scope: The library does not collect in this area.
1   Minimal Level: Includes few selections beyond very basic works.
2   Information Level: Includes works that introduce and define a basic subject; supports general library users through the first two years of college.
3   Study Level: Includes a wide range of basic works on a subject; supports independent research for general library users as well as graduate and undergraduate students.
4   Research Level: Includes major source material on a subject; supports research needs of doctoral students.
5   Comprehensive Level: Attempts to collect all significant works in a subject area; serves as a national or international resource.

The Western Library Network/OCLC Western Conspectus scale uses more levels (ten as opposed to six).

0   Out of Scope
1a   Minimal Information Level: uneven coverage
1b   Minimal Information Level: focused coverage
2a   Basic Information Level: introductory
2b   Basic Information Level: advanced
3a   Basic Study or Instructional Support Level
3b   Intermediate Study or Instructional Support Level
3c   Advanced Study or Instructional Support Level
4   Research Level
5   Comprehensive

School media centers have a mission revolving around the curriculum and therefore have a much more limited focus (Figure 3.5). The following are a couple of examples of how a school library media specialist may do a subject analysis of the collection.

Collection Mapping

K–12 schools sometimes prefer to map the collection to the curriculum. The table in Figure 3.5 serves to summarize the curriculum at the high school level in terms of library and information support. Information support is defined as the provision of information and library resources to students and staff from both the physical in-house collections and external sources made available through library services. Support also includes student instruction by school library media specialists and staff assistance in reference services.

Support Levels

Note the similarity to the Conspectus approach, tailored to the level of the school.

Figure 3.5. Subject Descriptions of a Senior High Collection

Classification	Description	Percentage of Collection	Percentage of Circulation	Goal	Comments
000s	Generalities	.8	.9	+	Computer science area growing.
100s	Philosophy and psychology	1.5	2.8	+	Paranormal phenomena, psychology, and ethics circulate heavily.
200s	Religion	.7	.6	–	World religions utilized in world culture classes.
300s	Social sciences	12.0	12.1	+	Criminology materials receive heaviest circulation.
400s	Language	.3	.1	–	Needs weeding.
500s	Natural sciences	2.9	2.4	+	Astronomy collection underutilized.
600s	Technology and applied sciences	5.8	6.6	+	Medicine selection used heavily by health classes.
700s	Fine arts and recreation	4.4	3.4	=	Art and sports books not circulating well.
800s	Literature	7.3	4.7	+	Literature classes are textbook driven; only advanced classes do literary criticism.
900s	Geography and history	10.9	10.4	+	Used heavily by world cultures classes.
AV	Audiovisual	8.0	9.2	+	Obsolete formats need replacements—records, filmstrips.
B	Biography	4.4	2.8	–	Students not reading biography unless related to class assignments.
F	Fiction	9.4	4.3	–	Students prefer paperbacks; hardbound fiction not circulating.
FAC	Faculty and professional	1.1	.5	=	Needs promotion.
PA	Paperbacks	15.2	13.3	=	Could use weeding and removal of some duplicates and badly worn titles.
PER	Periodicals (recent use only)	.4	3.2	=	Circulation is staff use only; student in-library use not represented.
REF	Reference	10.5	9.7	=	Overnight only.

1. Minimal library resources needed for students and teachers; basic resources are textbooks and specially purchased classroom resources.
2. Library resources needed to support one or two student projects per year plus some teacher resources; textbooks used as guides with some supplemental, teacher-developed units.
3. Library resources needed to support several student projects per year and classroom instruction; minimal textbook use; most units teacher-designed with local resources; some units include the instruction of core information skills by the school library media specialist.

Phase Levels

The language arts courses are designated with a "phase level" to aid in course selection. The levels identify courses for students who have various needs and abilities (for an example, see Figure 3.6):

Phase 2   Need to learn how to improve sentence writing skills, understand what they read, and talk about what they have read.

Phase 2–3   Can write a complete sentence and speak in front of a class; will learn to write a paragraph and improve speaking and writing skills.

Phase 3   Have average abilities in language arts.

Phase 3–4   Can think, write, and read analytically; college preparatory.

Phase 4   Will be challenged to think creatively and to produce superior work.

As you can see from these examples, a thorough subject analysis is time well spent, as it leads to a virtual roadmap of where the collection needs to expand or where fewer materials are needed or ones better focused to user needs, what sections of the collection need weeding, and where the library is on target.

Analysis of Collection by Format

This portion of the collection development policy is usually a narrative that deals with the formats collected and any special considerations for particular formats. Common formats include books, periodicals, newspapers, videos, CDs, DVDs, curriculum materials, mp3 files, and others. For example, an academic library might purchase local newspapers for those areas from which students come, including international newspapers. These may not be added to the permanent collection, but may be kept for a specific period of time such as six months.

It is also good practice to include here types of formats that are normally collected such as textbooks, laboratory manuals, games, theses and dissertations from other institutions, and aural recordings. Sometimes items may be purchased under special circumstances, which can be indicated if deemed

Figure 3.6. Example from a Senior High School Collection Mapping

Language Arts Courses	Grade Levels	Enrollment	Support Level	Type	Comments
English 9	9	48	1	Yr	Phase 2
Basic Grammar	9	145	2	Sem	Phase 2–3
Introduction to Literature	9	147	1	Sem	Phase 2–3
Grammar and Usage	10–12	46	1	Sem	Phase 2
Legends and Folklore	11–12	18	2	Sem	Phase 2
Basic Speaking Skills	10–12	28	1	Sem	Phase 2
Adventure Stories	10	49	1	Sem	Phase 2
Paragraph Writing	10–12	147	1	Sem	Phase 2–3
American Character	10–12	88	2	Sem	Phase 2–3
Short Stories	10–12	49	1	Sem	Phase 2
Techniques of Reading	11–12	45	1	Sem	Phase 3
Introduction to Composition	10–12	167	1	Sem	Phase 2–3
Public Speaking	10–12	82	2	Sem	Phase 3
Introduction to Research	11–12	83	3	Sem	Phase 3
Business English I	11	0	1	Sem	Phase 3
Applied Communications	11–12	56	2	Yr	Phase 3–4
American Literature	10–11	138	2	Sem	Phase 3
Mystery and Detective Literature	10–12	43	2	Sem	Phase 3
Contemporary Man	11–12	40	2	Sem	Phase 3
Business English II	11	10	1	Yr	Phase 3
College Vocabulary	11–12	48	1	Sem	Phase 3–4
Techniques of Research	11–12	15	3	Sem	Phase 3–4
Advanced Reading	12	35	1	Sem	Phase 3–4
English Literature	11–12	48	1	Sem	Phase 3–4
20th-Century American Writers	11–12	49	2	Sem	Phase 3–4
Humanities: Greek to Renaissance	11–12	38	2	Sem	Phase 4
Humanities: Renaissance to 20th Century	11–12	32	2	Sem	Phase 4
Advanced Composition	11–12	15	1	Sem	Phase 4

appropriate. For example, the library might purchase textbooks authored by the institution's faculty; if so, this would be an appropriate addition to the policy.

It is becoming more common for libraries to deal with web links in their policies. Generally there is a statement indicating that web links are selected for the library's website on the same basis as printed materials, meaning that the links are evaluated and selected for inclusion as part of the library's resources.

This is also the proper section to deal with the selection of materials in different languages. An academic library may state, for example, that only materials in languages taught by the university are acquired. A statement could also be made that the library supports faculty research in whatever language is required, although this is common only in large research libraries. A public library may make substantial purchases in Spanish or any other language prevalent in the community.

The library may wish to include government documents in this section, although they are not strictly a format as they come in various printed and electronic forms. If there is a substantial government documents collection, the library may want to include it as a section to itself, whatever makes the most sense in the particular situation.

Policies that recognize the quickly changing world of new technologies may indicate that the library will collect in new formats when feasible. A statement such as this will suffice when a new technology first comes along, but the new format should be incorporated into the policy as soon as possible, while still including the paragraph about new technology to cover the next new format.

Selection Aids

Selection aids vary with type of library and the collection. Never box yourself into having to use only the sources listed in that section, but rather use it to list the more common sources for selection in your type and size of library. A more thorough discussion of selection aids follows in Chapter 4.

Intellectual Freedom

This section of the policy contains a philosophy statement concerning intellectual freedom and procedures for handling complaints. Generally it is a good idea to include a copy of any complaint or reconsideration forms and letters in an appendix to the policy. Many libraries include the Library Bill of Rights (American Library Association, 2009).

Figure 3.7 is a sample form that library staff would give to a person who wants to challenge a particular work. One item that the library challenge form should always have is a question asking whether the person has read

Figure 3.7. Sample Challenge Form

Request for Reconsideration of Library Material

Author: _____

Type of Material: _____

Title: _____

Publisher (if known): _____

Request initiated by: _____ Telephone: _____

Street Address: _____

City: _____ Zip Code: _____

1. Did you read and examine the entire item? If not the whole item, what parts?

2. What do you feel might be the result of using this item?

3. For what age group would you recommend this item?

4. Do you feel there is any value in this item?

5. To what in the item do you object? (Please be specific.)

6. Have you had an opportunity to discuss the proposed use of this item with a staff member?

_____ Date: _____
Signature of Complainant

Please return this request to: *<insert name and contact information>*

You will be contacted about the decision by the *<insert proper person or group for your library>* within *<insert time frame>* weeks of the receipt of your completed form.

the work. Most libraries will not consider a challenge valid if the person complaining has not read the work.

Collection Maintenance and Weeding

Weeding or deselection needs to be performed in most libraries, with school and public libraries having to pay the most constant attention to this process. The collection development policy lays down the general guidelines for weeding based on the needs and collection purpose of the particular library. Evaluation criteria that are used in the weeding process should be listed here as well. More specific information about weeding criteria are presented in Chapter 7.

Gift Policy and Procedures

Although most libraries welcome gifts and donations in the form of materials or monetary funds, gifts should be accepted only with the understanding that they will be evaluated with the same criteria used for purchased materials.

Typical policies will state that the use and disposal of gifts will be at the discretion of the librarian in the interest of maintaining an appropriate and balanced collection. The library cannot assign a monetary value to any gifts but, for tax purposes, may give receipts showing the date and number of books donated. A gift to the library becomes library property and must be treated as such. Gifts can be one of the trickiest aspects of collection development. Some donors have collected unusual materials that may fit into the library's collection and be a real asset. Other donors may have a complete set of *Reader's Digest Condensed Books* or a set of magazines that the library does not need. Being able to sell or otherwise dispose of such unneeded materials has to be established upfront with the donor.

Replacements

This section of the policy deals with conditions under which the library will or will not replace stolen, lost, or damaged materials. A replacement is an item purchased to take the place of an identical title previously in the collection. It is usually the library's policy not to automatically replace all materials removed because of loss, damage, or wear. The need for replacement in each case is to be judged by such factors as:

1. existence of adequate coverage of the subject area, especially if more current materials are available;
2. demand for the specific title; and
3. appearance of the title in standard selection tools and bibliographies.

Special Collections

Almost all libraries have some type of special collection materials. For instance, in a school library it is often professional materials, which are necessary to promote professional development of the faculty and aid in the process of educational development and progress within the school. A school media center may have a policy such as: "Professional materials will be acquired and housed in a special area of the library. These materials will be available for checkout by the faculty and staff of the school. Requests for materials by teachers, other staff, and the administration will be given high priority."

Public libraries are likely to have special collections of local materials such as books by local authors, pamphlets and newspaper articles about local events, locally produced magazines, personal papers and diaries from prominent citizens of the area, and so on. This type of special collection requires a very different approach than the one described above.

An academic or special library may be the repository of special subject materials from a donor that may include personal papers, scrapbooks, diaries, and so forth. The library then may want to fill out a collection. For example, if a prominent author gave the library his or her personal papers, the library may try to obtain a complete set of the first editions of the author's novels to make the collection more valuable. These libraries will most likely have special collections librarians or archivists who will work with the collection development staff on such issues.

It is becoming more and more common for academic and some special libraries to create digital repositories of faculty and staff publications, which are often included in special collections for their creation, use, and maintenance.

Revisions

At the conclusion of the policy there should be an indication of the process for revisions. The policy cannot be useful if it is not revised often enough to keep it up to date with the needs of users, the curriculum of a school, and the needs of researchers and faculty in academic and special libraries. Depending upon the amount of change in what users need, a committee or task force should be assigned the responsibility of looking at the policy for small additions and deletions every year and a full revision at least every ten years.

As should be apparent by now, writing and revising a policy is a time-consuming process, which is the reason some libraries do not have one. However, if done correctly, the collection development policy should be a blueprint for the continuing development of the collection and a tremendous aid in explaining the kinds of materials purchased to users, boards, and administrators.

Vocabulary

Be sure that you understand the following terms or phrases:

cooperative collection development   curriculum mapping

digital repository   intellectual freedom

Library Bill of Rights   RLG Conspectus

WLN (OCLC Western) Conspectus Model

Activities

Form groups of four to five students based on type of library (academic, community college, medical, law, corporate, large research public library, medium-sized public library, branch public library, elementary school library, middle school library, high school library, etc.). Each group should select a reporter (to report to the class as a whole about their discussion) and a recorder (to take notes about the discussion). Discuss each part of the elements of a collection development policy with particular attention to what needs should be included for the type of library they are representing. Be sure to include your decisions on how to best approach the analysis by subject for your type of library. Report in the time frame chosen by your instructor.

Discussion Questions

1. Why go to the trouble of writing a collection development policy? What advantages can you see to having such a policy? Disadvantages?
2. If you were hired to do collection development for a library not having a written collection development policy, how would you proceed?

References

American Library Association. 2009. *Library Bill of Rights.* American Library Association. Accessed June 22. http://www.ala.org/ala/aboutala/offices/oif/statementspols/statementsif/librarybillrights.cfm.

Futas, Elizabeth, ed. 1995. *Collection Development Policies and Procedures.* 3rd ed. Phoenix, AZ: Oryx Press.

Gardner, Richard K. 1981. *Library Collections: Their Origins, Selection, and Development.* New York: McGraw-Hill.

Hoffman, Frank W., and Richard J. Wood. 2005. *Library Collection Development Policies: Academic, Public, and Special Libraries.* Lanham, MD: Scarecrow Press.

Johnson, Peggy. 2009. *Fundamentals of Collection Development and Management.* 2nd ed. Chicago: American Library Association.

Wood, Richard J., and Frank Hoffman. 1996. *Library Collection Development Policies: A Reference and Writers' Handbook.* Lanham, MD: Scarecrow Press.

Selected Readings

Coleman, Jim. 1992. "The RLG Conspectus: A History of Its Development and Influence and a Prognosis for Its Future." *Acquisitions Librarian* 4, no. 7: 25–43.

IFLA Section on Acquisitions and Collection Development. 2009. "Guidelines for a Collection Development Policy Using the Conspectus Model." International Federation of Library Associations and Institutions. Accessed June 22. http://www.ifla.org.sg/VII/s14/nd1/gcdp-e.pdf.

Lee, Hur-Li. 2000. "What Is a Collection?" *Journal of the American Society for Information Science* 51 (October): 1106–1113.

Tucker, James Cory, and Matt Torrence. 2004. "Collection Development for New Librarians: Advice from the Trenches." *Library Collections, Acquisitions and Technical Services* 28, no. 4: 397–409.

4

Selection Sources
and Processes

Overview

In this chapter you will learn the theories of selection and the sources and processes used by professional librarians in developing library collections. We also examine how the selection function is carried out in most libraries. Although selection inevitably involves a lot of work, when well done, it is one of the most interesting and indeed fun areas of librarianship. Another point to keep in mind is that in the future more and more digital content will be created by the library, and selection in that case means deciding what to preserve for the long haul.

Once a collection development librarian has in hand the results of a needs assessment and has consulted the library's collection development policy, it is time to select the resources to which the library's users will have access. As discussed in Chapter 3, a collection development policy should indicate the office or library positions that have responsibility for all or part of the collection. Most such policies include a statement such as the following: "The Library Director is responsible for the overall operation of the library, including the material that is in the collection. The Library Director will delegate collection management responsibility to the Adult Services Supervisor, the Children's/YA Services Supervisor, and the Reference Services Supervisor to fulfill responsibilities to acquire, catalog, and process materials." As appropriate and correct as this sort of statement undoubtedly is for indicating who is ultimately responsible, it doesn't provide much in the way of practical guidance for the person charged with developing a library's collection. In this chapter we attempt to fill that gap.

Considerations in the Selection Process

Bases for Selection

Because the selection process is naturally at the heart of the collection development process, as discussed in Chapter 2, it is imperative for the librarian to consider the needs of the library's user community. This is the great baseline criterion. If librarians are to address successfully the many challenges presented and the opportunities that are now available through the provision and proliferation of both print and electronic information sources, it is necessary to start from a clear understanding of the library's basic missions and goals. This is a basic necessity to establish the types and kinds of library resources and services that libraries should be offering to their users. As electronic resources are added to their collections, few libraries are likely to be sufficiently prosperous to maintain both their prior levels of acquisition of traditional print materials and the simultaneous acquisition of the newer, electronic forms of materials. You have to take into account what it is that the library's users actually use, as well as what they might want to use.

The selection decisions a collection development librarian makes therefore necessarily involve a form of intellectual triage. Deciding what items to acquire necessarily implies what items to forgo, what to cut, and what to keep. This process is best grounded on a philosophical basis, determined by a needs assessment rather than an ad hoc, item-by-item basis. The latter approach is one all too often utilized by many libraries, wasting valuable limited funds and causing patron dissatisfaction due to perceived limited choices of materials.

Approaches to the Selection Process

Traditionally, public libraries have selected and typically purchased large quantities of the latest best sellers in both fiction and nonfiction. Because of the predictability of a large portion of a public library's collection, some libraries have turned over much of the selection process to vendors, with library staff concentrating only on a small percentage of the collection that is of local interest or specialized materials (see, e.g., Hoffert, 2007: 40–43). Academic libraries have done the same except that they typically acquire their "best sellers" from more of an academic or programmatic perspective.

There has been and probably always will be a dichotomy in collection development philosophy between two schools of thought: "give them what they want" (exemplified by, to exaggerate a bit, the willy-nilly purchase of best sellers described above), and, for lack of a better term, "give them what they need." Early authors on the subject of collection development often favored the view that public libraries (in the broad sense of libraries whose collections are generally available to the public) were part and parcel of the education system of the United States, responsible for continuing education and elevation of cultural standards, and therefore it was the job of the selector to choose titles that would best continue the education of the library's users. Many times it was stated that a key part of the librarian's role was to bring great works to the attention of patrons by making them readily available.

In contrast, however, later academic authors and commentators in the library field began to view libraries as an important taxpayer-subsidized public benefit or utility, implying that it was necessary for the library to serve the wants, and not just the needs, viewed through the lens of the librarian, of its users.

In 1950, Helen E. Haines provided one of the best, and certainly most eloquent, descriptions of how the role of the librarian in selecting materials reflects the theory of the public library as a vehicle for education:

> Librarianship is the only calling that devotes itself to bringing books into the common life of the world. The materials librarians work with are the materials which furnish the understanding, knowledge, and reason that can inform the mind and direct the will to meet the challenge of the time, to fit ourselves to its compulsions, to discern and guide the forces that are shaping the future. The "great trade" of publishing and bookselling, though it is the oldest and most universal agency for bringing together the reader and the printed word, has not the same range of opportunity nor the same variety and intimacy of relationship to readers of all tastes, capacities, needs, habits, and levels of education. The spirit of delight and confidence in books, the receptive and adventurous attitude toward the new and experimental, the catholicity of lifelong friendship and understanding for literature, are attributes of librarianship more than of any other calling. And those attributes must be fused in a dynamic of social consciousness, of confidence and purpose, if librarians are to rise to their potential leadership in welding public understanding and unity for the building of a safer and better world. (p. 10)

This educational theory of the library selection or collection-building process goes considerably further back than the redoubtable Ms. Haines (1950: 15), as she recognized:

> When the first convention of librarians ever held met in 1853 in New York City, their purpose was concisely stated by Charles Coffin Jewett. "We meet," he said, "to provide for the diffusion of a knowledge of good books and for enlarging the means of public access to them."

Haines's classical position becomes very clear in one of her 11 principles for selection: "[W]hile demand is primarily the basis and reason for supply, remember that the great works of literature are foundation stones in the library's own structure and therefore select some books of permanent value regardless of whether or not they will be widely used" (p. 41). By 1950, though, when the second edition of her book was written, the idea of trying to provide for public wants was seeping in, but she and most others in the field still clung steadfastly and more or less successfully to the great books as the most proper literary domain for the library.

This approach to collection development continued to hold sway generally until the 1960s, when demands for public accountability became more prominent. Librarians found that they needed to pay more attention to the expressed wants and not necessarily the educational needs of users. At this point, many public libraries began to espouse the "give them what they want" theory of selection in a major way. This change in emphasis brought more copies of best sellers, popular magazines, and genre fiction into the public library. Whether the dismay of many in the profession, who feared the effects of perhaps neglecting classical literature and what are sometimes called the great books, was justified is difficult to determine and impossible to measure, especially with the multiplicity of other sources, the rise of mass-market bookstores, and so forth. Certainly, ameliorating many of the feared deleterious effects was the considerable rise in public support for libraries over much of the last third of the 20th century. Whether the anticipated relative scarcity of public resources for library purposes, likely to result from the stagnant national economy of the first decade of the 21st century, will result in any dumbing down effect due to possible misallocation of such scarce library resources remains to be seen.

The Way Forward

However all of that controversy may play out, with the World Wide Web's introduction of the phenomenon of the Long Tail, as discussed in Chapter 1, simply picking the hits (best sellers and other mass-market materials) can no longer be enough, if it ever was (or if anyone ever did only that, which seems highly doubtful). The web's allowance for the development of more niche markets for materials of interest only to small segments of the population has, in turn, made the selecting process even more difficult for the librarian, at least in the sense that the old dichotomy seems to have broken down. Now, we have to blend "what they want" with "what they need."

It appears self-evident that local priorities and needs, as limited by any local constraints (such as those vexing but all-important limitations on funding) are basic factors that have to be considered in selecting print or electronic resources. However, sometimes in the rush to meet patron and administration demands to become more electronic (and hence more modern), a vendor who shows up on the library doorstep with an attractive short-term deal on a particular product that holds out the promise of getting the library out of a current funding jam can become an alluring alternative to a carefully considered program. Timing of decision making is a matter of paramount concern. Making decisions too hurriedly can staunch a wound, but a series of hasty decisions can and usually does eventually lead to a collection structure best described as chaotic, a problem not only for the staff but also for those users who do not understand why the library's resources appear to lack coherence and consistency. It cannot be said enough: it is extremely important for librarians with collection development responsibilities to monitor user needs and priorities. This is especially true while negotiating the tricky and rapidly changing terrain of electronic vendors and products that promise comprehensive solutions.

Web 2.0 technologies are leading us into an age of recommendations rather than just information. Finding materials is no longer the big problem it may once have been for the library that could not afford all the old traditional reference books—rather the problem is choosing what to recommend among the millions of things now available through the Internet, be it books, serials, mp3 files, DVDs, and so on. Again, it comes back to the librarian's crucial need to know the requirements and preferences of the users as the library becomes no longer just a provider of selected materials but a prime source for the recommendation of the best materials.

Traditionally, librarians have been trained, and perhaps in recent years even more emphatically, based on the principles of everything from multiculturalism to freedom of speech (both important concerns, surely), to become in some ways informationally agnostic, reluctant to tell a user that one source is really better than another. While there may be good reasons supporting this sort of thinking, in today's highly technological environment, the job of filtering sources for the patron is becoming more and more the appropriate role of the librarian. Users can easily use Google and retrieve a thousand hits on their subject, but those hits may or may not be reliable. Filtering software of various types can help, but ultimately the librarian has the responsibility to help the user find what he or she needs. And collection development intersects with this need by ensuring that the library acquires the best tools, be they books, serials, access to electronic resources, and so forth.

How can we make that intersection a successful meeting of the library and its patron? Approaches to the selection process vary, and some degree of eclecticism in method is indicated. One is not enough. Some have traditionally tried to rely almost exclusively on published reviews, including tools such as the American Library Association publication *Choice*. Book reviews have always played an important role in the selection of library materials and can prove very helpful guides, especially for libraries with small staffs and little time for much in the way of independent consideration.

However, research has shown, and the reader of almost any daily newspaper today can easily confirm, that fewer and fewer book reviews are being published each year (Johnson and Brown, 2008: 105). But the past was never a golden age, as many worthy materials were never reviewed. That is why a "bright-line" rule, such as insistence that every book or resource to be acquired must have been the subject of a published review, is often a mistake. Certainly, many first efforts by authors, including now-famous ones, were never reviewed, and small and alternative press books have always had a difficult time getting reviewed by any but the most specialized publications.

There is, thankfully, some hope for the continued use of the published review as an acquisitions tool, with many reviews now available on the web. As with any web-only source, of course, authoritativeness can be a major problem. They need to be in the mix, however.

> The catch-all phrase for recommendations and all the other tools that help you find quality in the Long Tail is filtering. These technologies and services sift through a vast array of choices to present you with the ones that are right for you. . . . [T]he role of a filter is to elevate the few products that are right for whoever is looking and suppress the many that aren't. (Anderson, 2006: 108, 116)

To measure popularity there are methods besides the *New York Times* Best Seller lists. For instance, hits on web search engines can be a valuable approach and should not be ignored; but again, some caution is in order. Although most Internet search engines today produce results vastly superior to those of early search engines, there are still problems. Google, for example, measures relevance mostly by way of incoming links, not how recent those links are. Older webpages are more likely to come to the top in a Google search than a page that a scholar put up just last night. A user may require help to find the best page from a list of results.

Original digital content from the library, faculty, staff, business organization, and so on should be a part of the selection process as well. "Born digital" content has been correctly described as promising on the basis that in the future almost any library's most important content will be its unique content. But beware, as one commentator has noted, that "it is also a source of peril because many librarians lack the awareness and technological skills to actively select, collect, and preserve this content" (Coombs, 2007: 24).

Selection Criteria

General

Everyone likes to have some general rules to live by, and collection development librarians are no different. So here are some good ones to get started with:

1. Library materials are best selected on the basis of suitability for inclusion in the collection.
2. The collection should be an unbiased source of information that represents as many points of view as possible.
3. Subjects should be covered in a manner appropriate to the library's anticipated users' needs.
4. No material should be excluded from the collection because of the race, religion, gender, national origin, sexual preference, or political view of the author, the material, or the user.

No one can or should argue with much of this these days, but a short history of librarianship will quickly reveal that some of these rules were often considered revolutionary or even subversive. That they have a fine pedigree should not, however, allow them to become selection criteria to control what a library actually acquires (within the rules, of course).

So, if we have some general rules as set out above, what are some good, general criteria to govern a selection process within those rules? Fortunately, there are some ready to hand that have stood the test of time rather well. Haines (1950: 123) succinctly states that there are "three most important ways to judge a book: by immediate personal impression received from reading it; by judgment of its usefulness or value to others; [and] by dissection and appraisal of its intrinsic qualities." Within the parameters and with the caveats discussed along the way, the following general criteria should be considered when making selections for essentially any library's collection:

1. User needs and wants as evidenced by the library's own needs assessment.
2. Holdings in other libraries available to patrons and the availability of materials via interlibrary loan or other cooperative resource-sharing agreements.
3. Relationship of the proposed acquisition to the collection—does it fill a gap or meet a need, or is it simply something fun to have?
4. Suitability for the intended audience. This criterion obviously depends greatly upon the setting and clientele of the library.
5. Public attention, including critical reviews, web hits, movies, and other positive publicity for the title.
6. Relevance to community needs. Decisions on relevance should be based on the library's needs assessment, information and requests from library users, circulation and interlibrary loan information, plus any other sources of information that reflect possible user needs.
7. Price must obviously be considered by smaller libraries as an essential criterion. If you cannot afford the $200 art book on Van Gogh, what about a less expensive version in the $50–75 range? Librarians should always be on the proverbial lookout for the best resource that they can afford to satisfy user needs.

8. Like other big decisions having long-lasting impact (where to go to college, whom to marry, etc.), choice of formats of items must be considered carefully. Does the library have access to equipment to handle formats such as microfilm, DVDs, mp3 files, and so forth? These examples show how things change over time—who has a home film projector? Or a reel-to-reel audiotape player? DVDs may already be on the way out, and what might supersede the current Blu-ray format? We don't know at this moment, but what we do know is that something will.

9. Availability for purchase. Is the material still in print or is it easily obtainable from a secondhand dealer at a reasonable price?

Specific

For the selection of an item within the rules and meeting the general criteria, the work still needs to be considered more closely. The following specific criteria are typically used when making selections for the collection, in this case for nonfiction:

1. Published recently (public libraries and school library media centers), or not. Academic and special librarians may be looking for older materials for research purposes.
2. Reputation of author and publisher.
3. Authoritative reputation (this is a broader consideration than just technical accuracy).
4. Grammatical correctness, well-presented material, accurately annotated and logically organized. This obviously falls into the realm of judgment, and sometimes only a hands-on physical examination will do in determining whether an item meets this criterion.

These are really just examples of a few points that the selector should always consider. A collection development policy should also always include specific selection criteria for the number of formats and subject areas relevant to the library for which works are being acquired.

Electronic Resources

Electronic materials have become a major part of virtually every library's acquisition process and budget. Here, while the rules and criteria described above continue to have relevance and applicability, special criteria have to be considered. The following questions should always be asked when selecting electronic resources (Gregory, 2006: 18–20):

- Is the resource authoritative? Determining the accuracy of materials available through an electronic resource, particularly those derived from web resources, is critical to the selection and evaluation process. One of the strengths of the World Wide Web is the ease of publication and distribution of information to the world; however, this strength is also its greatest weakness since it essentially places the burden on the information user to determine and evaluate the source of the website's information (i.e., to do the very thing that collection development policies have traditionally attempted to do for libraries and their patrons over the years).

- Does the technology make the content of the electronic resource accessible in a manner that better serves users' needs than does an existing equivalent print resource that the library already maintains or could acquire, perhaps at a lower cost? Some electronic products may actually be more difficult to use than their print counterparts, but others will offer significant improvements in the ways that a user can search for needed information.

- Does the electronic resource fill current gaps in the print collection? Electronic products should not be acquired simply because they are available and attractive; rather, they should add needed resources to the library's collection.

- Does the electronic resource duplicate information or material that is already owned by the library? Due to the common practice of the bundling of electronic resources, libraries may sometimes find themselves forced to accept some duplication that would have never been contemplated or tolerated with print resources.

- Will the library replace a current print resource with an electronic resource, and what are the price ramifications of doing so? Some electronic resources do cost less, but only if the library also takes the print version. Some publishers require the library to pay for the print version to be eligible to subscribe to the electronic one. On the other hand, some electronic resources really do cost less than their print equivalent, and in the case of those that are frequently supplemented, such as tax or legal services and reporters, the savings in filing labor costs can be enormous. Some electronic resources carry an additional cost (above the price for the current version or issue) for access to their archives. In addition to price, one should also consider whether the electronic resource contains everything that is in the print version. Are all articles included in the electronic version? Are advertisements or illustrations deleted? Is the electronic product as well indexed as the print version? Is there an index at all or is there exclusive reliance on word searches, for example? Are any deletions in the electronic version important to your users?

- If the electronic resource is licensed and not available for purchase (see Chapter 7 for more on licensing issues), can the library continue to meet its current obligations to local or state consortia in regard to interlibrary loan or user access to materials if some materials are only available in restricted form? Although it is unlikely that the boilerplate license will allow interlibrary loans, sometimes it is possible to negotiate terms that allow such activity.

- Does the electronic resource require the purchase of additional computer hardware or software? Will it run on your current operating platform? For cost considerations, the selector may have to ensure that the format of an electronic resource is compatible with existing library hardware and software (unless equipment money is available to support simultaneous purchases of hardware).
- If an electronic product is selected, what format is the most appropriate to meet the library's needs? For example, would a CD-ROM product or an online product best meet the needs of the library and its users?
- Does your library have enough computer resources to handle the additional user traffic that this product would likely generate? For small libraries, adding an electronic resource can be a significant problem; they simply may not have enough computers or suitable space for patrons to access the new resource in a reasonable amount of time, particularly if the library must cease carrying print versions to be able to purchase the electronic equivalent. A large set of print books, such as a multivolume encyclopedia, might be expected to be used by a number of patrons at the same time, but if you only have one computer that can access a particular resource (or a number of electronic resources), only one person will be able to access the resource at a time.

Selection Teams

Instead of relying on individual selectors for the final decisions, many libraries today utilize a team approach, particularly for the selection of electronic resources or other big-ticket items. This approach is similar in some ways to the methods that many public libraries traditionally used to select audiovisual materials. Such teams should include members from both public services and technical services departments. Bringing together a team with both subject and technical expertise is the most effective method for selection of any material that is expensive and requires equipment or software for use. Each group's expertise and experience can be brought to bear, hopefully with the result that the selection does not turn out to be one that, owing to some technical difficulty or shortcoming, cannot be utilized as anticipated.

A carefully chosen team of no more than three to five members (any more than that and you have a conference or convention, not a team) can usually then manage subject matter considerations and technical matters, and gather patron and staff input as appropriate. The team can also be responsible for other related activities as well, for instance, for producing documentation and training sessions after a new electronic resource is acquired. In addition, by establishing a planning and reviewing cycle with specified actions to occur at regular intervals, the team can go a long way toward helping to bring order to a potentially chaotic process if the new product differs significantly from the old that it is replacing. Because electronic products are still used in a rather unstable environment (i.e., the personal computer), an electronic acquisitions team approach requires team members to be open minded and flexible. Change is a constant and selectors must be able to make decisions in environments that are often more murky than crystal clear.

In academic libraries, subject specialists and bibliographers will generally work best together as a team when considering big-ticket purchases. For less expensive electronic purchases, an individual bibliographer may need to work only with the person dealing with copyright and licensing issues. Yet another approach recently utilized in academic libraries (and some large public libraries) is to use the patrons themselves as a de facto selection team, letting user requests, ILL requests, and other expressions of needs determine items to be purchased.

Some libraries have a single librarian or maybe two that are in charge of selecting electronic materials. This may be the same librarian who is responsible for keeping up with the library's copyright, digital rights management, and licensing issues. This should be avoided, if possible, because while the difficulties of managing electronic resources should not be ignored, they should nevertheless not be allowed to become a paramount consideration in the selection process—something that can easily happen when those who have to struggle with them are also the ones charged with selecting them.

Selection Differences for Internet Resources

Although most selection criteria used for determining the appropriateness of print resources apply equally to Internet resources, a number of important distinctions need to be kept in mind:

1. The librarian is truly only selecting materials, not collecting them. Internet resources are likely to be housed on the library's computer only temporarily; the resources are merely accessed from the library's catalog or website.
2. The librarian may choose items that in print form were never considered for purchase. For example, the library may have acquired few pamphlets due to problems in cataloging, shelving, and making the items available. The equivalent publication on the web obviously does not present the same handling problems for the library.
3. Cost is not likely to be a factor, at least in terms of purchase price for the item, but the librarian must consider the overall cost of maintaining links to the resource. A resource that is constantly moving and requires constant URL maintenance and updating, either in the catalog or on the library's website, may well be so frustrating as to be deemed not worth the effort, even if the information it provides is of good quality.
4. Selection of Internet resources tends to take place at a sort of macro level, while most print decisions tend to be made at the micro level. That is

to say, Internet resources are typically chosen in a more generalized manner. Selecting Internet resources, therefore, can quickly lead to more duplication and can result in the need for users to examine more unneeded or inappropriate resources to get to the ones they actually need. It is also important to remember that by selecting a website, you are in effect selecting everything that is linked from that page, and not all of those links will necessarily be needed by your library's users.

5. On the other hand, while print resources are much more likely than online materials to be chosen without actual examination of the item but rather through reviews or approval plans, Internet resources will typically be chosen only after personal examination by the selector. However, a number of the traditional selection tools are beginning to include reviews of websites, so the practice of choosing Internet resources may tend to become, over time, more similar to the methods traditionally used for selecting print resources.

6. Some of the library's Internet resources may be actually created or published by the library itself, which is not often the case for traditional print resources.

7. Access is a critical issue. If the server on which the resource resides is overtaxed and therefore slow to respond, or if it is often not available at all, the resource will probably not be selected by the library; likewise, technical reliability problems, no matter how accurate and authoritative the information provided by the site may be, can become a paramount concern if significant difficulties are encountered. An additional access issue involves the number of users who may have simultaneous access to a single item. A single-volume print document may typically be accessed by only one user at a time, but the same resource, when made available on the web, may be accessed effectively by numerous if not an unlimited number of simultaneous users.

8. Archiving and preservation issues are obviously much more problematic with Internet resources than for traditional print materials. Quality websites come and go at the site owner's discretion (and sometimes whim), but a print resource, unless stolen, lost, or mutilated, will typically remain in the library's collection for a very considerable time.

Tools for Acquiring and Selecting Materials

Current Books and Serials

- All About Romance (http://www.likesbooks.com) is a site mainly intended for lovers of the genre, but librarians can access reviews of new books that are much more detailed than the genre usually receives in the mainstream review sources. There are staff reviews and reader reviews on this site.

- *American Book Publishing Record (APBR)*, published by R. R. Bowker (http://www.bowker.com/index.php/component/content/article/27), is designed specifically for librarians. *APBR* has approximately 10,000 new titles each month. It is arranged in three parts: the main section is organized by Dewey Decimal Classification number with the remaining adult fiction and juvenile fiction arranged alphabetically by main entry author or title.

- *American Reference Books Annual* (ARBAonline, http://www.arbaonline.com/) is produced by Libraries Unlimited. ARBAonline has approximately 18,000 reviews of reference works published since 1997. Written by librarians for librarians, ARBAonline's reviews cover reference sources from more than 400 publishers in over 500 subject areas. ARBAonline is updated monthly. More than 500 reviewers—all experts in their fields—provide thorough content evaluations that cover strengths and weaknesses of each reference resource and in many cases compare reference publications to similar titles, giving the librarian relevant information about titles that best fit their requirements.

- *Book Review Digest*, published by H. W. Wilson, provides excerpts from and citations to reviews of current adult and juvenile fiction and nonfiction. In recent years over 8,000 English-language books generally have been covered by the database each year. Concise, critical evaluations are chosen from 109 leading American, British, and Canadian periodicals in the humanities and social and general sciences, as well as library review media. Covering a wide range of review media and offering an enormous variety of reviews—all carefully excerpted to convey the diversity of critical opinion on a title—the digest is an excellent source for anyone needing to obtain information about new books.

- *Book Review Index (BRI)*, produced by Thomson Gale, contains references to more than 4,000,000 reviews of approximately 2,000,000 distinct book and periodical titles. The file dates from 1969 to the present and covers every review published in nearly 500 periodicals and newspapers. Each record includes the author and title of the work being reviewed, journal name, date of review, and page number. Document type indications are also included if the work is a children's book, periodical, children's periodical, young adult periodical, reference work, or young adult book. Approximately 500 periodicals and newspapers are currently indexed by *BRI* (retrospective coverage varies). *BRI* offers broad subject coverage due to the range of sources indexed. Subjects include the social sciences, the humanities, the sciences, business, the fine arts, and general interest areas.

- *Booklist* is published by the American Library Association (http://www.ala.org/ala/booklist/booklist.cfm) and is intended to provide a guide to current library materials in many formats appropriate for use in public libraries and school library media centers. The needs of small and medium-sized libraries receive special consideration in all selection decisions. All materials reviewed in the Adult Books, Books for Youth, and Media sections are recommended for purchase by libraries and media centers. No negative reviews are published. This recommended-only policy, in place since *Booklist*'s founding in 1905, has been adapted over the decades to reflect changes in the philosophy of public library service. Thus, materials are recommended for reasons relating to both quality and anticipated demand by library users.

- *Books in Print* (http://www.booksinprint.com/bip/) is produced by R. R. Bowker, and is available in print, CD-ROM, and web formats. The *Books in Print* database offers valuable information on more than 6 million U.S. book, audiobook, and video titles, as well as another 10 million international titles, making it the industry's largest bibliographic database. This is an indispensable resource for booksellers, publishers, and librarians. It offers reviews, tables of contents, full-text previews, cover images, author biographies, awards information, annotations, and much more. BooksInPrint.com Professional offers extensive bibliographic information on over 6 million in-print, out-of-print, and forthcoming book, e-book, audio, and video titles. BooksInPrint.com features over 220,000 tables of contents, 2.5 million annotations, and over 1 million reviews of titles by more than 370,000 publishers, as well as extensive cover images and author biographies.

- *Choice* is published by the American Library Association (http://www.ala.org/ala/acrl/acrlpubs/choice/home.cfm) and is the selection tool most commonly used by college libraries. *Choice* publishes nearly 7,000 reviews annually, spanning all academic disciplines. Reviews are written by teaching faculty and academic librarians, and they are generally the first professional postpublication reviews of scholarly works. *Choice* reviews books and electronic resources appropriate for libraries serving students at the undergraduate level, including community college or lower-division undergraduates. *Choice* selectively reviews graduate-level materials when they have value for advanced undergraduates or honor students. Strictly professional works are excluded, as are foreign-language materials and most reprints and undergraduate textbooks.

- Criticas Spanish Language Authors and Book Reviews (http://www.criticasmagazine.com/csp/cms/sites/LJ/Reviews/Spanish/index.csp) has the latest English-language review coverage of Spanish-language authors, book reviews (*criticas libros*), best sellers, and more from the editors of *Library Journal* and *School Library Journal*. In response to reader demand following the suspension of the hardcopy *Criticas* in February 2009, *LJ* and *SLJ* have resumed reviewing Spanish-language books for adults and children. Adult books will be reviewed monthly, and children's titles every other month. The reviews are written by librarians.

- *Guide to Reference* is published by the American Library Association (http://www.guidetoreference.org/index.html). The *Guide to Reference* is one of the cornerstones of the literature in reference for academic librarianship. The online edition makes use of the web's capacities to connect information sources; it also creates and links to content that makes it a center for learning about and practicing reference librarianship. *Guide to Reference* describes resources for academic libraries supporting curricula for undergraduate and graduate students, the research efforts of faculty and other academic staff, and the advanced information needs of the public. It is both selective and broad in coverage, identifying the best available reference sources in a range of academic disciplines.
- *Historical Fiction Review* (http://www.historical novel society.org/the-review.htm) is published quarterly by the Historical Novel Society. It is the best and most complete guide to the latest historical fiction in the world. Besides book reviews, the magazine also features author interviews, feature articles, and letters from subscribers.
- *Horn Book Guide* is published by Horn Book, Inc. It rates and concisely reviews over 2,000 titles in each semiannual issue—virtually every children's and young adult book published in the United States in a six-month period. Five indispensable indexes, including an extensive subject index, make the *guide* a primary resource for librarians, classroom teachers, booksellers, and professors of children's literature. The publisher also produces the Horn Book Guide Online, which offers access to a searchable database of over 70,000 book reviews from 1989 to the present.
- *Kirkus Reviews* (http://www.KirkusReviews.com) is available online and also biweekly in a print edition that has been published since 1933. *Kirkus* reviews more than 500 prepublication books each month, including fiction, nonfiction, children's, and young adult books. *Kirkus* does not review books that have already been published. *Kirkus* does, however, consider for review any previously unpublished, but already contracted, titles that are submitted in galley form at least three to four months before publication date.
- *Library Journal (LJ)*, published by Reed Business Information, devotes a large percentage of its pages to review sections that evaluate nearly 7,000 books annually, along with hundreds of audiobooks, videos, databases, websites, and computer systems that libraries buy. Books are selected for their potential interest to a broad spectrum of libraries. Only a few areas of publishing fall outside *LJ*'s scope: textbooks, children's books, very technical or specialized works, and books in languages other than English.
- *Magazines for Libraries* is published by R. R. Bowker (http://www. bowker. com/index.php/component/content/article/488), providing

essential information, useful statistics, and comparative data to help librarians support their collection decisions. *Magazines for Libraries* has more than 6,850 full-text reviews and recommendations from nearly 200 subject specialists. Libraries of all types can benefit from this critical evaluation of journals, magazines, and databases to create and maintain quality collections of all sizes.

- Mystery Ink (http://www.mysteryinkonline.com) reviews mysteries and thrillers as well as providing interviews with authors. This site is edited by David J. Montgomery, who writes about authors and books for the *Chicago Sun Times,* the *Philadelphia Inquirer,* the *Boston Globe,* and the *South Florida Sun-Sentinel.*

- *Publishers Weekly,* published by Reed Business Information, is the industry's leading news magazine, covering every aspect of creating, producing, marketing, and selling the written word in book, audio, video, and electronic formats. There are 51 issues per year, targeted at publishers, librarians, booksellers, and literary agents. Subject areas covered by *Publishers Weekly* include bookstores, book design and manufacture, bookselling, marketing, merchandising, and trade news, along with author interviews and regular columns on film rights, people in publishing, and best sellers. It attempts to serve all involved in the creation, production, marketing, and sale of the written word in book, audio, video, and electronic formats. It reviews 7,000 new books per year and is likely the large public library's primary selection tool.

- *Reader's Advisor* is published by Libraries Unlimited of the Greenwood Publishing Group and is now offered online (http://rainfo.lu.com/ product.aspx). Reader's Advisor Online is a sophisticated finding tool for reader's advisor practitioners. The content in Reader's Advisor Online is not available elsewhere. It includes all the volumes in Libraries Unlimited's well-known *Genreflecting* series, and contains selected essays from the *Readers' Advisor's Companion* and *Nonfiction Readers' Advisory,* and more. This site also aids book groups. As it refines searching to look for books, it is recommended as suitable for book groups.

- SF Site (http://www.sfsite.com) reviews the best in science fiction and fantasy, in print, audio, and other media, whether on the web, in print, or other formats. In addition to reviews, the site also contains interviews with authors and artists.

- *School Library Journal (SLJ)* is published by Reed Business Information (http://www.schoollibraryjournal.com/info/CA6409015.html). *SLJ* serves librarians who work with students in school and public libraries, reaching an audience of more than 100,000. The world's largest and most authoritative reviewer of children's and young adult content—principally books, but also including audio, video, and the web—the magazine and its website provide 38,000 subscribers with information indispensable in making purchasing decisions. In addition to its reviews, *SLJ*'s news, features, columns, and departments deliver the perspective, resources, and leadership tools necessary for its readers to become indispensable players in their schools and libraries. *SLJ*'s reviews are written by librarians working directly with children and young adults in schools or public libraries, library school educators, teachers of children's literature, and subject specialists. They evaluate books in terms of literary quality, artistic merit, clarity of presentation, and appeal to the intended audience. They also make comparisons between new titles and materials already available in most collections and mention curriculum connections. Grade levels are assigned by reviewers based on their expertise with readers.

- *Serials Review* is a quarterly peer-reviewed scholarly journal for the international serials community published by Elsevier (http://www.elsevier.com/wps/find/journaldescription.cws_home/620213/description#description). Articles focus on serials in the broadest sense of the term and cover all aspects of serials information; regular columns feature interviews, exchanges on controversial topics, book reviews, and conference reports. *Serials Review* includes all aspects of serials management: format considerations, publishing models, statistical studies, collection analysis, collaborative efforts, reference and access issues, cataloging and acquisitions, people who have shaped the serials community, and topical bibliographic studies. The journal also examines emerging and changing standards, methods of delivery, innovations, and a multitude of other issues that contribute to the essence of understanding, managing, and publishing serials in a comprehensive, complex, and global environment.

- *Ulrich's International Periodicals Directory* is published by R. R. Bowker (http://www.ulrichsweb.com/ulrichsweb/prodDescriptions.asp). Ulrichsweb.com contains authoritative information about more than 300,000 serials of all types from around the world—academic and scholarly journals, peer-reviewed titles, online publications, newspapers, and other resources. The *Ulrich* records provide details such as ISSN and title, publisher, online availability, language, subject area, abstracting and indexing coverage, a database searchable by table of contents, and full-text reviews. *Ulrich's* is an important tool for reference, research, and serials management. This database provides information on virtually every active and ceased periodical, annual, irregular publication, and monographic series published throughout the world, plus thousands of newspapers.

- *Voice of Youth Advocates (VOYA)* is owned by Scarecrow Press and published bimonthly. The journal addresses librarians, educators, and other professionals who work with young adults and is the only magazine devoted exclusively to the informational needs of teenagers.

In addition to the previous sources, many websites and blogs by librarians and book lovers may be helpful in selection. One example of this type of site is BookBitch (http://www.bookbitch.com). Stacy Alesi, the creator of the site, also has a blog and a Facebook page that have reviews and discussion of new books. Many more such sites are available on the web, with more being added all the time.

Antiquarian and Out-of-Print Books and Serials

- AcqWeb Directory: Rare and Antiquarian Book Vendors (http://www. library.vanderbilt.edu/law/aqs/pubr/rare.html) contains a list of websites of rare and antique booksellers.
- Advanced Book Exchange is owned by AbeBooks, Inc. (http://www. abebooks.com/docs/RareBooks/). This site offers scarce first editions of sought-after signatures. AbeBooks offers an array of rare, valuable, and highly collectible books. The Rare Book Room is the entrée into this remarkable collection, regularly featuring a selection of the booksellers' most precious items. The Collector's Corner features a Rare Bookseller Directory, articles from the newsletter, information on book care as well as book fairs and events, links to Easton Press (all leatherbound books), and a collection of first editions for sale.
- Alibris (http://www.alibris.com) is an excellent source for used books, textbooks, CDs, and DVDs. If a work has gone out of print before the library could obtain it, Alibris is a good place to begin searching. Bibliocity has recently joined with Alibris to make this site an excellent one for rare as well as used materials.
- Amazon.com (http://www.amazon.com) covers a wide range of used and rare materials through its website. The out-of-print searcher can look for books using many options, including publication date and format. Search results can be limited by collectability and condition.
- Biblio, Inc. has a direct link for rare books (http://www.biblio.com/ ltd/). Biblio brings together over 5,500 independent booksellers from around the world and offers millions of select rare, old, used, antique, and out-of-print books from the 18th–20th centuries including rare photography books, old adventure and art history books, children's classics, rare historical fiction, literary criticism, rare antique military history, paleontology, poetry, and much more.
- Bibliofind (http://www.amazon.com/gp/browse.html?node=299899011) has combined with Amazon.com to provide millions of rare, used, and out-of-print books through the online bookstore.
- BookFinder.com (http://www.bookfinder.com/about/) is a one-stop e-commerce search engine that searches over 150 million books for sale—new, used, rare, out of print, and textbooks. It saves you time and money by searching every major catalog online and letting you know which booksellers are offering the best prices and selection.

- Powell's Books (http://www.powells.com/rareandcollectible.html) carries about 9,000 volumes in their rare book collection. They offer an advanced search (with the options to limit for first edition or signed editions), rare book basics, and trivia; browsing by category or author is available.

Electronic Resources

To make good selection decisions regarding electronic materials, you will first need to gather a group of titles with review information using both a local and global information perspective. Therefore, it is important to determine a set of resources to be used to gather titles and then to apply criteria to select among various materials having a similar subject matter focus. The selector will be looking for tools, such as the following, that can help answer a variety of questions:

- *Current Cites* (http://lists.webjunction.org/currentcites) is an electronic newsletter that contains useful reviews of numerous electronic resources as well as print sources in various areas of information technology.
- *eReviews* (http://www.libraryjournal.com/article/CA6635801.html) is a section of the *Library Journal* website where Cheryl LaGuardia, Research Librarian, Widener Library, Harvard University, reviews newly released or updated electronic resources. Her reviews are both descriptive and evaluative.
- *iGuides* (http://www.iguides.org) is a web-based directory of web resources and Internet guides. It is a human-edited Internet resource with, by editorial policy, each review, listing, and article being reviewed by an editor. It organizes the guides and resources by broad subject areas, from Arts and Humanities to Health to Transporters and Inductors, along with many additional topics.
- *Infomine* (http://infomine.ucr.edu) is one of the best sites for getting announcements of academic-quality Internet resources. Nearly all academic disciplines are represented.
- *Intute* (http://www.intute.ac.uk). This directory, produced in the United Kingdom, is one of the few such directories to have a published collection policy. Selectors are subject specialists, so the resources are generally of high quality. The future of *Intute* is uncertain after July 2011.
- *NewJour* (http://library.georgetown.edu/newjour/NewJourWel.html), an electronic discussion list, can help you identify new electronic journals.
- *Scout Report* (http://www.scout.wisc.edu/Reports/ScoutReport/Current/) is a weekly electronic publication produced both as a website and a weekly e-mail that provides reviews of valuable resources on the web.

General Review Sources Online

The following is just a sampling of the sources that are available on the web to help in selection. Although the focus of these websites is on print sources, some popular electronic products are reviewed.

- Amazon.com (http://www.amazon.com) provides access from its web- site to various lists of best books, videos, CD-ROMs, and other materi- als. The selector also has access to peer reviews and standard review media. Some selectors find the peer reviews from readers to be helpful; they feel that the peer reviews may be more in touch with the materials that their users are likely to want or like.
- Barnes and Noble (http://www.barnesandnoble.com) offers services similar to those of Amazon.com, including peer reviews of materials. This site has links to resellers of books with the ability to order through the Barnes and Noble website.
- *BookWire* (http://www.bookwire.com) contains reviews and links to other review sources such as the *Boston Book Review* and *Hungry Mind Review.*
- Borders (http://www.borders.com). The website of this book chain is noteworthy for its reviews and links to the *New York Times Book Review.*

A large number of blogs and other online reviewing sources are available on the web. Some of these are more authoritative than others. "Over the past 15 years, the book review landscape has changed seismically. Reviewing is no longer centralized, with a few big voices leading the way, but fractured among numerous multifarious voices found mostly on the web. In turn, read- ers aren't playing the captive audience any more" (Hoffert, 2010: 22). Readers are busy talking about books on the web through a number of sites. Some of these sites may be helpful to selectors, at least in getting a popular opinion of books that may or may not be covered by one of the more authoritative review sources.

Other Selection Means

In addition to being reviewed in more or less traditional ways, whether in print publications or on the web, electronic resources often lend themselves well to other means of evaluation, including the following:

- Trial offers: Vendors of electronic resources may allow you to mount or link to their materials without cost for a trial period. After the trial period, one must either purchase or license the materials to continue using them. Trials are often advertised through e-mail and library web- sites. Thus more users are likely to try the products and offer advice to the selector than is likely to be the case for traditional print materials.

Some libraries (and publishers) limit trial offers to staff use, but others open them up to their entire user population so that feedback from users, along with usage statistics, can be utilized in the final selection decision process. You will want to make sure that the trial conditions are equivalent to the actual use conditions that would apply if you purchased or licensed the product and that you do not receive a poor demonstration version.

- Demonstrations: Vendors will often be willing to come to your library and demonstrate their electronic products to you. Again, be sure that the conditions of the demonstration are as close as possible to what they would be if the product were purchased or licensed. For example, you don't want to see a demonstration of a web product at 8:00 a.m. on Monday when web traffic would probably be much lower than on, say, Wednesday at 3:00 p.m. Trade shows at library conferences are also a good way to get the feel of the product. Librarians can use the demonstrations at trade shows to hone in on the particular systems that they would like to see demonstrated to the entire library staff locally.

- Visits to other libraries: Another way to gauge the usefulness of a product is to visit a similar library that already has the product and to see it in action there. This approach also provides the opportunity to talk with that library's staff about the product and their experience with it. To be really useful, the library that is visited should have a technological setup and user base similar to yours.

- Vending machines: Some public libraries are experimenting with rental kiosks for new DVDs. Such kiosks are popping up in many locations. Library users can insert their money and make their selections. The libraries thus have the latest materials without having to do any selection, and as with drink and snack vending machines they may get a small percentage of the take. Other libraries make them free to users with the swipe of their library card. Library selectors can then concentrate on educational and other "more serious" titles.

Open Access Movement

Another consideration in the selection process involves open access journals, which make scholarly publications available online at no charge, and have greatly reduced the cost of publication while at the same time greatly increasing the distribution and availability of information. Public libraries should be aware of the new opportunities for selection of titles that previously may not have been within their budget.

All of the major library professional associations have issued statements in support of open access, including the Association of Research Libraries, the Association of College and Research Libraries, and the International Federation of Library Associations and Institutions. Other prominent organizations that support open access include the Budapest Open Access Initiative, the Scholarly Publishing and Academic Resources Coalition, the Public Library of Science (PloS), and many others.

A few examples of open access journals include *First Monday,* which began publication in 1996 and was one of the first peer-reviewed open access journals (http://www.firstmonday.org). PloS publishes two open access journals, *PloS Biology* and *PloS Medicine,* and has announced two new journals, *PloS Computational Biology* and *PloS Genetics.* To see a list of open access publications, go to the Directory of Open Access Journals (http://www.doaj.org).

In open access publishing, the standard commercial copyright contract has been modified in one of several ways. In one model used by many electronic journals, the author retains copyright and the journal simply obtains first publication rights. Many examples of this copyright modification can be found at Directory of Open Access Journals. Another popular model used by many open access journals, including the PloS, is called the Creative Commons Attributions License (http://creativecommons.org/licenses/by-nc-sa/1.0/).

Another way to look at open access materials is to look at what is actually delivered to users. Open access repositories that are sometimes viewed as "green" are not peer reviewed before being made available and are often not the final version that would be published in a peer-reviewed journal. The American Society for Information Science & Technology (ASIS&T) Digital Library, which is managed by Wiley Blackwell, allows authors to put their last version of the article in an institutional repository or on their own website. The edited article, which has been peer reviewed, is only available from the Wiley Blackwell site, in pay-per-view if the user is not a member of ASIS&T. So-called gold open access repositories only have peer-reviewed articles.

It is still too early to know how widespread and successful the open access movement will prove to be, but currently it offers new opportunities for libraries to add electronic journals to their collections without hurting their pocketbooks.

Selection in today's libraries involves not just the traditional factors and criteria, but a number of new technical and cost factors as well. The tendency of vendors to bundle or package various resources, titles, and images has changed much of the selection process from a title-by-title approach to an aggregate approach. This change involves some new decisions about the tolerable amount of duplication, consideration of differences in search engines, analysis of differences in ease of use of the product, and other similar factors. Open access electronic journals provide another source of resources for librarians to select for their libraries without any additional costs beyond their existing networking and telecommunications costs. Nevertheless, the librarian's role and judgment in the selection process remains important, including the increasing use of teams, especially in connection with the acquisition of electronic resources and materials. Various emerging technical issues may be better addressed through a team approach incorporating members having both subject matter and information technology expertise.

Vocabulary

authoritativeness	born digital content
collecting versus selecting	collections
Creative Commons	open access journals
open access repositories	PloS review sources
selection teams	

Activity

Divide the class into several groups. There should be one group for each of the major types of libraries. Each group should assume that they have been hired to be the professional staff of a brand new library, and they must select the opening-day collection. What review sources and other resources would you use to select titles or particular subject areas in the new collection? Justify your procedures.

Discussion Questions

1. What is a collection? Consider collections in their broadest sense and then narrow to library collections.
2. Would you ever select a book for your library for which you could not find a review or a favorable review? What factors might influence your decision?
3. What do you think about using reviews from websites such as Amazon. com? How reliable are such reviews? Should they be treated the same way as, for example, a review in *Booklist*?
4. Do best sellers or graphic novels belong in the academic library collection? Why or why not?
5. Assume that a needs assessment has determined that your library needs more foreign language material, predictably in Spanish, but also in several of the Eastern European languages (Polish, Hungarian, and Czech). How would you go about searching for titles in the various languages, most of which you do not speak or read yourself? What criteria would you use for selection of titles in these languages?
6. From the perspective of having a well-balanced collection, should a librarian feel compelled to select a certain number of titles from the Holocaust denial literature? Why or why not?

References

Anderson, Chris. 2006. *The Long Tail: Why the Future of Business Is Selling Less of More*. New York: Hyperion.

Coombs, Karen. 2007. "Digital Promise and Peril." *Netconnect* (Summer): 24.

Gregory, Vicki L. 2006. *Selecting and Managing Electronic Resources*. Rev. ed. New York: Neal-Schuman.

Haines, Helen E. 1950. *Living with Books*. 2nd ed. New York: Columbia University Press

Hoffert, Barbara. 2007. "Who's Selecting Now?" *Library Journal* 132 (September 1): 40–43.

———. 2010. "Every Reader a Reviewer." *Library Journal* 135 (September 1): 22–25.

Johnson, Liz, and Linda A. Brown. 2008. "Book Reviews by the Numbers." *Collection Management* 33, nos. 1/2: 83–113.

Selected Readings

Austenfeld, Annie Marie. 2009. "Building the College Library Collection to Support Curriculum Growth." *Collection Building* 34 (July–September): 209–227.

Bailey, Charles W. 2007. "Open Access and Libraries." *Collection Management* 32, nos. 3/4: 351–383.

Bielke-Rodenbiker, Jean. 2004. "Review Sources for Mysteries." *Collection Management* 29, nos. 3/4: 53–71.

Chen, Shu-Hsien Lai. 2002. "Diversity in School Library Media Center Resources." In *Educational Media and Technology Yearbook*, Vol. 27, edited by Mary Ann Fitzgerald, Michael Orey, and Robert Maribe Branch, 168–187. Englewood Cliffs, CO: Libraries Unlimited.

Chu, F. T. 1997. "Librarian-Faculty Relations in Collection Development." *Journal of Academic Librarianship* 23 (January): 15–20.

Crawford, Gregory A., and Matthew Harris. 2001. "Best-Sellers in Academic Libraries." *College and Research Libraries* 62 (May): 216–225.

Dick, Jeff T. 2009. "Bracing for Blu-Ray." *Library Journal* 134 (November): 33–35.

Dilevko, Juris, and Lisa Gottlieb. 2003. "The Politics of Standard Selection Guides: The Case of the *Public Library Catalog*." *Library Quarterly* 73 (July): 289–337.

Donatich, John. 2009. "Why Books Still Matter." *Journal of Scholarly Publishing* 40 (July): 329–342.

Downey, Elizabeth M. 2009. "Graphic Novels in Curriculum and Instruction Collections." *Reference and User Services Quarterly* 49 (December): 181–188.

Fenner, Audrey, ed. 2004. *Selecting Materials for Library Collections*. Binghamton, NY: Haworth Information Press. Copublished as *Acquisitions Librarian* nos. 31/32 (2004).

Gherman, Paul M. 2005. "Collecting at the Edge—Transforming Scholarship." *Journal of Library Administration* 42, no. 2: 23–34.

Gregory, Cynthia L. 2008. "'But I Want a Real Book': An Investigation of Undergraduates' Usage and Attitudes toward Electronic Books." *Reference and User Services Quarterly* 47 (Spring): 366–373.

Guedon, Jean-Claude. 2008. "Mixing and Matching the Green and Gold Roads to Open Access—Take 2." *Serials Review* 34, no. 1: 41–51.

Hiebert, Jean T. 2009. "Beyond Mark and Park: Classification Mapping as a Collection Development Tool for Psychiatry/Psychology." *Collection Management* 34 (July–September): 182–193.

Hoffert, Barbara. 2007. "Who's Selecting Now?" *Library Journal* 132 (September 1): 40–43.

Jobe, Margaret M., and Michael Levine-Clark. 2008. "Use and Non-use of *Choice*-Reviewed Titles in Undergraduate Libraries." *Journal of Academic Librarianship* 34 (July): 295–304.

Koehn, Shona L., and Suliman Hawamdeh. 2010. "The Acquisition and Management of Electronic Resources: Can We Justify the Cost?" *Library Quarterly* 80 (April): 161–174.

Kopak, Rick. 2008. "Open Access and the Open Journal Systems: Making Sense All Over." *School Libraries Worldwide* 14, no. 2: 45–54.

Lee, Hur-Li. 2000. "What Is a Collection?" *Journal of the American Society for Information Science* 51 (October): 1106–1113.

McCulloch, Emma. 2006. "Taking Stock of Open Access: Progress and Issues." *Library Review* 55, no. 6: 337–343.

Mulcahy, Kevin P. 2006. "Science Fiction Collections in ARL Academic Libraries." *College and Research Libraries* 67 (January): 15–34.

Neal, Kathryn M. 2002. "Cultivating Diversity: The Donor Collection." *Collection Management* 27, no. 2: 33–42.

O'English, Lorena, J. Gregory, and Elizabeth Blakesley Lindsay. 2006. "Graphic Novels in Academic Libraries: From *Maus* to Manga and Beyond." *Journal of Academic Librarianship* 32 (March): 173–182.

Pool, Gail. 2007. *Faint Praise: The Plight of Book Reviewing in America*. Columbia: University of Missouri Press.

Randall, William M. 1931. "What Can the Foreigner Find to Read in the Public Library?" *Library Quarterly* 1: 79–88.

Rathe, Bette, and Lisa Blankenship. 2005. "Recreational Reading Collections in Academic Libraries." *Collection Management* 30, no. 2: 73–85.

Strothmann, Molly, and Connie Van Fleet. 2009. "Books That Inspire, Books That Offend." *Reference and User Services Quarterly* 49 (Winter): 163–179.

Sullivan, Kathleen. 2004. "Beyond Cookie-Cutter Selection." *Library Journal* 129 (June 15): 44–46.

Van Orden, Phyllis J. 2000. *Selecting Books for the Elementary School Library Media Center.* New York: Neal-Schuman.

Van Orsdel, Lee C., and Kathleen Born. 2008. "Periodicals Pricing Survey 2008: Embracing Openness." *Library Journal* 133 (April 15): 53–58.

Wagner, Cassie. 2010. "Graphic Novel Collections in Academic ARL Libraries." *College and Research Libraries* 71 (January): 42–48.

Willinsky, John. 2003. "The Nine Flavors of Open Access Scholarly Publishing." *Journal of Postgraduate Medicine* 49, no. 3: 263–267.

5

Acquisitions

Since some library information science programs do not include a separate course on acquisitions, it is important to include the basics in a collection development textbook. Because there is so much material to cover, Chapters 5 and 6 should be taken as an overview and not an in-depth coverage of acquisitions equivalent to a semester-long class.

Overview

Library acquisition processes have changed immensely over the last two decades. Most of the changes involve electronic processes and resources, both of which have changed the library more than any other period since the invention of the movable-type printing press. Although the process and the format may be electronic instead of print, the concept of acquisitions remains the same: acquiring (in any format) the materials that library users need.

In a nutshell, library acquisitions can be simply described as the process of locating and then acquiring the materials previously identified through the collection development processes.

> Acquisitions departments are responsible for getting the materials needed by library users, in the most appropriate format and in the most efficient manner. Formats and methods change, but the responsibility and the functions of acquiring library materials remain at the core of the acquisitions department. (Wilkinson and Lewis, 2003: 9)

The Principal Goal of Library Acquisitions

Virtually every library would lack a raison d'être without the existence and use of its resources by those persons who used to be referred to as patrons and nowadays, more accurately perhaps, as users (or in some contexts even customers). Thus, a library's acquisitions activities should be structured to respond to its users' wants and needs. Stating something that will come as no surprise to anyone who has ever worked in any capacity in a library,

Daniel Melcher (1971: 1) noted in his longtime bible for library acquisitions, *Melcher on Acquisition*:

> Fundamentally, the wants of any library's users are easily stated. They want what they want—now. They want it when it is being reviewed, talked about, displayed in bookstore windows, or offered in coupon ads. If you haven't got it yet, but it is in the bookstore across the street, they don't see *why* you haven't got it. If it's in the library but not yet cataloged, they don't see why that should prevent you from letting them take it out. If last year's issues of X magazine have been reported in the bindery for the past six months, they don't see why you send the issues to the bindery before the bindery is ready to bind them.

Melcher was writing in 1971. To say his conclusion remains just as true in this day of instantaneous web communication and electronic access to materials over the Internet is a significant understatement. If it is possible for items to be wanted faster than now, that is when users will want the newest books, as well as the DVDs and other formats that can spread quickly through the Internet. Any library that receives public support disregards the public's wishes at peril to its continued existence. Any technical or special library that fails to keep itself current risks irrelevancy in the eyes of its constituency. Even a library that views itself primarily as an archival resource and repository must ultimately be responsive to user needs, so the never-ending, never-done work of the collection development and acquisition staffs of virtually any library has to accelerate to keep abreast of new items and to order them in advance of publication for authors or subjects that are known to be needed by or even just popular with the library's users. This is thus the central goal of acquisitions: matching the library's resources (once simply described as its collection, but now a much broader range of materials) with the library users' needs and wants.

The Nature of Library Resources

Library resources may be deftly, if not very precisely, described as all print and print-alternative published matter, with "published" being a looser concept today than the traditional idea of what a printer does or what scribes once did. Here we are less concerned with format than with the conditions surrounding their acquisition and use. From this viewpoint, we can distinguish three basic classes of information items:

1. Those that are owned by the library
2. Those that are leased by the library
3. Those that are accessed electronically by the library (or its users)

The acquisition of items in each of these classes is subject to varying procedures and commercial and legal controls, usually depending on whether one is referring to physical ownership or usage rights. Acquisition of items falling into each class will carry with it certain imperatives, which must be understood clearly if the library is to allocate its resources most efficiently and effectively.

Owned materials are those acquired by the library through purchase and exchange or obtained free, obviously including the wide range of traditional materials. Regardless of whether the library paid cash, traded, or obtained the materials gratis, the common element is that they are now owned by the library and are under its control. Although there remain legal and institutional restrictions on what the library may do with these materials, the copyright aspects of which are discussed in detail in Chapter 9, basically these are materials that may be managed by the library and its staff.

Leased materials are items under the temporary physical control of the library, which are acquired through contractual arrangement with the actual owner of the material. Public libraries in particular often find it advantageous to lease current, popular books under what is usually referred to as a McNaughton plan from a library vendor. In addition, all types of libraries from time to time lease databases (typically on CD-ROM or magnetic tape suitable for mounting on the library's computer information system) on a contractual basis. The library pays for the use of these materials in accordance with a contract between the vendor and the library. In a sense, such materials are similar to serials, since updates, additions, or completely revised versions are supplied at intervals according to the contract. If the library should stop paying the fees, some contracts provide for the return of the original, while others render the information inaccessible past a certain date. Some vendors allow continuing access to materials previously leased. The applicable lease agreements can be very complicated and may include restrictions on where the materials can be used (such as a particular building or computer) and to a specified group of users (such as the faculty and staff of a particular institution).

Larger libraries and library consortia are generally the ones acquiring on-site databases, which are leased for a specified time and price. In addition to the periodic leasing costs, the library must also budget for the operational costs of initially setting up and then running the database and making it available to users.

Accessed materials are those that involve purchasing the right to view (and sometimes download or print) electronic materials through an aggregator. The large serials vendors now generally aggregate collections of electronic publications (often referred to in the library science literature as the "big deals") and lease the right of access to these materials. So that libraries do not have to negotiate with each individual electronic publisher, the aggregator attempts to add value by putting together a package of electronic databases, periodicals, or other such materials. The library then purchases the package, which is not the same as ownership of the materials but rather the right to access them for the term of the contract.

The traditional ownership paradigm often infects the acquisition librarian in subtle ways that can result in the library acquiring contractually based items on quite disadvantageous terms, especially given the often high cost of the items. Acquisitions librarians must be careful when considering the impact of license restrictions on future use of their collections (Schaffner, 2001). For instance, digital packages frequently include less desirable items that must be accepted in order to get the items the library actually wants. There also may be unexpected restrictions that apply as soon as the shrink-wrapped software package is opened. Recent court cases in a number of jurisdictions upholding the validity of "shrink-wrap licenses" certainly make vigilance in this regard a necessity for all libraries in the future.

Budgetary constraints having often significantly reduced purchasing capacity for many libraries, it has become increasingly common for electronic document delivery to substitute for purchasing hard copy. Whether or not the library pays the costs involved, in such situations the purchased material does not belong to the library, with the concomitant loss of control. In addition, the price may include both fees and royalties. Some libraries fund these unpurchased materials from their collection development budgets. Others require users to pay some or all of the fees. Still others have developed some kind of hybrid arrangement where they may fund a certain amount of materials for a patron over a specified period or ask a patron to pay, for example, $5 per document whereas the actual cost may be in the $10–$20 range. All such arrangements create an element of uncertainty as to exactly how much should be budgeted for purchases and how much for costs of electronic access.

Sources of Library Materials

Libraries and Publishers

Despite the large number of books and other materials purchased each year by libraries, most publishers do not consider libraries their primary market. That role still belongs to retail bookstores, including such marketers as Amazon. com. As a result, bookstores enjoy the benefit of huge discounts from publishers, often ranging up to 50 percent, while libraries generally are offered something in the range of 10–20 percent. Serial publishers are notorious for almost never giving libraries a discount (except for the popular magazines), and all too often academic publishers charge libraries more than individual subscribers, sometimes significantly more, despite libraries generally being the major customer for their academic titles. In the United States this has led to considerable antagonism between librarians and serial publishers.

Library Vendors: Domestic and International

Libraries generally acquire materials directly from publishers, booksellers, and vendors or jobbers. Although not all publishers will deal with third-party library vendors (generally publishers of reference materials), the majority of library materials can be obtained through a vendor that specializes in selling to libraries. They are called by a variety of names including dealers, suppliers, agents, booksellers, and jobbers. These vendors allow libraries to deal with just a few companies while ordering library resources published by hundreds of organizations. There are major overall vendors, such as Baker and Taylor, and smaller vendors that deal with specific types of materials, formats, or materials from outside the United States, often from a specific country or in a specific language (Figure 5.1). These specialized vendors can be located by consulting sources such as *American Book Trade Directory* or *Literary Market Place*. There are also vendors, such as EBSCO, that specialize in serial publications and electronic databases.

In addition to the benefits of one-stop shopping, libraries favor the use of vendors because of the array of other services that they can offer. A librarian can expect a vendor to provide access to databases with bibliographic information, including title, author, publisher, price, and ISBN (International Standard Book Number) or ISSN (International Standard Serial Number). In addition, many vendors will ship the books to the library already cataloged and prepared for the shelf. Libraries can also get pricing trends for books and serials to help them in planning their budgets.

Online bookstores such as Amazon.com and Barnes and Noble are being utilized increasingly by libraries for popular titles needed quickly or for out-of-print materials (see Out-of-Print Purchasing). Some libraries are even ordering books demanded by users and having them shipped directly. When finished, the user then brings the book to the library. Local brick-and-mortar bookstores may also be a good source of materials needed quickly. If an extremely popular book blindsides the library, buying a few copies at a local bookstore can help the library quickly satisfy user desires. Some libraries use specially issued credit cards for such purposes.

In addition to firm orders (materials that are ordered title by title), there are a number of ways to save the librarian's time and ensure that books and other materials are already in the library when needed. These may be summarized as follows.

Mass Gathering Plans

As most medium-sized to large libraries cannot afford enough librarians who specialize in collection development to individually select every title, a number of mass gathering plans have been devised over the years to collect most of the standard materials that a library needs so that the librarians can work on areas of special interest, as well as the kinds of "gray" literature,

Figure 5.1. Major Library Vendors

Vendor	Type of Library Generally Serviced	Vendor's Specialty
Baker and Taylor	Public and academic	Books, DVDs, CDs and other major formats
Brodart	School media centers and small public	Books, DVDs, CDs, popular magazines
Elsevier	Academic and special	Academic journals and scientific and technical books
EBSCO	All types	Serials and subscription databases
Follett	School media centers and public	Books, DVDs, CDs, and other major formats
H. W. Wilson	All types	Subscription databases and printed indexes
Harrasowitz	Academic and special	Books and other publications from European countries with an emphasis on German language materials
Ingram	All types	Popular materials
Proquest	Academic and special	Subscription databases
SWETS	Academic and special	Serials
Wiley Blackwell	Academic and special	Serials, digital libraries of various scientific and technical publications
Yankee Book Peddler	Academic	Academic books, but can supply almost anything

Note: This is meant to be a representative sample, not a complete list of vendors. A more comprehensive list with web addresses can be found on the accompanying CD-ROM.

association literature, and international publications (to name a few) that are not readily available by one of the following methods:

- Approval plans are frequently used by academic or large public librar-ies. Titles are shipped from a wholesaler or vendor on approval accord-ing to a profile set up by the library and vendor. Libraries can return items, but it is important to the vendor that returns be kept low, so profiles are generally revised to the point that few items are returned.

- McNaughton plans are heavily used by public libraries. These are rental or lease systems for popular works that a public library will need multiple copies of in order to meet the anticipated demand.
- Standing orders and blanket orders are similar in that, in both cases, the library commits to purchasing everything sent by a publisher or vendor, provided the materials match the terms of a formal agreement. A standing order is generally placed for a series, while a blanket order is placed with a particular publisher for a subject field, a grade level, or a particular country's publications.

Serials

Scientific journals began in the 17th century to disseminate research among members of a few scientific societies and, needless to say, this process grew and grew until serials are now a large percentage of the budget of most academic and research libraries. The term *serials* covers scholarly journals, newspapers, conference proceedings, popular magazines, annual publications, and anything published in a series, including some government documents. They may exist in print, electronic, or even multimedia formats. Serials may be published on a regular basis, be it daily, weekly, biweekly, monthly, quarterly, yearly, or even biennially. Much to the professional cataloger's and any library shelver's dismay, serials can also be and often are published on an irregular basis; they can merge and split and change titles, sometimes only occasionally or seemingly on a yearly basis. It takes a special person to love working with serials, and the fact that such professionals fortunately exist does nothing to obviate the censure due to serials publishers for their haphazard ways.

A crisis in the serials field owing to skyrocketing costs that began in the 1970s continues today. Year after year, serial prices have grown exponentially, requiring a larger and larger percentage of library resources budgets. In the late 1970s, libraries began trying to cut the cost of their serial subscriptions to preserve a reasonable percentage of the acquisition budget for book purchases. In the 1990s and continuing today the pressure to lease more and more electronic serials and databases has likewise put pressure on the library resources budget for nearly all types of libraries (Figure 5.2). Some journals are available in print and electronic form with different pricing schemes, but other electronic journals are free with a paid subscription to the print version. Sometimes there is a relatively small supplemental cost to have both electronic and print. No generalizations can be made, and getting the best deal for the money has never been more necessary for acquisitions librarians to create a balance between electronic, multimedia, and print resources.

One of the remaining issues surrounding electronic serials is who will maintain perpetual archives, so that the journal will always be available. Some serial publishers promise this, but in today's world of mergers and

Figure 5.2. Representative Pricing Samples for Electronic Serials

Model	Category	Example
FTE	Approximate use	$3,000 for schools under 5,000 FTEs
Book budget	Approximate use	$3,000 for schools below $100,000 book budget
Simultaneous users	Approximate use	$1,495 for four simultaneous users
Number of documents	Approximate use	$20 per document
Number of abstracts	Approximate use	$0.20 per abstract
Number of downloads	Approximate use	$1.00 per record downloaded; view for free
Number of views	Approximate use	$0.50 per view
Number of faculty	Approximate use	$100 per faculty member
Personal copy price	Approximate use	$100 for individual copy
Usage last year	Approximate use	Pay fixed amount now, next year's price based on use
Institution type	Approximate use	Public library, high school, ARL, community college prices
Price per computer	Approximate use	$3 per computer
LAN price	Approximate use	$500 price for a LAN
WAN price	Approximate use	$1,000 price for a WAN
Unlimited site license	Approximate use	$7,000 unlimited use within defined site
Purchasing paper copy	Discount	20% off for purchasing paper and electronic
Purchasing web copy	Discount	90% off for purchasing CD and web
Multiyear discount	Discount	5% off for purchasing 2 years
Multisite discount	Discount	5% off for multisite purchases
Multicopy discount	Discount	5% off for purchasing multiple copies of same product
Prepub discount	Discount	5% off for buying before publication
Consortium discount	Discount	20% off for 20 sites participating
Multiple database discount	Discount	5% off for purchasing more than 10 products at once

Figure 5.2. (continued)

Model	Category	Example
Early purchase incentive	Discount	5% off if you purchase without a trial
Country discount	Discount	Developing country discount
Free	Sponsored	No charge
Remote usage surcharge	Value added	$500 to add a remote campus
Ownership surcharge	Value added	$15,000 for outright purchase of the data for a site
Hard disc surcharge	Value added	$500 to download data onto a hard disc
Software maintenance fee	Value added	To ensure technical support and software updates
Update frequency	Value added	4 updates yearly for $1,000; 12 updates $2,000

Note: ARL = Association of Research Libraries; FTE = full-time equivalent; LAN = local-area network; WAN = wide-area network.

consolidations, whether these agreements will mean anything in the future remains to be seen. Research and academic libraries are looking for long-term solutions to the crisis in scholarly publishing in several ways. JSTOR and SPARC are just two of them.

JSTOR

JSTOR is a project that was initiated by the Andrew W. Mellon Foundation to provide academic libraries with back runs of important journals in electronic form. It combines both academic and economic objectives. The academic objective is to build a reliable archive of important scholarly journals and provide widespread access to them. The economic objective is to save libraries money by eliminating the need for every library to store and preserve materials.

The JSTOR collections are organized by discipline—economics, history, philosophy, and so on. The first phase involved 100 journals from 15 fields. For each journal, the collection usually consists of all issues from the first up to about five years before the current date.

JSTOR was established in August 1995 as an independent, not-for-profit organization. Libraries are charged to access its database, but the fees are set lower than the comparable cost of binding and storing paper copies of the journals. JSTOR has straightforward licenses with publishers and subscribing institutions. By emphasizing back runs, JSTOR strives to avoid competing with publishers, whose principal revenues come from current subscriptions rather than back numbers.

SPARC

Scholarly Publishing and Academic Resources Coalition (SPARC) was founded in 1998 as a direct result of discussions involving the future of scholarly publishing. Libraries had, as noted earlier, experienced huge increases in journal costs, particularly in the sciences, technology, and medicine. At the same time, libraries were experiencing flat or declining budgets. Libraries responded with yet another round of serials cancellations. "Both the high prices and steep annual increases have forced libraries to cancel thousands of journal subscriptions, prompting publishers to raise prices higher to make up the loss" ("SPARC and Chemists," 1998: 1).

SPARC was formed to work with scholarly societies and scholars to create new journals that could be sold for less money while still maintaining high-quality input, in direct competition to established commercial publications. These journals are frequently priced at least 50 percent below the cost of commercial counterparts and are sometimes essentially free. SPARC is also working with academic societies that have in the past 20 years or so given up the publishing aspect of their journals to big commercial publishers, to take back their publications and lower costs to subscribers. (Of course, some of these societies have been living off the royalties earned from the commercial publishers, making this a difficult decision for many.)

Government Publications

Government publications come in all the formats previously discussed, but there are significant differences in the acquisition process. The challenges of selecting government documents are similar to those of selecting other types of materials, but obtaining publications from government offices does offer special problems for acquisition or document librarians. A large percentage of the material published throughout the world comes from local, state or provincial, national, and international agencies and governments. Issuing bodies may change or regroup with no notice and little record. Their publications vanish or reappear with new titles and frequencies, making acquisition as much a matter of luck as the application of specialized training, experience, and diligence. Historically, the most effective method for acquisition of state and local documents has been through direct agency contact, and the usual method of acquisition of U.S. federal documents has been either through the Federal Depository System or the Government Printing Office. Currently, more and more government documents are being made available only on the web.

Library Consortia

Consortia are groups of libraries that come together for various purposes. They can be large, such as OCLC and its regional networks SOLINET or AMIGOS, or more localized consortia covering parts of states, such as TBLC and SEFLIN in Florida. The purchasing power of library consortia should not be ignored. Early consortia were based on cooperative collection development and then cataloging, but now library consortia are also acting as middlemen in purchasing electronic resources. Consortia are often able to get lower prices than libraries negotiating licenses alone. Particularly for smaller libraries, consortium staffs will probably have more experience in negotiating license agreements to be able to get the kind of concessions needed for resource sharing. Larger libraries will probably have staff members that deal with licensing agreements, but the impact of a large number of libraries may allow them to get a better deal than negotiating alone.

Out-of-Print Purchasing

All libraries may find themselves needing to purchase a title that is no longer in print. Even classic titles that no library should be without can be out of print or sometimes out of stock indefinitely, meaning that the publisher does not want to declare the title out of print but has no more copies to sell at present. Thus, the acquisitions librarian is sent into the secondhand or even antiquarian book market. The library may need to replace a lost or mutilated item, or a new area of interest may evolve where both current and older titles are needed for the collection. Academic librarians may need to serve a new academic program and thus need to collect titles not on the current market. And, of course, special collections librarians mostly work in this environment.

Acquiring out-of-print materials is labor intensive and often expensive, but it is a very worthwhile endeavor to keep older titles available to users. A user may go down to the local bookstore and buy a new best seller, but an out-of-print book will lead them to the library. It is really too early to tell whether e-books will have a major impact on keeping titles available longer, but it is possible that at some point in the near future e-books may make getting and replacing older titles easier.

Another way that the new digital technology is helping in acquiring formerly out-of-print titles is through print-on-demand publishing. Generally, titles are scanned onto a disc and printed on demand when they are requested. Random House has been a leader with its "backlist extension plan," which is essentially on-demand publishing. Academic librarians have been acquiring dissertations in this manner for a long time. However, the process is less expensive and quicker with new technologies, making it likely that more publishers will use it in the near future.

The University of Michigan's Undergraduate Library in Ann Arbor now provides books on demand in a library setting, as it was the first university library to install an Espresso Book Machine, which produces perfect-bound, high-quality paperback books on demand, in this case out-of-copyright books from the university's digitized collections. The books are available to researchers, students, and the public at a cost of about $10 each.

Before going into the out-of-print market, the first step is to make sure that the book is really out of print. It is not unheard of that a library vendor will report that a book is out of print when it really is still available. There are a number of reasons why this may happen, including the following:

- Academic titles that may be used as textbooks sometimes change publishers, with the original publisher selling the rights to the title to another publisher. An order from the vendor may result in an out-of-print response because they may not refer the order to the new publisher.
- A title can be out of print from the publisher's standpoint, but copies may still be available from some vendors that stocked the title earlier and have not sold all their copies.
- Mistakes do happen since inventory is usually based on ISBN or other standard numbers that can be transposed or otherwise incorrectly keyed.

Public libraries may want to consider carefully whether to buy out-of-print books, as they will not come with the usual library discounts. The books are often used and may be marked or otherwise show wear and tear. Book jackets are often in bad shape or missing altogether. The search and purchase of out-of-print titles may not fit neatly into a single year's budget cycle.

The availability of out-of-print materials through Amazon.com and other online sources has taken a lot of the guessing out of a title search and may make the cost more competitive and the purchasing process more timely for the library's fiscal year. To entirely forgo the out-of-print market can lead to serious gaps in the collection.

Gifts and Exchanges

Within the context of acquisitions and collection development as discussed in earlier chapters in this book, the 800-pound gorilla always in the room, sometimes mentioned, occasionally ignored, is the ever-increasing costs of materials and the funding problems those costs engender. Financial resources are always limited, and thus those involved in the selection process are under pressure to make the best possible choices and selections, or to get the "most bang for the buck." Sometimes, though, acquisitions are not made through selection but are instead received from other sources. This section looks at gifts and donations to the library.

Gifts can be a double-edged sword for collection development librarians. Accepting gifts from library supporters can enrich a library's collection by providing otherwise unattainable resources, but if care is not taken in weeding out redundant, unnecessary, or improper materials, librarians run the risk of alienating those inclined to bestow such gifts on the library. You don't have to contemplate gifts within the field of collection development for very long to discover the conundrum they can present. The collection development position can become a very critical one when gifts are involved because the librarian must always respect the interface of the library with its users and benefactors.

At their best, gifts can lead to the development of a special collection that can make the library's name a household word for scholars, and maybe even the public as a whole. This can be a laudable goal for any library, but who's lucky enough for that to happen? You may think that all of the great special collections have been set up already. Well, this is not necessarily the case. Perhaps a famous writer grew up in your public library's town, remembers the library fondly, and wants some of his or her materials to form the basis of a special collection that represents either the author's work and life or subjects in which the author is interested. This can be a good thing, but, on the other hand, the most well-intentioned gift may not always fulfill a library's collection development goals. For example, what library needs a donation of someone's 50-year collection of *National Geographic Magazine* when the library has its own complete set? What if many of the donated items feature torn pages, squashed bugs, and coffee ring stains?

How do libraries end up with these kinds of gifts? Often, gifts are bestowed following the death of a family member who once treasured these items, and the person's heirs think the library is the perfect recipient. In other cases, certain well-off individuals want to see their materials cataloged and protected for future generations to enjoy. These sorts of situations can be tricky for the library because such donors may have other materials that the library would love to have, but that aren't presently featured on the donor's gift list. Collection development librarians must keep in mind that for the common in-kind donation, it is important to express clearly to the donor that, although gifts are welcome, not all gifts can be added to the library's catalog.

So when you are faced with a gift that doesn't meet your library's collection development goals, you will need to consider a few alternatives before heading to the dumpster if good relations with donors are to be maintained. One such alternative is a Friends of the Library used-book sale. Donors may welcome the knowledge that the library might still realize a benefit from their donation through sale of the materials, and the library can use the money to buy items that it desperately needs. An added benefit is that the work in question may find a home with a new owner who will value it as much as the previous owner did.

Wilkinson and Lewis (2003: 178) present an excellent philosophy for a library to adopt in accepting gifts:

Libraries need clear policies describing the types of materials they will and will not accept. Larger libraries may have collection development policies that describe the collection priorities of the institution, and these are helpful to gifts personnel who deal with donors. Developing descriptions of the types of materials that are not wanted is equally important, if not more so, than describing the subject areas in which the library collects materials. For example, some libraries will not accept recent newspapers, popular magazines, paperback fiction, or textbooks, while other libraries want those types of materials.

In general, libraries normally add only a small percentage of the materials given to them, which means that they can and do have large numbers of items to dispose of in some manner, and they can't all wait for the annual book sale. First, consider whether these sorts of materials may be given to other libraries, either for their collections or to be sold at their Friends' book sales. Recycling gift materials is another possibility, though this may not necessarily be the best option with a donor's family collection, for instance. Recycling books also poses some practical problems, such as the need to remove bindings or glossy paper not being accepted by the recycling agent. A good alternative for many libraries is to establish an arrangement with a used-book dealer whereby the dealer buys items the library does not want at a fixed price per volume (or pound). Increasingly, libraries are even offering some of their more interesting but unwanted materials on Amazon.com, CraigsList, and eBay to bring funds into the library that can then be used for new materials.

Responsibility for Handling Gifts

The responsibility for handling gifts usually resides, naturally enough, in the library's acquisitions department. Sometimes in a small library setting, however, the director is the public face of the library, and so will undertake this responsibility, at least with the initial acceptance of gifts, passing them on to acquisitions or collection development for final decisions as to the dispensation of items—keep, sell, give away, etc. When performing this sort of triage for donations that duplicate library holdings, when time permits, check to see which copy of a title is in better physical condition—the gift item or the book currently on the shelf—and keep the best one.

Many acceptance policies depend on the size of the library and the amount of donations that they are likely to receive from donors over a given period of time. In a research institution, there will probably be a librarian whose responsibilities include the active solicitation of gifts. Part of this person's job is to know the kinds of collections that exist in libraries in the local area, as well as throughout the state and the nation, so that accepted items that are not necessarily appropriate to the receiving library can be given a "good home" elsewhere.

More important, this person's responsibility is to cultivate relationships with those persons who will make decisions about the placement of their potential gift items. Establishing such contacts can be difficult, but narrowing your objectives to those potential donors with some ties to your institution, those who have already offered donations, or those who live in the area and utilize the library's services will boost the possibilities of success. The successful negotiation of a large or important gift may also require the involvement of higher administration. Obtaining useful gifts for the collection is, however, not an impossible task. *College & Research Libraries News* features a column in each issue about important donations received by university and research libraries. Keep in mind, however, that successful solicitation of the types of gifts featured in this column generally require coordinated work among varied members of an institution's staff.

Before Accepting and Adding Materials to the Collection

In addition to determining whether the materials proposed for donation are appropriate for your collection, the physical condition of the materials must be assessed. Gifts can bring mold and mildew plus the possibility of insect and/or small rodent infestations into the library. Unless questionable materials are perceived as obviously valuable owing to known age, provenance, or rarity, it is better to err on the side of caution. Always ask about where the items have been stored.

Books that have been stored in an attic or basement are candidates for mold, mildew, and/or infestation. Mold can be a serious problem for paper-based and even microfilm collections because, given a warm humid environment, just a small amount of mold can build up quickly. In addition to having to wipe each book to remove the mold, staff with allergy problems may also become ill. A gift of medical periodicals from a lab may bring with it droppings from white mice used in experiments, which can wreak havoc on the collection, not to mention the nerves of staff members. The most likely problem, though, is insect infestation because insects will often hitch a ride in or on the boxes containing gifts. This is how cockroaches, silverfish, and larder beetle larvae (the proverbial bookworm) typically get into a library, and they can eat their way through any collection. Cockroaches seem to target the glue used in bindings and book lice will eat the starch and gelatin sizing on paper. The problem is not just the initial damage but also the potential damage of insect progeny.

So, if the library receives a lot of gifts, it is best to have a separate room to store the materials initially, away from the general collection, to minimize potential damage arising from infestations in the donated materials or the containers they arrive in. Although good remedies exist for all of the aforementioned problems, getting rid of mold and insects is always harder than examining the acquired items thoroughly before introducing them to areas where the general collection materials are located (which includes the acquisition and cataloging areas as well as the stacks and reading rooms).

Beware Gifts with Strings Attached

Although donations can be useful to libraries in many ways, as indicated earlier, some donors do not want to stop with simply giving materials to a library but may also try to place burdensome restrictions on their gifts, such as requiring the items be housed in a particular collection or certain prominent locations. Some may even want the books back if they are ultimately judged inappropriate for the collection (Kertesz, 2001). As Morrisey (2008: 169) explains:

> Just keep to the motto that what you do for one donor you should do for all. Most libraries will not accept every book unless it fits with the collection development profile of the library. Stipulations that donors want can't be abided by unless there are separate funds to help with the set up of a special collection. Your collection development policy should address these issues.

Other times, the donor may simply want a bookplate put in the materials indicating their gift or in memory of a loved one who may have been the original owner of the materials. This kind of string-attached is not so difficult to deal with and is often accommodated by the library as an effective "marketing" tool to encourage gifts and donations in kind.

Legal Issues Involving Gifts

A more complete discussion of general legal issues involved with collection development and acquisition can be found in Chapter 9; however, a review of those issues relating specifically to gifts warrants inclusion here.

Tax Matters; Appraisals of Gifts

Donors to college and university, school and public, and nonprofit libraries designated by the Internal Revenue Service can claim a deduction for the value of their gifts on federal income tax returns (subject to certain limits depending generally on the income of the donor). If the donation is valued at more than $250, a written acknowledgment of the gift must be provided. Value is the key to the amount of the tax deduction available to a donor, and the valuation must be provided by an outside agency, not the library; thus usually the library will often not know how much the donor may be claiming. The library should provide in all cases a written acknowledgment describing the items given if the donor wishes one. If a donor wishes an appraisal of the value of the gift, the library should, at most, provide a list of people who are qualified to perform an evaluation, but there must be no relation between the library and the appraiser.

Copyright Issues with Manuscripts, Letters, and Works Published by the Donor

Copyright issues with unpublished materials can be problematic for libraries. When negotiating with the donor of such materials, it is critical to determine who in fact holds the copyright to the materials. For example, the copyright of a letter resides with its author, not the person who received the letter and may be donating it to the library. In the case of a donation of letters and manuscripts after the death of the author, the author's estate or a relative may now hold the copyright. In this situation, a written document that describes what can and cannot be done with the materials becomes most important. It should cover such questions as these:

- May future authors quote from the materials?
- May a user of the library publish a single or several letters as a part of a biographical work?
- If the materials contain photographs, can a user of the collection reproduce one or more photographs as a part of a work being written for publication?

The library needs answers to these questions, and perhaps others, depending on the nature of the items being donated, so that it can inform users as to how the donated collection may be used and also be able to direct users to the proper source to obtain permission for a specific use. Libraries should prefer to receive a grant of the copyright when they receive such materials, but that may or may not be possible for all donations of unpublished materials that they may desire to add to their special collections.

Exchange Programs

Exchange programs among libraries can involve either unwanted older materials or the exchange of new materials. Public libraries may have arrangements with libraries in poorer areas to provide duplicates or other unwanted materials to them at little or no cost. Research libraries are the ones most often involved in the exchange of new materials, and they may especially be involved in exchange programs involving hard-to-obtain international publications and serials. In the case of academic libraries, the library or its university may have serials titles published by the university that can be offered to other libraries in return for similar publications from their organizations or countries. These programs are often used to obtain materials from less-developed countries where it is sometimes difficult to order or even know about the existence of such publications. Wilkinson and Lewis (2003) mention that often exchange programs can be part of a public relations effort to get a university's scholars' materials out to a wider audience or to improve the university's public image.

Items received pursuant to exchange programs are often treated as gifts because they need to be examined to see if they belong in the collection, and to determine whether there are signs of mold or of insect manifestations, etc., before adding them to the collection.

This chapter has only scratched the surface of acquisitions processes and concerns. Your library and information studies program may have a separate acquisitions course, but if not, it is hoped that this chapter at least gives the student an idea of the kind of work involved in the acquisition of library materials.

Vocabulary

appraisal   approval plans
blanket orders   bookplates
exchange program   firm orders
gray literature   JSTOR
manuscript   McNaughton plans
memorial gifts   restricted/unrestricted donations
serials   SPARC
standing orders

Discussion Questions

1. Suppose that you have been using a vendor (books or serials) that is no longer in business, how would you go about selecting a new vendor? What features or services would be the most important to you in making that decision?

2. Some library administrators argue that acquisitions is basically a business process and someone with an undergraduate business-related degree can do the job better and cost the library less in salary than hiring a professional librarian. Do you agree or disagree? Why? Why not?

3. Someone at the circulation desk refers a potential book donor to you as head of acquisitions. After a brief discussion, you realize that this might be a gift of manuscripts worth over a million dollars, but the materials do not initially strike you as materials that fit the library's current collection development plan. How do you proceed?

4. Your local community is known for being very generous with your library with both donations of money and materials. The only problem

is that a large number of the gifts are not deemed to be useful enough to add to the library's collection. How do you deal with the donations?

5. If your library and information studies program does not have one, would you like to see a course in acquisitions, separate from collection development? Do you feel that there are enough professional skills to be learned in this area to justify a separate course?

References

Kertesz, Christopher J. 2001. "The Unwanted Gift: When Saying 'No Thanks' Isn't Enough." *American Libraries* 32 (March): 34–36.

Melcher, Daniel, with Margaret Saul. 1971. *Melcher on Acquisition.* Chicago: American Library Association.

Morrisey, Locke J. 2008. "Ethical Issues in Collection Development." *Journal of Library Administration* 47, no. 3/4: 163–171.

Schaffner, Bradley L. 2001. "Electronic Resources: A Wolf in Sheep's Clothing?" *College and Research Libraries* 62 (June): 239–249.

"SPARC and Chemists to Collaborate on New Reduced-Cost Journals." 1998. *ARL: A Bimonthly Review* 199: 1–2.

Wilkinson, Frances C., and Linda K. Lewis. 2003. *The Complete Guide to Acquisitions Management.* Westport, CT: Libraries Unlimited.

Selected Readings

Abel, Richard. 1995. "The Origins of the Library Approval Plan." *Publishing Research Quarterly* 11 (Spring): 46–56.

Ballestro, John and Philip C. Howze. 2005. "When a Gift Is Not a Gift: Collection Assessment Using Cost-Benefit Analysis." *Collection Management* 30, no. 3: 49–66.

Bostic, Mary. 1991. "Gifts to Libraries: Coping Effectively." *Collection Management* 14, nos. 3/4: 175–184.

Cassell, Kay Ann. 2008. *Gifts for the Collection: Guidelines for the Library.* The Hague: International Federation of Library Associations and Institutions.

Chadwell, Faye A. 2010. "Good Gifts Stewardship." *Collection Management* 35 (April–June): 59–68.

Dali, Keren, and Juris Dilevko. 2005. "Beyond Approval Plans: Methods of Selection and Acquisition of Books in Slavic and East European Languages in North American Libraries." *Library Collections, Acquisitions and Technical Services* 29, no. 3: 238–269.

Eaglen, Audrey. 2000. *Buying Books: A How-to-Do-It Manual for Librarians.* 2nd ed. New York: Neal-Schuman.

Farrell, Katherine Treptow, and Janet E. Lute. 2005. "Document-Management Technology and Acquisitions Workflow: A Case Study in Invoice Processing." *Information Technology and Libraries* 24 (September): 117–122.

Fowler, David and Janet Arcand. 2003. "Monographic Acquisitions Time and Cost Studies: The Next Generation." *Library Resources & Technical Services* 47 (July): 109–124.

Gagnon, Ronald A. 2006. "Library Vendor Relations from a Public Library Perspective." *Journal of Library Administration* 44, nos. 3/4: 95–111.

Heller, Anne. 1999. "Online Ordering: Making Its Mark." *Library Journal* 124 (September 1): 153–158.

Hellriegel, Patricia, and Kaat Van Wonterghem. 2007. "Package Deals Unwrapped . . . or the Librarians Wrapped Up? 'Forced Acquisitions' in the Digital Library." *Interlending and Document Supply* 35, no. 2: 66–73.

Hill, Dale S. 2003. "Selling Withdrawn and Gift Books on eBay: Does It Make Sense?" *Journal of Interlibrary Loan, Document Delivery & Information Supply* 14, no. 2: 37–40.

Holley, Robert P., and Kalyani Ankem. 2005. "The Effect of the Internet on the Out-of-Print Book Market: Implications for Libraries." *Library Collections, Acquisitions and Technical Services* 29, no. 2: 118–139.

Kulp, Christina, and Karen Rupp-Serrano. 2005. "Organizational Approaches to Electronic Resource Acquisition: Decision-Making Models in Libraries." *Collection Management* 30, no. 4: 3–29.

Lam, Helen. 2004. "Library Acquisitions Management: Methods to Enhance Vendor Assessment and Library Performance." *Library Administration and Management* 18 (Summer): 146–154.

Leonhardt, Thomas W. 1997. "The Gift and Exchange Function in ARL Libraries: Now and Tomorrow." *Library Acquisitions: Practice and Theory* 21: 141–149.

Leonhardt, Thomas W. 1999. "A Survey of Gifts and Exchange Activities in 85 Non-ARL Libraries." *Acquisitions Librarian* 22: 51–58.

Prabha, Chandra. 2007. "Shifting from Print to Electronic Journals in ARL Libraries." *Serials Review* 33, no. 1: 4–13.

Quinn, Brian. 2001. "The Impact of Aggregator Packages on Collection Management." *Collection Management* 25, no. 3: 53–74.

Roberts, Elizabeth Ann. 2008. *Crash Course in Library Gift Programs: The Reluctant Curator's Guide to Caring for Archives, Books, and Artifacts in a Library Setting.* Westport, CT: Libraries Unlimited.

6

Budgeting and Fiscal Management

Overview

In this chapter we look at some of the budgeting and fiscal issues involved with library acquisitions, including fund allocations. There is a section dealing with bookkeeping and very basic accounting terms and procedures. Although most acquisitions departments will have a bookkeeper, it is important to understand the terminology enough to be able to read a financial spreadsheet. Being too dependent upon the bookkeeper to interpret fiscal information can lead to a multitude of problems, but simply understanding the basic terminology goes a long way to helping the acquisitions librarian or supervisor feel more comfortable with budgeting and accounting for library funds.

As the budget is the major planning document of a library, the resource budget is the plan for the acquisition of all library resources.

> Financial planning . . . takes a great deal of care. There must be clear justifications as a defense against those who see their own expectations deferred. One budget action might, for example, be the establishment of a postal fund to cover deliveries of materials borrowed through a cooperative, or funds to cover the photocopying of articles from cancelled journals. All such adaptations must be planned as proper extensions of collection development rather than simply being allowed to happen. Coping with change is always traumatic, and the immediate needs tend to overshadow longer-term considerations. Thinking through the consequences of each action will help to minimize later problems, and ensure that the library continues to provide the best possible service consonant with the available budget. (Martin, 1995: 44–45)

As we have noted, today's typical library budget is concerned not only with the purchase of books, serials, and other print materials but also with access

101

to electronic materials, cooperative resource sharing, and direct document delivery. Issues involving nontraditional assets often devolve into debates of access versus ownership. Switching or evolving away from the traditional mission of acquiring ownership of physical materials to a primary concern with information access requires a comprehensive approach, including the review and redevelopment of library mission and goals statements, and therefore a collection development policy that reflects those statements and specifies the ways in which the collection's evolution is to be handled.

First, there is a need to define properly just what services, such as document delivery, will in fact mean in the future for the library's users and how the new forms of access will be implemented and funded. For instance, if you plan to rely on access as opposed to ownership of certain materials, this implies that those materials may be owned by another library. With respect to physical materials, it is axiomatic that all libraries cannot rely exclusively on access—some library somewhere does need to be the owner and to maintain the materials. Such a library cannot be expected to be one whose patrons have so little use for the materials that sharing them is not problematic. Cooperative resource sharing efforts need planning and careful implementation—and to succeed they require supportive budgeting.

As indicated earlier, librarians must consider the overall effect of relying on external services to supply needed materials and decide whether such a move is sufficiently consistent with the library's priorities. Access, of course, can mean merely access to bibliographic records, in which case further action remains necessary to retrieve the wanted materials and is likely to incur further costs. It can also mean direct access to the materials themselves, traditionally through physical interlibrary loan, and today most likely in an electronic format (which itself may be costly and may even require purchase of the print version before electronic access is available). The paperless future aside, electronic formats usually indicate a need to print or download the information for use. Access can also mean the ability to utilize the resources of other libraries, whether by way of a shared library card for borrowing or simply through permitted use in the other library.

Accountability

The postwar prosperity of the 1950s and 1960s can be seen today as the halcyon boom years for collection development. Difficult though it may be to believe in these days of limits, back then it often seemed that librarians could not spend money on materials fast enough to keep up with the flow of funds. Those days are long gone and, one must believe, never to return. Since the late 1970s, with the widespread recognition of the limits to growth and the imposition of both budgetary and tax limitations, accountability has become more important for libraries than ever before. Today, librarians may not assume and must be able to prove that they are using taxpayer or organizational monies in the wisest manner.

Accountability is a broad concept and means not simply setting up a budget that adequately reflects institutional goals and objectives, although that is important, but also the continuous monitoring of the budget and purchasing activities to see that the library's goals and objectives are actually being met. Too often, this process does not run smoothly or according to plan; there may be midyear budget cuts or pro-rations, institutional freezes on purchasing, or even the release of newly added funds near the end of the fiscal year with new restrictions on use, even requiring a prompt expenditure before they are lost for the year. All of this requires that the budget itself, and the process by which it can be changed, be appropriately flexible and able to deal with all sorts of issues on typically short notice.

Types of Budgets

A budget may be simply defined as a plan for the expenditure of funds over the period of time those funds are anticipated to be available. Most libraries have a parent organization, whether it is a governing board or board of trustees, a governmental entity (often with divided executive and legislative functions), or other similar entity that either exercises direct control or has significant influence on budgetary matters. The parent organization may also be responsible for entities other than the library and may therefore develop a number of different budgets with various procedures. The type of budget used by the parent entity must necessarily have a direct effect on how the library develops and uses its resources budget.

Budgets for libraries typically fall into one of four general categories: (1) an object of expenditure or line-item budget, (2) a lump-sum budget, (3) a program budget, or (4) a formula budget (being particularly the province of many academic libraries). A short summary of each type of budget in the library context may be useful.

A *line-item budget* is just what its name implies, essentially a listing of objects of expenditure with dollar amounts on each line, which add up to the total available for expenditure. Some line-item budgets are rather broad in terms of categories for the lines, and others are much more detailed. The process for a line-item budget is usually incremental, each line changing from year to year (or other budget period) by amounts based upon examination of changes in particular data or criteria from one year to the next, as opposed to establishing a linkage between the budget amounts and stated objectives or long-range plans. When broad categories are used, the overall budget that the library receives may have, for example, a designated resource budget but with few fixed categories, thereby allowing the library professionals to break down the budget lines according to internal criteria or schemes they may have developed, for example, between adult and children's materials, non-fiction and fiction, books and serials, electronic resources, and so on. This broad line approach is obviously best from the library perspective. Where the lines are more specific, concerns quickly arise in determining whether funds can be moved from one line item to another, without running afoul of either legal or institutional rules and practices.

A *lump-sum budget* is also a fairly clear-cut device that usually provides for the allocation of a specified amount of money to an organization or entity as a whole. Lump-sum budgeting allows administrators maximum flexibility in expenditures but obviously provides very limited built-in accountability to the parent organization. Library directors may elect to similarly pass on lump sums to the library resource budget and other budgets or, to better address the accountability problem, may convert the overall amounts into internal line-item budgets for each department.

A *program budget* is intended to take into account the actual cost of undertaking the purpose of the budget. Often such budgets try to force a continuous link between planning of activities and budgeting for them, and thus relate organizational objectives more directly to the expenditures necessary to meet those objectives. This type of budget approach can be described as nonincremental and often makes use of the zero-sum or zero-based budgeting approach, meaning that financial considerations are returned to the first dollar or zero amount rather than using the previous year's expenditures and allocations as starting points.

A *formula* (or *formula-driven*) *budget* is a method of allocating available resources on the basis of objective quantitative criteria, based either on history or formulaic projections. It has obvious appeal to the scientist and is the type most likely to be found in higher education contexts, and therefore is often used in resource budgets of university and college libraries. Budget formulas vary greatly in their complexity, from relatively simple allocations of a certain percentage of available monies per student credit hour to the division of earmarked funds based on complex mathematical formulas. However they are computed, at least in the higher education arena, most formula budgets can be seen as essentially enrollment driven. Many academic libraries use formulas based on relative numbers of undergraduates and graduate students, absolute number of faculty, subject areas of emphasis at the institution, the presence and number of doctoral degree programs, and so on. Formula budgets have the look and feel of greater objectivity, especially when compared to seemingly arbitrary lump-sum budgeting, but it is in the setting up of the formula and its determining criteria that external factors such as politics can come into play.

For instance, in a state appropriations context, if doctoral programs are heavily favored in the formula (i.e., if their presence yields a higher overall appropriation, as they usually do), then the result of the formula should be that the resource needs of doctoral degree-granting departments receive more attention in the library resources budget than a department that may have huge numbers of undergraduates, but few or no graduate students.

Budget Scenarios

The first requirement in developing a resource budget is to define the programs involved. The traditional library programs are set out below along with concerns for electronic media, document delivery, and interlibrary loan. The listing provides a framework for deciding what kinds of materials should be purchased or accessed and how. The general emphasis here is on the ways that the library could acquire materials, but the same principles are involved whether the materials are acquired or accessed.

1. Direct purchase
   - Publisher
   - Dealer/jobber/vendor
2. Approval plans and blanket orders
3. Subscriptions
   - Direct
   - Vendor
4. Standing orders
   - Publisher
   - Vendor
5. Gifts and exchange
   - Books
   - Periodicals
6. Preservation
   - Binding and mending
   - Other preservation measures
7. Leasing and access (to include document delivery and interlibrary loan costs)
8. Replacements
9. Multiple copies

Setting Budget Priorities

As any library sets out to define (or redefine) its budget, it has to set some priorities. Although they extend across the total library budget, here we are most concerned with priorities affecting library materials expenditures and their equivalents:

1. Basic needs
   - Mission related
   - Primary community
   - Ongoing
   - One-time
2. Type of material
   - Monographs
   - Serials
   - Audiovisual and electronic products
   - Government documents
   - Microforms
   - Electronic services
3. Special needs
   - Research related
   - New programs
   - Retrospective needs
   - Replacements
4. Budgetary settings
   - Steady-state budgets
   - Decreasing budgets
   - Increasing budgets
   - Special funds

A budget is one of the most important planning documents that a library has. The budget translates the organization's mission and goals into dollar terms. To be able to effectively budget for library materials, you must fully understand the political realities under which your institution must function plus any legal restraints on the expenditure of its funds. Materials and personnel are the two largest portions of the library's operating budget. To be in charge of collection development and acquisitions means being responsible for the expenditure of a large percentage of the overall library budget.

Gathering Information for a Library Materials Budget Request

The quest for information begins with what you already know. Existing records show where you are now and give a preview of the future. Since you usually begin preparing a budget request for the next year shortly after the beginning of the current fiscal year, the latest complete records will be for the previous fiscal year (for a sample budget, see Figure 6.1). The current year may also provide information about any trends in orders or price changes. In a sense, the request is prepared as part of a three-year cycle, and information is often sought as to the library's requirements for a further year beyond the

Figure 6.1. Typical Public Library Materials Budget ($)*

Area	Books	Standing Order	Serials	Electronic	Media	Total	% of Total
Adult							
Reference	13,000	17,800	5,000	13,700	400	49,900	19.63
Nonfiction	44,200	0	0	0	2,600	46,800	18.41
Business	4,000	2,500	3,200	3,000	1,200	13,900	5.47
Careers	2,000	450	1,900	1,900	700	6,950	2.73
Serials	0	0	20,000	32,200	0	52,200	20.54
CDs/DVDs	0	0	0	0	11,000	11,000	4.33
General fiction	28,000*	0	0	2,000	0	30,000	11.80
Mystery	2,000*	0	0	400	0	2,400	0.94
Romance	1,200*	0	0	400	0	1,600	0.63
Paperbacks	2,000	0	0	0	0	2,000	0.79
McNaughton	[6,500]	0	0	0	0	[6,500]	
Large print	3,400	0	0	0	0	3,400	1.34
Subtotal	89,600	2,950	30,100	40,800	15,500	170,250	66.99
Young Adult							
Nonfiction	3,100	0	500	0	0	3,600	1.42
Fiction	6,000	0	0	0	0	6,000	2.36
CDs/DVDs	0	0	0	0	3,900	3,900	1.53
Subtotal	9,100	0	500	0	3,900	13,500	5.31
Children							
Reference	2,200	0	1,100	1,800	0	5,100	2.01
Nonfiction	3,100	0	0	0	0	3,100	1.22
Fiction	5,000	0	0	0	0	5,000	1.97
Picture books	6,100	0	0	0	0	6,100	2.40
CDs/DVDs	0	0	0	0	1,200	1,200	0.47
Subtotal	16,400	0	1,100	1,800	1,200	20,500	8.07
Grand Totals	128,100	20,750	63,900	20,400	21,000	254,150	100.00
% of Total	50.40	8.16	25.14	8.03	8.26	100.00	

*E-books are included in the book budget for each category of fiction and nonfiction.

one that will be affected by the next budget. Trends and changes are therefore of vital importance when looking into the future. We can extrapolate only from what we already know about the near past and what is happening currently. Many vendors provide information about book and serials prices and projected increases. *Library Journal* publishes such information about serials every April.

The end result of the budgeting process seldom matches exactly any initial distribution among categories. There are many reasons for such differences:

- Materials may not have been published either in the expected quantities or by the expected times.
- Shipping, postal, or other strike action may have disrupted the normal flow of supply.
- Prices may have increased more than allowed for in the original projection.
- Any price increases were probably unevenly distributed and have had more impact on some areas than on others. In the budget in Figure 6.1, an increase in serials costs was offset somewhat by restricting the amount spent on books.
- Unexpected vacancies or other work pressures may have reduced the output of selectors.
- A special donation may have added to the workload and skewed the original distribution.
- Unforeseen events may have increased the demand for replacements or duplicate copies.
- Financial crises may have reduced or increased the original budget.

Substantial year-end encumbrances may exist for material requests processed late in the year. (Encumbrances represent the cost of orders that have been placed but not yet received.)

Consortium Purchases

All purchases may not be the sole responsibility of a particular library. More and more purchases, especially of electronic resources, are being made through consortia. A study focused on OhioLINK concludes:

By evolving from individual- to group-based licensing we can dramatically expand the information licensed per dollar spent and expand usage far above that possible through individual library action. We can significantly reduce the annual rise in licensing costs versus individual library action. These are good and necessary achievements that we should not sell short nor fail to maximize. (Sanville, 2008: 13)

However, it always behooves the librarians charged with the responsibility for selection and retention plus those who oversee the budget to determine if the library is really getting what it needs from consortium purchases. The library may be getting more resources for its dollars, but it is still important to make sure that the library and its users are getting the right materials. Thus, deciding when to join and leave "big deals" through a consortium is both an economic and a collection management decision.

Bookkeeping Terminology 101

It is now time to turn to the practical business of receiving and paying for shipments of materials or for licenses to access materials. The first thing that happens is that you get an invoice for materials either in the shipment or, for electronic materials and serials, through the mail. Once the materials have been checked against the purchase, it is time to approve the invoice for payment.

But what if something is missing? When the company is notified of the problem, they may issue the library a credit memorandum in the amount of the missing item to speed up payment of the invoice. The invoice might be for thousands of dollars while the missing item costs only $10.00. Then, depending upon arrangements with the company, the item is either reordered or sent later.

As the acquisitions librarian begins to handle this nitty-gritty end of the collection development process, it might seem that morphing into a CPA would be advisable. Not so, but you do need to understand a little about the terminology and the methodology underlying financial statements. The main thing to keep in mind is that what you need most is to become comfortable with the vocabulary. Here are some terms that will be typically encountered:

The Accounting Vocabulary of the Acquisitions Process

accountability	accounts payable	accounts receivable
appropriation	approval plan	audit
blanket order	bookkeeping	budget
budget categories	cash-basis accounting	contingency fund
cost accounting	credit memorandum	double-entry accounting
encumbrance	endowment funds	line-item budget
lump-sum budget	operating budget	program budget
purchase order	requisition	standing order
subscription	voucher	zero-based budgeting

An ordinary dictionary will see you through most of these terms, but it is important in the context of encumbering and paying for acquisitions not to assume that you know what they mean, so some research and reading is advisable. While it is beyond the scope of this work to delve deeply into the intricacies and medieval origins of accounting, a little familiarity with the double-entry system traditionally used by accountants generally may be helpful.

Double-entry accounting requires that each transaction be recorded in at least two accounts, resulting in a debit to one or more accounts and an offsetting credit to one or more accounts. This method thus provides for checking accuracy because the sum of all debits should equal the sum of all credits. Modern personal finance software does not usually require double-entry accounting, but often actually performs and simply hides it from the user, presumably to prevent confusion. But in large entities like universities, accounting systems are clearly based on the double-entry system, and the librarian must be able to understand it generally in order not to misapprehend, for example, moneys actually available.

Basically, accounting for money may be seen as an equation. When revenue equals expenses, the following equation applies:

assets = liabilities + equity (the investment in the enterprise)

Of course, revenue does not usually exactly equal expenses. So, the accounting equation becomes:

assets = liabilities + equity + (revenue − expenses)

In double-entry accounting, this equation must always be true, for any time period. Then the accounts are said to be in balance. If the accounts are not in balance, you know an error has occurred. For accounts to remain in balance, a change in one account must be reflected through a change in another account.

These changes are made by accounting entries, called debits and credits. Whether one uses a debit or credit to increase or decrease an account depends on the account's normal balance. Asset and expense accounts have a normal balance of debit. Liability, revenue, and capital accounts have a normal balance of credit. On an accounting ledger, debits are recorded on the left side and credits on the right side for each account. Since the accounts must always balance, for each transaction a debit will be made to one or several accounts and a credit made to one or several accounts. The sum of all the debits in connection with any transaction equals the sum of all the credit entries. After each transaction, therefore, the sum of all the accounts with a debit balance must equal the sum of all the accounts with a credit balance.

In the acquisitions context, the librarian must keep in mind that when an item is paid for, there are always two accounting entries, a credit to the cash asset account (the moneys available for purchase) and a debit to the book asset account. If the library uses an encumbrance system, the debit will be to that account, reducing the encumbrance to balance the cash credit amount. Knowing at least this little bit will help you to read and better understand the financial statements and account balance information you may receive. It is not the librarian's job to design or make entries in the library's accounting system, but having a general idea of the intricacies and basic theory involved will make you more knowledgeable about the effects of each day-to-day financial transaction and how to read and understand the library's financial statements and accounts.

Activity

In groups of three to five students, manipulate the budget in Figure 6.1 based on the situations described below. Assume that you have the authority to make changes to the budget allocations, but must still make the overall budget balance. You may or may not want to create line items below the level in Figure 6.1 to ensure that particular types of materials are not overlooked.

1. The mayor's office calls and needs information concerning endangered wildlife in your state. A quick check of the library collection does not bring to light anything newer than 2000. Given the interest by the mayor in this subject, it is a good assumption that others may come to the library looking for such materials. At present there is no allocation for such materials since your nonfiction allocation is already encumbered, but there is still money in other categories of your budget. What do you do to solve the immediate need? How will you budget for this in the future?
2. A digital camera club gets permission to meet in the library and attendance is huge. It seems everybody has received a new digital camera for Christmas and interest is high in photography, printing of digital images, and their permanent storage. After the first meeting some of the attendees tell the circulation librarian that the library collection is outdated, and they would really like to be able to borrow some more recent books, especially on digital photography. They ask if there are current magazines that deal with digital photography. How would you handle this situation?
3. A community meeting reveals that new residents want and need materials in several Slavic languages. At present the library has a collection of English and Spanish materials, but no other languages are represented. The library has no employees with language skills in any of the Slavic languages. How should the library respond to this new need?
4. A local church group protests the low numbers of pro-life materials in the library. They claim that the library holds a substantial number of items about abortion, but not items that reflect their views. How should the library respond?

References

Martin, Murray S. 1995. *Collection Development and Finance: A Guide to Strategic Library-Materials Budgeting.* Chicago: American Library Association.

Sanville, Tom. 2008. "Do Economic Factors Really Matter in the Assessment and Retention of Electronic Resources Licensed at the Library Consortium Level?" *Collection Management* 33, nos. 1/2: 1–16.

Selected Readings

Anderson, Douglas. 2006. "Allocation of Costs for Electronic Products in Academic Library Consortia." *College and Research Libraries* 67 (March): 123–135.

Bailey, Timothy P., Jeannette Barnes Lessels, and Rickey D. Best. 2005. "Using Universal Borrowing Data in the Library Book Fund Allocation Process." *Library Collections, Acquisitions, and Technical Services* 29, no. 1: 90–98.

Canepi, Kitti. 2007. "Fund Allocation Formula Analysis: Determining Elements for Best Practice in Libraries." *Library Collections, Acquisitions, and Technical Services* 31, no. 1: 12–24.

Clendenning, Lynda Fuller, J. Kay Martin, and Gail McKenzie. 2005. "Secrets for Managing Materials Budget Allocations: A Brief Guide for Collections Managers." *Library Collections, Acquisitions, and Technical Services* 29, no. 1: 99–108.

Gerhard, Kristin H. 2005. "Pricing Models for Electronic Journals and Other Electronic Academic Materials: The State of the Art." *Journal of Library Administration* 42, nos. 3/4: 1–25.

Hallam, Arlita, and Teresa R. Dalston. 2005. *Managing Budgets and Finances: A How-to-Do-It for Librarians and Information Professionals.* New York: Neal-Schuman.

Martin, Murray S., and Milton T. Wolf. 1998. *Budgeting for Information Access: Managing the Resource Budget for Absolute Access.* Chicago: American Library Association.

Schmidt, Karen, Wendy Allen Shelburne, and David Steven Vess. 2008. "Approaches to Selection, Access, and Collection Development in the Web World." *Library Resources and Technical Services* 52 (July): 184–191.

Smith, A. Arro, and Stephanie Langenkamp. 2007. "Indexed Collection Budget Allocations: A Tool for Quantitative Collection Development Based on Circulation." *Public Libraries* 46, no. 5: 50–54.

Walters, William H. 2007. "A Regression-Based Approach to Library Fund Allocation." *Library Resources and Technical Services* 51 (October): 263–278.

Wu, Eric FuLong, and Katherine M. Shelfer. 2007. "Materials Budget Allocation: A Formula Fitness Review." *Library Collections, Acquisitions, and Technical Services* 31, nos. 3/4: 171–183.

7

Assessment and Evaluation of the Collection, Including Deselection (Weeding)

Overview

In this chapter we look at various methods to evaluate or assess your library's collection with an eye toward determining when and how to weed out or deselect items and materials. Every library needs to periodically assess its collection. Determining what you have, what you don't have, what you need, and what to keep is a central component in the collection development process that is often ignored in favor of acquisitions. While public librarians and school media specialists usually instinctively understand that they must do a lot of weeding to keep their collections current and circulating, it is an issue in academic, archival, and other special libraries as well. The missions of public and school libraries require almost constant remaking of their collections to reflect changes in tastes and needs and to replace quickly worn out or lost components of their collections. Academic and special libraries often need to assess their collections to ensure inclusion of the materials most needed by their institution's researchers and students.

Since collection evaluation and assessment are usually studied together with weeding in most library school curricula, some students may think the terms are nearly synonymous, but they should not be so viewed. Indeed, evaluation or analysis of a collection does not necessarily imply weeding at all. Assessment can result in a determination that certain materials currently in the collection ought to be deselected or weeded, but there are many other reasons to assess a collection apart from weeding. A quick example will suffice: an academic library may be interested in assessing its materials in a particular subject area, for example, early modern European history, because the university's history department is actively considering and needs to make a case for adding a PhD program in that specialty to its curriculum. Such an assessment would inevitably lead not to deaccession or weeding but rather to the need to purchase additional materials on the subject.

Likewise, special accreditation reviews of programs in many disciplines (such as those conducted by the Association to Advance Collegiate Schools of Business, or the American Library Association) almost always require a written analysis assessing the adequacy of the library's support of and collection in the particular program subject area or discipline being reviewed prior to an initial or continuing accreditation visit by the reviewing agency. Libraries are also part of the review process as part of regional accreditation generally conducted by accrediting entities for the institutions of which they are a component (e.g., Middle States Association of Colleges and Schools, New England Association of Schools and Colleges, North Central Association of Colleges and Schools, Northwest Association of Accredited Schools for primary and secondary schools and Northwest Commission on Colleges and Universities for postsecondary institutions, the Western Association of Schools and Colleges, and the Southern Association of Colleges and Schools), which typically entails an overall assessment of the library's collection.

Evaluating or Assessing the Collection

Collection assessment and evaluation necessarily include a number of different activities and processes. First, a comprehensive description of the library's existing resources at a particular point in time will need to be developed. This description will include not only an assessment of past and current collecting strengths but also a determination of what the library's future collecting strengths should be. Increasingly, the overlap in full-text resources among vendors must also be considered, as bundled resources often contain titles that are already owned or licensed by the library. An assessment project also evaluates the effectiveness of the library's collection in supporting the mission and goals of the organization of which it is part, and it should lead to a plan of action detailing how the library's collection development activities should proceed in order to obtain the best match between the collection and the mission and goals of the library.

A large library will seldom decide to evaluate its entire collection in one project, instead choosing areas within the collection for evaluation. Of course, some areas will present more difficulties than others. Interdisciplinary study fields can be particularly difficult—"Women's Studies is problematic for collection developers because of its interdisciplinary nature, its lack of commercially published materials, and its various user populations" (Bolton, 2009: 221). Other more traditional disciplines may not reach across so many fields and so may be better defined particularly in the library's classification scheme, but still be too large for a single project. A large academic library, for instance, would probably not choose to evaluate the history collection in one project, but would probably break it up by geographical area, such as American history or British history. The moral of the story here is simple: in any collection evaluation project, limit what you try to capture to the resources you have available to hand.

Getting Started with Evaluating a Collection

In carrying out the collection evaluation process, librarians have traditionally sought to gather both qualitative and quantitative data. While not an end in itself, such gathering is important. The following areas should be looked at and determined:

- Circulation statistics, with an emphasis on frequency of usage of particular items
- Title count
- Median age of items in the collection, within categories
- Shelf observation conducted by subject experts
- Holdings checked against standard lists and bibliographies
- Interlibrary loan requests
- User surveys conducted and focus groups organized to discuss library holdings and perceived adequacy

The information garnered using these methods can be equally important in evaluating both print and electronic resources. An important aspect of the evaluation process is the consideration of all formats of materials and how they fit into the library's overall collection. Some special characteristics of electronic collections need to be considered in their evaluation and assessment. Specifically, information and data need to be collected and analyzed in the following areas:

- Type of Internet connection used by the library itself and that used by patrons to access the library remotely
- Capabilities and distribution of computer workstations and printers provided in the library building
- Internet and other network service costs, including the costs associated with remote dial-in capabilities
- Webpage and database hits, searches, printing, and the like

Although vendors may be able to supply statistics for the use of their networked resources, the proliferation of federated or metasearch software means that these statistics require additional study to determine the true usefulness of particular sources to patrons because of the very nature of the federated search. In addition, not all vendors report usage statistics in the same way, so care always has to be taken when comparing across vendor products.

Evaluation Methods

We will look at the major methods of collection evaluation, out of the numerous methods available. Almost none of these is right for every situation, and perhaps not absolutely so for any situation, but they may be considered tried and true. Sometimes a mix of at least two of the methods may make for a better result and more accurate and useful evaluation.

Checklists Method

In 1849, Charles Jewett at the Smithsonian Institute engaged in the first recognized use of what has come to be called the checklist method of evaluating a collection. This, the oldest method still in general if not widespread use, may be considered subject-matter specific and involves using bibliographies or lists of notable books in specific subject areas. Several standard subject area lists have been developed over the years.

Obviously, picking the checklist or bibliography that is right for your particular library or situation is critical. While the checklist method generally involves use of a standard bibliography or other authoritative work, the bibliographies appearing in theses and dissertations in particular subject areas are also good sources to check against. In evaluating undergraduate libraries, student papers may also be checked to see if the materials cited are available in the library, as students may have used other libraries to conduct their research. The basic premise here is to determine whether the student paper could have been written solely utilizing the student's home library's collection. To the extent this is determined not to be the case, the collection can be seen as arguably less than fully adequate.

A popular bibliography for use in evaluating college and university libraries is *Resources for College Libraries* (*RCL*), published by the Association for College and Research Libraries. A comprehensive and valuable list, it nevertheless provides an excellent example of the caution needed in picking a checklist, and indeed a problem with the checklist system generally. For instance, if the library has previously used *RCL* in connection with its purchasing and acquisitions decisions (which many naturally do), using the same list to evaluate your collection presents obvious inbreeding problems, as it were. In such a situation the evaluating librarian would be well advised to find other bibliographies for evaluation purposes. And while a good plan might involve using *RCL* for evaluation purposes initially and then using the results for deselection purposes, the next time an evaluation is performed another resource must be used as the checklist. Otherwise, the collection runs the risk of likely becoming narrower than desirable.

A more up-to-date and faster checklist approach would involve evaluating your collection using an online database such as WorldCat with assessment software for research libraries (Perrault, 1999: 47–67) or a product such as

Follett's *Titlewave* for public libraries. Again, however, caution is important, and use of another checklist the next time would likely be desirable.

Circulation and Interlibrary Loan Statistics

Circulation statistics can be a valuable evaluation tool. This approach involves looking at the number of times that particular items have been checked out within a given period. Obviously, these sorts of statistics can inform the collection development librarian in numerous ways, for instance, about which subject areas enjoy the greatest circulation and the percentage of titles in a particular subject that are checked out at the same time or, conversely, the number of books on a particular subject waiting on the shelves at a given time.

In the mid-1990s, Carpenter and Getz (1995) studied the subject areas contained in a broad curricular field (economics) to try to determine just which books published in a given year did not circulate. Their premise was that a book held by libraries that did not circulate was a collection error, just the same as a failure to have a book on hand that was needed was an error. They labeled these noncirculating books as "type II errors," and classified as "type I errors" those books not purchased by the library but obtained through interlibrary loan, often more than once. Carpenter and Getz emphasized the importance of the often ignored type II error, which indicates a waste of resources that could be used to remedy type I errors, while advocating the use of both of their derived error statistics in evaluating any collection.

As indicated in the Carpenter and Getz study, interlibrary loan statistics can be an excellent source of data when evaluating a collection as these records can, almost by definition, show the titles that users have needed that were not available in the library when they needed them.

Citation Analysis

On the college and university level, citation analysis can be a useful tool. This approach involves a study of the bibliographies from faculty publications, student dissertations and theses, or other student work to determine how many items (or what percentage of items) cited in these bibliographies are in fact available in the college or university library. The purpose of this type of study is to determine whether the academic work produced by the college's faculty and students could have been written using primarily materials in the institution's library. While the citation analysis approach is most often used and generally best suited to colleges and universities, high school media centers may use this technique as well when students are asked to write major research papers. Worth examining is a study by Ashman (2009: 112–128) of the research objectives of citation analysis studies published between January 2005 and March 2008. Not all deal with analysis of a collection, but this study provides the reader with a good feel for the many effective uses of citation studies.

With particular relevance to the evaluation of electronic resources, a number of technology-aided methods of collection assessment are available:

1. Scripted user surveys or assessments: To conduct this type of assessment, the library's users of electronic resources are provided contemporaneously with their session a pop-up box (or some other similar method) onscreen, allowing them to rate the value of the resource used to resolve their particular information need. This type of user survey at the point of actual use of an electronic resource can prove valuable (although patron complaints can be expected to outnumber compliments and praise, and some correcting for this factor has to be made).

2. Transaction log or web log analysis: This is an arguably more objective, if not necessarily adequately qualitative, approach that can provide data for analysis of user transaction activity at a website or in interaction with an electronic resource. Some electronic resource vendors provide library licensees with useful statistics on resource usage both on a regular basis and upon request. These statistics can be used to make decisions concerning the desirability of database renewal as well as revealing the number of simultaneous users of the electronic resource for which the library may need to provide. Examples of statistical data that can be gathered include number of queries per specific database, number of sessions, number of menu selections, number of items available to be examined, citations displayed, and the number of times users were denied access because the maximum number of simultaneous users was exceeded. Such statistics, unfortunately, do not usually provide much information concerning the relative usefulness of a resource and whether the patron received exactly the information that was desired, but they can provide some information about how, and how often, the particular product is being used; that information can then be supplemented through one or more of the qualitative assessment techniques.

Network Usage Analysis

Network usage analysis measures the use of web-based services by collecting network or by terminal use, which can provide important information, such as the load on the library's network server or router, user access points, and numbers of users both simultaneously and in the aggregate. This information showing network load and capacity can also indicate what services are being used and how frequently.

Vendor-Supplied Statistics

For networked electronic resources, the vendors can supply the library with a great deal of statistics on the use of the particular resource. Often these statistics are not comparable across products and almost certainly are not comparable across vendors. Given that the statistics provided to libraries are nonstandardized, librarians must be careful not to compare apples with oranges when making decisions based on those data. Vendors should be able to supply librarians with statistics in a form that the library specifies, but at present that is not usually the case. It generally falls to the libraries to attempt to keep their own statistics if they are to make purchasing and retention decisions based upon statistical data; however, most libraries do not have the staff to keep thorough statistics across products and vendors.

Generally the best assessments will involve at least two and sometimes even three different methods. Using more than one method tends to rid the assessment of most of the biases that inevitably work their way into an evaluation using only one method. In research terms, the use of such multiple methods is called triangulation.

Deselection or Weeding the Collection

While evaluation of a collection does not ineluctably lead to deselection or weeding, in public libraries and school media centers evaluation and weeding typically do go hand in hand. As noted above, all libraries must inevitably engage in some weeding to keep the collection in good shape for users. This is true even for libraries with significant archival missions, where multiple copies and editions can come to clog the shelves.

The definitive modern work on deselection is *Weeding Library Collections: Library Weeding Methods*, by Stanley J. Slote (1997), who has published several editions of this important text on weeding. Based on a lifetime of research, Slote (1997: xix) draws an important distinction between the basic parts of a library's collection, what he refers to as the core collection, and the library's "weedable" collection. Different types of libraries will naturally exhibit different distributions of their core and weedable components. For example, an academic library will usually consist primarily or mostly of core materials with only a relatively small number of items in its weedable collection. Public libraries and school media centers, by contrast, will typically have just the opposite proportions. To gain a more thorough understanding of weeding and the various methods of doing it, Slote's *Weeding Library Collections* remains the most authoritative source and is highly recommended, especially in regard to a primarily print collection.

Why Weed?

As noted earlier, virtually every library needs to weed or deselect. Slote maintains that there are no less than seven very good reasons to weed any collection:

1. To stimulate circulation
2. To save space
3. To save time
4. To enhance appeal
5. To establish credibility
6. To respond to community needs and interests
7. To make room for new technologies and formats

Let's look at each of these reasons.

Circulation

Weeding has been shown time and again to be one of the best ways to stimulate circulation, especially in public libraries, as overcrowded shelves discourage browsing by users. Crowding also tends to make particular items difficult to find, a problem in academic libraries as well. To illustrate, Figure 7.1 shows a small section of a bookcase that most likely could benefit from significant weeding. Even if these groaning shelves contain nothing but items central to the library's core collection, only if the library's shelves are uncluttered will users easily be able to find what they want, thereby improving the tendency for patrons to check out more items.

Figure 7.1. Shelves in Need of Weeding

Space

Weeding can naturally save space on the shelves. Shelf space in any library should generally be seen as a finite (and certainly expensive) resource, so why waste valuable space on items that do not circulate or are outdated? Weeding provides the necessary room for needed materials that are more likely to circulate than those deselected.

Time

Weeding saves time for both librarians and users and can make the library more appealing to users. Items can be shelved more easily and accurately and located faster on shelves that are not overcrowded.

Appeal

Ridding the collection of damaged or unattractive materials makes a better impression on users, and making the library more appealing simply makes it more likely to be used. People, for whatever reasons, do tend to judge books by their covers. And from the library staff side, uncluttered shelves make for a more pleasant work environment, presumably resulting in improvements in the quality and accuracy of their work.

Credibility

Weeding helps the library establish credibility with its patrons. A bloated collection crammed on the shelves is not necessarily a good collection. Indeed, often quite the opposite is the case. It is more important to have items that users actually need and that are up to date to satisfy current users' needs.

Community Needs and Interests

A well-weeded collection tends to send a message to users that the library is concerned with keeping up with the community's needs and is in touch.

Making Room for New Technologies

Hand in glove with making shelf space available is the idea that in today's electronic resource environment, not all the library's space need be devoted to maintenance of a large, traditional print collection. Where unlimited building funds are not available to provide needed additional space, trimming the print collection can be a necessary step.

Issues That Discourage Weeding

If weeding is such a good idea and so basic to any good library's collection, why isn't it high on everybody's to-do list? Slote (1997: 5–6) lists five factors that have a tendency to discourage weeding:

- Emphasis on numbers: Numbers of books and other items are time-honored criteria used in standards of accreditation as well as internal reports and decision making. Administrators in institutions of all kinds often try to avoid being overly subjective in their decision making through reliance on seemingly objective statistics and numbers. This leads to far too many key library decisions makers viewing more materials as necessarily better, and thus discouraging their librarians from too much weeding.
- Time constraints and professional work pressure: There is never enough time to do everything that needs to be done, in a library or anywhere

else, and this limitation often makes weeding difficult to schedule. Proper deselection is correctly seen as a professional library function, but this does not mean that volunteers cannot assist in getting the job done.

• Public displeasure: Especially in the case of tax-supported libraries, if the general public becomes aware that the library seems to be throwing away valuable books, serious objections will almost inevitably arise. The same holds true in academic libraries where faculty typically hold strong opinions respecting the value of particular works and materials. Generally, this displeasure and consternation occur when a collection has not been weeded regularly and then too much has to be done in a relatively short time (see, e.g., St. Lifer and Rogers, 1997). "Weeding is politically incorrect. Citizens go nuts when they find out that libraries discard thousands of books each year" (Manley, 1996: 1108). This reaction puts an additional burden on library staff to explain what they are doing and that it is consistent with the library's goals and mission, a burden that doing nothing might be seen as avoiding. Some of these problems can be overcome if another library that wants and needs the items can be found. When a major weeding is underway, part of the process should involve a search for likely recipients for deselected items.

• Sanctity of the collection: Libraries are traditionally and rightfully seen as repositories of the ideas on which civilization itself is based, and such thoughts can cause many people to develop and express deep emotional as well as intellectual arguments to support keeping a collection fully intact. Certainly the great effort that likely has gone into establishing a collection can be seen as being unjustifiably rendered something of a waste. But not every library has the mission and goals of the great library at Alexandria, and trimming a collection should not be allowed to be viewed as the equivalent of a great fire endangering the world's intellectual patrimony. At best, a library collection will always have items that are lost, stolen, mutilated, and so on, so no collection ever really remains fully intact. Education of the public about the goals of deselection and weeding are the best answer here.

• Conflicting criteria: Libraries are often faced with the dilemma that many good books do not seem to be needed by the library's users, but many poorer quality items, including those that seem unrelated to the collection or the library's mission and goals, circulate frequently. Who wants to throw away a printed compilation of Christopher Marlowe's plays? But who will likely read them if the library supports a technical or trade school curriculum? These kinds of situations can lead to paralysis in the weeding process, especially where the library is not archival. Look to the nature and goal of the library and its public as the best touchstones as to what to keep and what to discard.

When and Who Should Weed?

When to weed is easy: often, if not always early, in order to give items sufficient time to prove their worth. But it is important to weed routinely. Problems with the public over weeding generally occur when the library has let weeding go for a long period and then needs to remove a large number of items. To avoid this, set up a schedule by subject area to ensure a continuous and thorough approach to weeding. If your library has a collection of e-books, they should also be included in your weeding projects with the same criteria as for printed materials (fortunately, these resources will not have appearance issues to be considered). Items that are returned to the library should be checked for damage. Such materials may need to be weeded or replaced. When new editions are acquired, it is a good idea to check for earlier editions that then need to be weeded.

As to whether to consider the weeding process as strictly a professional job, weeding this way can be a big mistake. Yes, the responsibility must ultimately be a professional one, but all staff can and should have a role in keeping the collection properly weeded. Pages and shelvers should be instructed to pull damaged and worn items when shelving or accessing materials. Library assistants should do the same when checking in materials or retrieving items on hold. Librarians should evaluate their assigned sections of the collection on a routine basis. Everyone should take responsibility for some aspect of assessing the collection as they are working with it for the benefit of users in the stacks.

Determining What to Weed

Besides the criteria of appropriateness to the library's collection, usage, and so on, and assuming that an item meets the library's collection assessment standards, or if multiple copies of an item exist, selecting particular items that need to go is important. Condition matters, so besides looking at the cover, flip through the material to make sure that the pages are in reasonable condition and not loose. Also check the binding to see if it is loose. If you have someone on staff who does repairs, it can be sent for repair, or it can be weeded if the condition is bad enough. In an academic library, you might be more likely to send it to be rebound. In public and school media centers, there is a feeling that rebound books are not popular with patrons, so in that environment, if repairs will be extensive, weeding is likely indicated. Stained, moldy, or mildewed items should also be strongly considered for weeding. Water damage, mold, or mildew in all events require removal of the affected items from the stacks promptly upon discovery, as mold and mildew can quickly spread, flulike, through an entire collection.

Even if the material passes all the physical and appearance tests above, particularly if you are working in a school media center or public library, check to see when the item last circulated. In such a library, adult fiction that has not circulated for two or three years has probably passed its prime. Multiple copies should certainly be weeded and a decision made as to whether even one copy remains useful. Without being too judgmental, it is a good idea to keep at least one copy of items generally recognized or regarded as classic literature. Although the circulation and use of these works may be sporadic, users rightly expect any good library to have copies of them.

For nonfiction, along with circulation data, you need to be concerned with whether the information contained in the work remains valid and current. Computer books are notorious for being outdated almost as soon as the ink is dry; histories, however, have a much longer shelf life. Many libraries work out a plan based on the classification scheme indicating when every subject area in the library should be weeded. This is usually a very satisfactory approach.

While academic and research libraries are much more conservative in their weeding or deselection processes and practices, weeding is still necessary. For instance, items may be required for particular classes, which will usually result in multiple copies being ordered to be held in reference room reserve. After some period, when the course ceases to be offered or the professor who required the readings retires, it may be that only one copy is needed. Care should be taken in deselecting seemingly outdated materials in research library contexts. Consider such questions as whether to keep materials with dated information in case someone later wants to undertake a history of the subject as opposed to weeding them to keep students from using the old materials instead of the newer, more up-to-date works. Here, consultation with relevant faculty members in the field can be a good approach.

The continuous review, evaluation, and weeding (CREW) method has been used in libraries since 1976. It is specifically targeted to small and medium-sized libraries. The heart of the method is a series of criteria based on the Dewey Decimal System. There are differences in its instructions according to the average subject needs of these libraries.

The CREW method gives six general criteria for considering weeding an item from the library's collection, summed up with the acronym MUSTIE:

M = Misleading—factually inaccurate

U = Ugly—worn beyond mending or rebinding

S = Superseded—by a new edition or by a much better book on the subject

T = Trivial—of no discernible literary or scientific merit

I = Irrelevant to the needs and interests of the library's community

E = Elsewhere—the material is easily obtainable from another library (Larson, 2008)

The website for the Texas State Library and Archives Commission (http://www.tsl.state.tx.us/ld/pubs/crew/) provides a manual for the CREW method (Larson, 2008). The website also has PowerPoint slide shows and other teaching materials to further understanding and answer questions about the CREW procedures. Specific sections of the CREW manual deal with children's materials and reference materials. The heart of the manual gives specific guidelines for each part of the collection by the Dewey Decimal classification.

A Note on the Typically Negative Public Reaction to Weeding

A study by Nikkel and Beltway (2009) describes an interesting event: the decision to severely weed and ultimately discard what many considered one of the best library collections of science fiction and fantasy in the country. A considered decision was made by the library to weed the collection. Following that, the remaining collection did not contribute significantly to the academic curriculum of the university and was therefore eliminated. In the introduction to their study, Nikkel and Beltway (2009: 195) pose a number of interesting questions relating to the philosophy underlying the deselection process:

> What happens when once actively used special collections are neglected and become underused or ignored? Do we as librarians maintain them in their current state in the hope that they will somehow receive the recognition they deserve or because they represent a significant investment of time and resources that we are loathe to do away with?

Although almost 5,000 works were weeded, the collection was largely saved, ultimately because of protests from outside the university, and a new specialized collection policy for science fiction and fantasy was developed to help improve the library's collection in the area and rationalize future acquisitions. While academic libraries usually feel less pressure to bow to public opinion, if for no other reason than that the public may lack a feeling of ownership, public libraries, with their typical dependence on public and tax funding, much more routinely have to deal with the experience of strongly expressed public displeasure when users do not understand why the library is suddenly discarding thousands of books. These stories hit the media relatively often, more than occasionally accompanied by unhappy visuals of dumpsters crammed to the rim with what appear to be perfectly useful books, presumably purchased at considerable public expense. Famously, the San Francisco Public Library aroused a firestorm of public criticism in the

1990s when the collection was heavily weeded before moving into a new library building. The problem, as usual, was that the library's collection had not been weeded systematically over a fairly long period of construction, with the result that a much larger than usual number of books and serials needed to be removed from the collection.

Conclusion

Faye Chadwell (2009: 77), in an article published in *Collection Management*, sums up the future of collection building and assessment very well:

> As we move forward and make more progress in the transition from print to digital, it is clear that it is going to be easier and easier to determine the impact that our collection building has on our users' daily lives. It is also going to be imperative that we keep our users' developmental, education, and entertainment needs in mind—more that we ever did in the print realm. If libraries and collection managers wish to compete with other user-focused services, we need to enlist our users regularly in collection building and collection management activities that once were mediated by library staff. We may risk losing relevancy in our users' daily lives if we do not.

While most librarians are book lovers at heart, and therefore usually keen to do selection, developing and maintaining a quality collection requires a commensurate ability to undertake the considerably less fun jobs of continuous evaluation and deselection. These tasks are just as critical to the development of a quality library collection as acquisition of items in the first place. Sufficient time to do the job right must be scheduled or found. Doing so, and then evaluating and weeding the collection properly, on a systematic and regular basis, will save you much grief and trouble. Just as no garden can prosper if left unweeded, so will a library collection inevitably fall into disrepair, if not outright ruin, if methodical and careful approaches to deselection are not undertaken.

Vocabulary

citation analysis	CREW
interlibrary loan	MUSTIE
network usage analysis	regional accreditation
resource sharing	specialized accreditation
transaction logs	triangulation
WorldCat	

Discussion Questions

1. Assume that you have just been hired to handle collection development and you are instructed to evaluate your new library's existing collection. What methods would you use and why would you choose those particular methods? First put your answer in the context of a particular type of library and provide a hypothetical collection size, and then describe how you would proceed.

2. Assume that you have just taken a position as the sole librarian or collection development librarian in a public or school library that has not, from all appearances, been weeded for some considerable time. How would you proceed? Describe any public relations, consultation, and so on that you would do. Assuming that you have support for weeding, how would you organize and proceed with such a project? What would the differences be in your procedures if the library were an academic or special library?

Activity

Divide up into groups of three or four students. Visit any type of library that has a book collection and choose a range of call numbers to examine. Have at least one shelf for each student in the group. In a large library, the classification area should be stated narrowly enough so that you have no more than two shelves per person. Examine each title on your shelves and decide if it needs to be weeded, repaired, replaced, or simply put back on the shelf. Use the rest of your group as a committee for tough decisions. (Your professor may wish to know which libraries the class will be using so that this activity can be cleared with the appropriate librarians.) Report back to the class as a whole the problems you had making decisions and how your group went about trying to address the issues.

References

Ashman, Allen B. 2009. "An Examination of the Research Objectives of Recent Citation Analysis Studies." *Collection Management* 34 (April–June): 112–128.

Bolton, Brooke A. 2009. "Women's Studies Collections: A Checklist Evaluation." *Journal of Academic Librarianship* 35 (May): 221–226.

Carpenter, D., and M. Getz. 1995. "Evaluation of Library Resources on the Field of Economics." *Collection Management* 20, no. 1/2: 49–89.

Chadwell, Faye A. 2009. "What's Next for Collection Management and Managers? User-Centered Collection Management." *Collection Management* 34 (April–June): 69–78.

Larson, Jeannette. 2008. "CREW: A Weeding Manual for Modern Libraries." Austin: Texas Public Library and Archives Commission. Accessed January 20, 2010. http://www.tsl.state.tx.us/ld/pubs/crew.

Manley, Will. 1996. "The Manley Arts: If I Called This Column 'Weeding,' You Wouldn't Read It." *Booklist* 92 (March): 1108.

Nikkel, Terry, and Liane Beltway. 2009. "When Worlds Collide: Dismantling the Science Fiction and Fantasy Collection at the University of New Brunswick, Saint John." *Collection Management* 34 (July–September): 194–208.

Perrault, Anna H. 1999. "National Collecting Trends: Collection Analysis Methods and Findings." *Library and Information Research* 21, no. 1: 47–67.

Slote, Stanley J. 1997. *Weeding Library Collections: Library Weeding Methods.* 4th ed. Englewood, CO: Libraries Unlimited.

St. Lifer, Evan, and Michael Rogers. 1997. "City Rebukes Philadelphia Library on Weeding Practices." *Library Journal* 122 (May 15): 12.

Selected Readings

Adams, Brian, and Bob Noel. 2008. "Circulation Statistics in the Evaluation of Collection Development." *Collection Building* 27, no. 2: 71–73.

Banks, Julie. 2002. "Weeding Book Collections in the Age of the Internet." *Collection Building* 21, no. 3: 113–119.

Bobal, Alison M., Margaret Mellinger, and Bonnie E. Avery. 2008. "Collection Assessment and New Academic Programs." *Collection Management* 33, no. 4: 288–301.

Dilevko, Juris, and Keren Dali. 2004. "Improving Collection Development and Reference Services for Interdisciplinary Fields through Analysis of Citation Patterns: An Example Using Tourism Studies." *College and Research Libraries* 65 (May): 216–241.

Fenner, Audrey. 2004. "The Approval Plan: Selection Aid, Selection Substitute." *Acquisitions Librarian* 16, nos. 31/32: 227–240.

Feyereisen, Pierre, and Anne Spoiden. 2009. "Can Local Citation Analysis of Master's and Doctoral Theses Help Decision-Making about the Management of the Collection of Periodicals? A Case Study in Psychology and Education Sciences." *Journal of Academic Librarianship* 35 (November): 514–522.

Franklin, Brinley, and Terry Plum. 2008. "Assessing the Value and Impact of Digital Content." *Journal of Library Administration* 48, no. 1: 41–57.

Fundy, Gerri, and Alesia McManus. 2005. "Using a Decision Grid Process to Build Consensus in Electronic Resources Cancellation Decision." *Journal of Academic Librarianship* 31 (November): 533–538.

Haycock, Laurel A. 2004. "Citation Analysis of Education Dissertations for Collection Development." *Library Resources and Technical Services* 48 (April): 102–106.

Hiott, Judith, and Carla Beasley. 2005. "Electronic Collection Management: Completing the Cycle—Experiences at Two Libraries." *Acquisitions Librarian* 17, nos. 33/34: 159–178.

McAbee, Sonja L., and William L. Hubbard. 2003. "The Current Reality of National Book Publishing Output and Its Effect on Collection Assessment." *Collection Management* 28, no. 4: 67–78.

Metz, Paul, and Caryl Gray. 2005. "Public Relations and Library Weeding." *Journal of Academic Librarianship* 31 (May): 273–279.

Nisonger, Thomas E. 2008. "Use of the Checklist Method for Content Evaluation of Full-Text Databases." *Library Resources and Technical Services* 52 (January): 4–17.

Pancheshnikov, Yelena. 2007. "A Comparison of Literature Citations in Faculty Publications and Student Theses as Indicators of Collection Use and a Background for Collection Management at a University Library." *Journal of Academic Librarianship* 33 (November): 674–683.

Roy, Loriene. 1994. "Weeding." In *Encyclopedia of Library and Information Science* 54, Suppl. 17: 352–398. New York: Marcel Dekker.

Samson, Sue, Sebastian Derry, and Holly Eggleston. 2004. "Networked Resources, Assessment and Collection Development." *Journal of Academic Librarianship* 30 (November): 476–481.

Singer, Carol A. 2008. "Weeding Gone Wild: Planning and Implementing a Review of the Reference Collection." *Reference and User Services Quarterly* 47 (Spring): 356–363.

Slote, Stanley J. 1997. *Weeding Library Collections: Library Weeding Methods.* 4th ed. Englewood, CO: Libraries Unlimited.

Smith, Rochelle, and Nancy J. Young. 2008. "Giving Pleasure Its due: Collection Promotion and Readers' Advisory in Academic Libraries." *Journal of Academic Librarianship* 34 (November): 520–526.

St. Clair, Gloriana. 1999. "Assessment: How and Why." In *Virtually Yours: Models for Managing Electronic Resources and Services,* edited by Peggy Johnson and Bonnie MacEwan, 58–70. Chicago: American Library Association.

8

Cooperative Collection Development and Resource Sharing

Overview

In this chapter we explore how libraries enhance their services to users by means of cooperative collection development (CCD) activities and participation in resource sharing consortia. There is evidence that cooperation among libraries to share resources goes back a long way, at least to the first half of the 13th century, when monasteries developed what we would today recognize as union catalogs of manuscripts to aid in their scholarly activity. As interesting as that might be, however, we focus on CCD and other resource-sharing activities in the 20th and 21st centuries.

Many librarians have dreamed of rebuilding the Library of Alexandria, which supposedly contained all the classical world's learning, by linking the collections of research libraries around the world to create the ideal, complete, and comprehensive research library. While the result remains well short of that ideal, libraries are nevertheless digitizing and making research materials available through the web. The Institute for Museum and Library Services, along with its granting agencies, has financed a large number of digitization projects so that research libraries can make their unique or rare collections available on their own campuses and also worldwide through the web. At no time in the past have various technologies combined to make the dream so close to being obtainable. Earlier CCD initiatives focused more or less exclusively on the acquisition of materials, but more recent projects center on user access to materials (Burgett, Haar, and Phillips, 2004: 2).

Library Consortia

As noted above, the history of library cooperation can be traced back to medieval monasteries. But it was the 19th century that witnessed the development of union catalogs, which allowed libraries to know what other libraries owned and became a key to early successful resource sharing and CCD efforts. Neither CCD nor resource sharing work well if libraries do not know what other libraries own.

Today, all types of libraries engage in consortial activities.

> Academic, public, special, and even K–12 school libraries face numerous challenges such as diminishing funds, limited space and staff, outdated assessment policies, print resources as opposed to nonprint resources, and technology concerns. In an effort to address these challenges, libraries have turned to various collaborative endeavors. One such endeavor has been the development of consortia. A library may belong to several consortia simultaneously depending upon the needs of the library and the mission of the consortia. (Kinner and Crosetto, 2009: 419–420)

There are many reasons for a library to belong to a consortium, but here we focus on the library's collection and getting needed resources to users.

The development of consortia is primarily a phenomenon of the mid-20th century. Following World War II and the beginnings of the Farmington Plan, librarians began to realize the strength that would come from combining their resources to build collections, union catalogs, and, today, digital libraries. The Farmington Plan was a post–World War II CCD plan that was conceived because of the difficulty of getting scientific information from other countries during the war. Individual research libraries agreed to accept responsibility for collecting scientific information or a specific subset of scientific information (physics, chemistry, etc.) from a particular country or area of the world. The Farmington Plan flourished when a growing amount of money was being put into libraries because of the space race and other competitions in science. When that money began to dry up, not all libraries involved could afford to continue their commitments. The Farmington Plan eventually fell apart in the 1970s, becoming something of a footnote in the history of CCD.

Cooperative Collection Development Defined

In library and information science, the generally accepted definition of cooperative collection development is "cooperation, coordination, or sharing in the development and management of collections by two or more libraries entering into an agreement for this purpose." Some CCD agreements focus primarily on the reduction of overlap, particularly for expensive, specialized materials. Other projects seek to expand resources and may require that a pool of money be created for new purchases. Another spin on CCD emphasizes the human element. Burgett, Haar, and Phillips (2004: 4) define CCD as "multiple libraries coordinating the development and management of their collections with the goal of building broader, more useful combined collections than any library in the group could build individually."

CCD projects have achieved positive results in spite of many false starts and even some complete failures. Their progress, however, is elusive since their products are difficult to measure and opinions vary as to the relative success of the programs. Yet the recognizable benefits of numerous collaborative library projects cannot be disputed. Even though many CCD projects have not always met librarians' expectations, CCD in the aggregate has demonstrated tangible progress.

All libraries should ideally be able to provide locally all items that are in heavy demand by their users. However, some types of materials may be used only occasionally by the patrons of a particular library. For these materials, the library can provide access in ways other than directly purchasing them. It is for these types of materials that CCD programs can come into play.

Benefits and Challenges of Cooperative Collection Development

Benefits

- Reducing unnecessary duplication by working together to create a plan for the acquisition of expensive materials. Every library will need to own the basics to cover undergraduate students' needs, particularly in the case of academic libraries, but more expensive materials needed for research by faculty and graduate students can be shared among the consortium members. This service requires a means of delivery from one campus to another.
- Enlarging the pool of materials available to users through cooperative purchasing plans is a natural result of a CCD plan involving all the members of the consortium.
- Working together on technological solutions for keeping track of and making electronic resources available to the membership has been very important in the past as it is the technology that has allowed easy access to the catalogs of the member libraries and sending resources from one campus to another.

Challenges

- Reductions in budgets can hurt consortial activities of any type. Hard times for library cooperation inevitably occur when there is an economic downturn and budgets and staffs are reduced. Ironically, cooperation, which should logically be viewed as a money saver, thrives during good times and suffers during the bad times.

- Maintaining local interests can generate problems for libraries participating in consortial programs. At all times, libraries tend to spend their money so as to protect local interests first and then use remaining funds for any costs of cooperation, including purchasing books, serials, and other library resources to meet the goal of the consortium or CCD agreement.
- Personal conflicts can seriously affect cooperation. As one so often finds in any cooperative effort, people and personal conflicts are often the biggest problems leading to failure in a consortium or CCD. Egos can snuff the candle all too easily in any cooperative agreement. One library, for instance, may feel that they are doing all the work and all the lending and that other libraries are simply taking advantage of them. In fact, it is often the smaller libraries that can feel disadvantaged as they get comparatively swamped with requests from other libraries.

Consortial and Access Relationships

Although libraries will mostly continue to purchase materials independently to meet their own users' needs, there is a growing and promising trend toward buying within a consortial framework. While no one would suggest that this is an ideal way of replacing individual library-based acquisition programs, it does offer a significant level of improvement over independent selection choices at a time when library budgets are strained to meet even the most basic needs. Other alternatives involve looking at the areas where the members of a consortium provide unique resources and adapting acquisition programs accordingly.

To a large degree, the actions taken by an individual library will reflect the ways in which it cooperates with other libraries. Where there is a close relationship, each library will consider the effects of its policy changes on the cooperative. Where the relationships are looser, each library will tend to follow its own path, regardless of the consequences for the group. The likely future financial environment suggests that librarians would be well advised to look carefully at the benefits of cooperative activity and to seek ways in which to meld them into their collection strategies.

In the past few years, there has been significant CCD activity in Florida, particularly in the state university library system. Some cooperative purchases can be seen in the databases available through the shared online system. Also, Florida's new distance education initiative has led to consortial buying of access to the *Encyclopaedia Britannica*, OCLC's FirstSearch, and other products. In addition, Sunlink provides public school media specialists an opportunity for CCD based on a statewide database of holdings. The ability of this database to allow sharing of MARC records and the development of shared catalogs (or Internet access to standalone catalogs) has greatly increased the ability of librarians in Florida to initiate CCD programs at all levels.

CCD can be especially useful when a group of libraries come together and indicate the areas or subject specialties that they intend to collect in depth. This allows purchases of materials that are not heavily used to be better planned. For example, if one library takes responsibility for collecting materials on the Arthurian legend, another library in the group will probably not purchase expensive, research-oriented materials in that area but would instead purchase popular, best-seller, or course-related materials. The second library would then rely on the first library for research materials relating to the Arthurian legend.

CCD projects proceed from the premise that in a constrained economic climate, libraries can no longer expect to build superior or even adequate collections independently. If each library proceeds unilaterally as inflation forces it to acquire ever smaller portions of the published universe, it risks unnecessarily duplicating many little-used materials that its users could borrow from other libraries. Conversely, it may fail to acquire many other items not readily available elsewhere. By coordinating acquisitions, libraries can maximize their aggregate purchasing power even as their individual financial situations decline. They can better position themselves to build broad-based collections by identifying resources that need to be held by only one or perhaps a few libraries and provided to the others through document delivery. Each library can continue to acquire core resources for its clientele while redirecting its remaining funds toward intensive purchasing in predetermined fields. It will then be able to share materials in these fields with consortial partners and rely on the partners to build and share intensive collections in other fields.

Interlibrary Loan

Some CCD programs rely heavily on traditional interlibrary loans since the very essence of CCD hinges on the ability to share resources. Of course, you can have resource sharing without CCD (e.g., conventional interlibrary loan), but the focus of ILL is almost the opposite of collection development, since it by definition necessarily involves accessing what you do not have. Certainly, interlibrary loan is likely to remain an integral part of most libraries' information services for the foreseeable future. The major cloud on the horizon concerns electronic materials and whether libraries will continue to have the same fair use rights to share electronic materials. Under even the best scenario, however, the role of interlibrary loan will probably change as libraries take into account the newer electronic methods of information delivery. There will be differences between what can be accomplished by document delivery services or databases and by the traditional sharing of printed resources.

The cost differentials between various information service patterns have not yet been fully explored. What is appropriate in one setting may be inappropriate in another. A library must take into account such differences in setting up its budget. Borrowing from another library makes sense when the original library is unable to purchase or obtain the item, when the item is rare or scarce, or when the patrons of the original library would infrequently use the item. When libraries are part of a consortium that provides courier services to minimize delays in the materials reaching the patron, interlibrary loan may be an attractive alternative for items not in heavy use.

Conclusion

CCD is very useful for most libraries. After an intensive evaluation and analysis of the Ohio consortium named OhioLINK, Kinner and Crosetto (2009: 436) concluded that the benefits of "being a member of an academic consortium are immeasurable. From sharing resources to assistance in purchasing products to collection development support, membership perks continue to grow." They also pointed out that for CCD to work, all participants have to operate cooperatively. If libraries only cooperate to further their own, insular needs, the consortium is naturally less likely to succeed.

Vocabulary

consortium	cooperative collection development
interlibrary loan	OCLC
resource sharing	SunLink

Case Study

The area surrounding a medium-sized city in South Carolina has three small private universities. In the 1970s the three came together in a consortium to provide better services and collections for graduate students in education, the liberal arts, and business. Each university library took primary responsibility for one of the subject areas, attempting to acquire what the students of all three institutions would require in that area. The resources included books, audiovisual materials, serials, and, of late, e-books and electronic databases. Each university had programs in all three areas of study that are included in the consortial agreement for CCD and document delivery.

Given the current recession, all three universities have suffered financially, but one in particular has suffered a large decrease in its foundation moneys. This institution is responsible for the business collection. The university's administration has asked the library to take a substantial cut in its acquisitions budget to the point that the library cannot fully meet its obligations to the consortium. Maintaining its current commitment in the electronic databases for all three institutions is particularly problematic. All three libraries are scheduled to meet in two weeks.

Divide into three groups, one for education, one for liberal arts, and one for business. Each group is assigned one of the institutions and should prepare a response that addresses the following:

- Is the consortium still viable? What difference may it make if the cost of each institution's purchases on behalf of all three is roughly equal? Is some redistribution possible that the institution in financial trouble could accommodate?
- How can the three institutions as a whole strive to maintain the business collection?
- Prepare a one-page memorandum that the libraries would submit to their higher administration that explains how the situation can be resolved.

Discussion Questions

1. Do you know or can you find references to CCD agreements in your state? Are they a part of the services of a library consortium or are they individual agreements among libraries? If you cannot find specific examples, are there consortia or other library activities that could result in CCD in the future?
2. Compare and contrast interlibrary loan with CCD.
3. Do you believe that participation in a consortium is advantageous to all libraries? Why or why not?

References

Burgett, James, John Haar, and Linda L. Phillips. 2004. *Collaborative Collection Development.* Chicago: American Library Association.

Kinner, Laura, and Alice Crosetto. 2009. "Balancing Act for the Future: How the Academic Library Engages in Collection Development at the Local and Consortial Levels." *Journal of Library Administration* 49 (May–June): 419–437.

Selected Readings

Allen, Barbara McFadden. 1999. "Consortia and Collections: Achieving a Balance between Local Action and Collaborative Interest." *Journal of Library Administration* 28, no. 4: 85–90.

Atkinson, Ross. 2003. "Uses and Abuses of Cooperation in a Digital Age." *Collection Management* 28, nos. 1/2: 1–20.

Connell, Ruth R. 2008. "Eight May Be Too Many: Getting a Toe-Hold on Cooperative Collection Building." *Collection Management* 33, nos. 1/2: 17–28.

Croft, Janet Brennan. 2005. "Interlibrary Loan and Licensing: Tools for Proactive Contract Management." *Journal of Library Administration* 42, nos. 3/4: 41–53.

Gammon, Julie A., and Michael Zeoli. 2003. "Practical Cooperative Collecting for Consortia: Books-Not-Bought in Ohio." *Collection Management* 28, nos. 1/2: 77–105.

Hazen, Dan. 2005. "Better Mousetraps in Turbulent Times? The Global Resources Network as a Vehicle for Library Cooperation." *Journal of Library Administration* 42, no. 2: 35–55.

Hoffert, Barbara. 2006. "The United Way: Will Public Libraries Follow Academics as They Take Collaborative Collection Development One Step Further?" *Library Journal* 131 (May 1): 38–14.

Hruska, Martha, and Kathy Arsenault. 2000. "Back to the Future: Building a Florida Library Research Consortium." *Collection Management* 24, nos. 1/2: 79–85.

Irwin, Ken. 2008. "Comparing Circulation Rates of Monographs and Anthologies of Literary Criticism: Implications for Cooperative Collection Development." *Collection Management* 33, nos. 1/2: 69–81.

Perrault, Anna. 2000. "The Printed Book: Still in Need of CCD." *Collection Management* 24, nos. 1/2: 119–136.

9

Legal Issues in Collection Development

Overview

In this chapter we examine several of the major legal questions and issues relevant to collection development activities. For electronic resources in particular, both statutory law and the applicable judicial decisions have not begun to cover all the potential issues of the acquisition of intellectual property in a form other than on the printed page. This chapter is not intended to make lawyers out of librarians, but will introduce you to a number of these important issues to better inform you as to how to recognize those issues and how best to proceed when you are confronted with them. Recognition of the problem is the all-important first step. Sometimes you can take the next step yourself, but consultation with the library's attorneys to make sure that you are proceeding in the way that they feel is appropriate may also be indicated, especially in terms of developing general policies, in final review of contracts, and so on.

In this chapter we also explore a number of diversity and disability issues as they have legal ramifications for library collection and management. Some of these issues are legal in nature and can be technical, but others involve simple common sense, whether they are interactions with new arrivals in this country whose command of English is less than fully adequate or simple accommodations to make users with special needs feel more welcome and comfortable in using the library. American society has always been diverse and is becoming more so all the time. By 2003, roughly 40 percent of all schoolchildren could be considered to belong to one or another ethnic minority recognized by the federal government (U.S. Census Bureau, 2005).

Legal issues are always implicitly and often directly connected to collection development activities. The most obvious areas are copyright and licensing. These concepts have become more important as more and more of any collection's materials are received or made available in electronic form. In this connection, digital rights management (DRM) software and hardware also present important questions for the collection development librarian. This chapter is intended to provide some answers and suggestions as to how to resolve those questions. Another and more traditional legal issue with which many collection development librarians must regularly deal involves the legal aspects of handling gifts and donations to the library; there are questions of rightful ownership to resolve and meeting the donor's typical desire to obtain allowable income and estate tax deductions for donations to qualifying libraries.

Librarians are usually comfortable when selecting materials that represent cultural and ethnic differences because this is easily and generally considered as simply the right thing to do with respect to the provision of information, and not done because it might or might not be deemed politically correct. However, they may find it much more difficult to not practice self-censorship when selecting materials dealing with political, social, and moral issues that do not represent their own beliefs.

Copyright and Licensing

Copyright became a collection development issue as long ago as the time of the invention of the moveable-type printing press. With the arrival of a practical way to print and make available written materials and manuscripts relatively quickly and cheaply, moving intellectual property from the hands of the Church to the populace at large (at the least the portion of the populace that could read), laws began to be made to protect authors from the unauthorized mass reproduction of their works. Copyright may be described as a governmentally created right granted to the creators of literary works to protect their individual interest in their work through prohibiting the printing, publishing, importing, or selling of multiple copies of a work without their permission, that is, the permission of the work's creator or a person to whom he or she has sold or given that right; in essence, it functions as a protection from unauthorized mass reproduction and commercial sale. From the author's or creator's point of view, this may seem exceedingly fair, but copyright laws can also be viewed as a serious limitation or restriction on something arguably more important and central to the role of libraries and librarians—the unfettered dissemination of information.

Copyright developed in a Western historical perspective in conjunction with the Renaissance and at about the time of the initial rise of the nation-state, a time when any individual's rights, such as they were, were essentially the prerogative of monarchs, who could dispense or withhold those rights essentially at pleasure. Thus, when the Constitution of the United States in Article I provided that Congress has the power "to promote the progress of science and useful arts, by securing for limited times to authors and inventors the exclusive right to their respective writings and discoveries," it reflected an intention of civilized societies to move away from arbitrariness to the exercise of governmental power for rational purposes. This short but powerful statement in the Constitution is the basis for all of our nation's laws dealing with copyright and intellectual property. It is well thought out and carefully drawn, and reflects a view that access to information is an inherent right and not a matter of royal or other governmental dispensation and favor. In the United States, copyright has thus always been meant to reflect a balance between the rights of authors or inventors and the public good.

As a method for releasing the "fettering" tension naturally created by copyright laws (i.e., the restriction on resource sharing imposed by the rights of authors to be compensated for or otherwise to restrict the use of their work through limitations on copying), libraries have long served as the established method to effect the dissemination of information on a mass basis, normally free of charge to the library patron, essentially through the purchase and maintenance of authorized copies of works. This dissemination is the quintessential application of what is usually referred to in copyright circles as the "first sale doctrine," enshrined in U.S. copyright law, which states that the owner of a legally obtained copy of a work has complete control over that physical copy. The owner can use it, read it, lend it, suppress it, or even burn it, but any additional copying of that work is regulated by the copyright laws. Thus, owners of a physical item may basically do anything they want with the work, except copy it.

The development in the last third of the 20th century of fast and cheap photocopying eventually evaporated many of the physical limitations on making copies, and new problems for librarians quickly arose. For instance, while only a single copy might be made for any given patron, the aggregate number of copies was potentially extremely high. In fact, the volume of photocopying became so great by the 1980s that copyright holders felt that their rights were being significantly violated, and that the rules of copyright in the United States had to be—and they eventually were—adjusted to reflect the new realities.

For librarians today, and for collection development librarians in particular, new forms of electronic resources, scanning equipment, and optical character reader software have intensified exponentially the potential problems in this area, both for libraries and for copyright holders. The rapid growth of online and electronic resources also affects our laws and commercial relationships. The copyright issues implicated by the digital medium's ease of use and access have elicited a response from the owners and publishers: restrictions on the use of electronic resources through DRM systems incorporated into licensing agreements required of users of electronic resources as a condition for obtaining access. The development of increasingly powerful and sophisticated communications networks and associated information resources will continue to have a significant impact on intellectual property rights in the United States and around the world.

The basic philosophy underpinning copyright laws in the United States was well articulated by the U.S. Supreme Court in a case decided in 1984:

> The monopoly privileges that Congress may authorize are neither unlimited nor primarily designed to provide a special private benefit. Rather, the limited grant is a means by which an important public purpose may be achieved. It is intended to motivate the creative activity of authors and inventors by the provision of a special reward, and to allow the public access to the products of their genius after the limited period of exclusive control has expired. (*Sony Corp. of America vs. Universal City Studios*, 1984)

Presently, under the Copyright Term Extension Act of 1998, which was enacted in part to bring U.S. law more into line with the tenets of the World Intellectual Property Organization, copyright protection in the United States extends for the life of the author plus 70 years. The 1998 law also provides that works with so-called corporate authorship and works that are anonymous or pseudonymous are protected for 95 years after date of first publication or 120 years after creation, whichever comes first. Prior to passage of the act, works published in 1923 would have passed into the public domain at the end of 1998; these works will now remain out of the public domain until 2019.

It should be noted that the copyright law also provides copyright protection to unpublished (i.e., not printed for sale) works as well as published ones.

Under U.S. copyright laws, as well as the laws of most European countries, there are stated exceptions to the exclusive rights granted to copyright owners, and these exceptions are critical for libraries. In the United States these include the following:

- The right anyone possesses to use and reproduce materials in the public domain, for example, works created by U.S. federal government employees, works never copyrighted, or works that have passed beyond the copyright protection period.
- Fair use (within the meaning of the copyright laws) of copyrighted materials for the purpose of research, teaching, journalism, criticism, or even parody.
- Archival preservation rights for libraries, that is, the right to photograph, archive, or otherwise copy, in order to protect or preserve the work.
- Copying for interlibrary loan for the use of another library's patrons.

Drawing the line between creators' and users' rights has always presented lawmakers with a vexing and complicated problem. Producers of works, as well as patentable inventions, must be encouraged to risk creating something new while still making their work available in some form to the public; if their work risks becoming free for the asking (i.e., if there is no copyright protection), the author or producer may be encouraged to the public detriment to keep it a secret—the avoidance of which result has always been a major justification for the copyright laws. But users of materials also have needs, and they enjoy certain rights that the copyright laws recognize. The proper balancing of these interests forms the basis for any discussion of the extent and nature of the copyright laws.

The Digital Millennium Copyright Act (DMCA), passed by Congress in 1998 in conjunction with the Copyright Term Extension Act, contains a number of special restrictions specifically applicable to electronic resources. For instance, the law prohibits the "circumvention" of any effective "technological protection measure" utilized by a copyright holder to restrict access to the copyrighted materials. In other words, no breaking of password protections or encryptions is allowed. The DMCA also prohibits the manufacture of any device, or the offering of any service, that is primarily designed to defeat such a protection measure. Thus, so-called digital rights management systems are protected in the United States through the provision in the DMCA of legal remedies against both actions taken to avoid or defeat DRM systems and the suppliers of circumvention technologies and equipment intended to allow persons to do just that. This anticircumvention clause presents a major legal concern that libraries have with DRM systems. Under the DMCA, anticircumvention appears to be an absolute offense (i.e., either a crime or a civil offense) no matter the reason why the circumvention occurred; within the European Union, however, rights holders must allow bona fide uses that are exceptions to the exclusive rights of the copyright holders, regardless of how those rights may be protected. Thus the balance in Europe may be fairly said to be in favor of the user, not at the stage of sanctions for circumvention, but rather at the earlier stage of the very exercise of the exception constrained by a technical measure.

Upon the widespread introduction 40 years ago of the practical and inexpensive-to-operate photocopying machine, many librarians had to become intimately familiar with copyright law and its provisions regarding hard copies of works. In this century librarians must become accustomed to dealing with copyright issues in connection with the electronic delivery of information services. At first glance it might be relatively easy to consider that the same restrictions should apply to electronic materials as those applicable to hard copies, that is, no copies of material not in the public domain beyond those needed for fair use, archival, or interlibrary loan purposes. But the restrictions applicable to electronic resources can extend much further. This is because the restrictions are effected through licensing agreements, which are really extensions not of copyright law at all, but of the application of principles of contract law.

Licensing issues are dealt with extensively in the balance of this chapter. But it is important to keep in mind that the Internet and the web did not introduce libraries to the concept of resource licensing. For instance, OCLC, Dialog, and other online mainframe systems have for many years required libraries to enter into network resource license agreements. But CD-ROM acquisitions, quickly followed by Internet and web resources such as electronic journals and other full-text resources, have opened the proverbial Pandora's box of issues and problems for libraries in the area of copyright and licensing.

Distance education also has increased the strain on libraries in regard to copyright and licensing issues, although the Technology, Education and Copyright Harmonization Act of 2002 updated copyright law to broaden instructors' legal use of copyrighted materials in online instruction at accredited, nonprofit educational institutions.

Creative Commons Licenses

A different approach to copyright involves the relatively new concept of Creative Commons licenses. The Creative Commons website (http://creativecommons.org/choose/) provides the templates for each of their four types of licenses. In granting such a license, the copyright holder retains the rights to his or her work but is able to specify ways that the work can be used or distributed without the user first having to seek copyright permission from the holder. Many researchers, artists, musicians, and scholars would rather see their materials used than restricted, so long as their authorship is appropriately acknowledged. The Creative Commons license ensures that the author gets credit for the material used, but does not make the user jump through legal hoops to use it. The license therefore seeks to encourage, not discourage, use.

The Creative Commons licenses are of four types:

1. Attribution
2. Share alike
3. Noncommercial
4. No derivative works

The *attribution license* allows others to copy, distribute, display, or perform the copyrighted work and make derivative works based upon it, but only if they give credit in the way the copyright right holder specifies in the license. The *share alike license* allows others to distribute derivative works only under a license identical in effect to the license that governs the original work. The *noncommercial license*, as the name indicates, allows others to copy, distribute, display, and perform your work and derivative works based upon it, but only for noncommercial use. The *no derivative works license* allows others to copy, distribute, display, and perform only exact copies of the copyrighted work, but not any derivative works based upon it (http://creativecommons.org/about/licenses).

Now let's examine the principal ways in which DRM and licensing interact with library uses of materials.

Fair Use

> One of the most important tools for users of copyrighted information in the United States, often called the safety valve of copyright, has always been the doctrine of *fair use*. A highly simplified definition of *fair use* states that it "permits the reproduction, for legitimate purposes, of material taken from a copyrighted work to a limited extent that will not cut into the copyright holder's potential market for the sale of copies." (Schlosser, 2006: 12; emphasis in original)

Educational institutions rely heavily on fair use to bring materials other than textbooks to students.

The Copyright Law of 1976 brought together and formalized in statutory form numerous court decisions to distill four basic factors to be considered when determining what constitutes permissible fair use:

- The purpose and character of the use
- The nature of the copyrighted work
- The amount and substantiality of the portion used
- The effect of the use upon the potential market for the copyrighted work

The most ubiquitous and easiest to apply of these criteria has tended to be the amount and substantiality criterion, which can be observed and measured objectively. Fair use has been the refuge for all who step up with some loose change or a debit card to use a copy machine. The limited copies allowed for research, teaching, and so on have traditionally worked more or less satisfactorily. But many of the traditional fair use rights (or in a slightly more limited way, the "fair dealing" requirements in the U.K. and Canada) that libraries have enjoyed in respect to print materials are not necessarily ensured in the new age of electronic information. Contracts for the acquisition and utilization of electronic resources have become increasingly common and at the same time have become more complex. This is an area where acquisitions librarians generally have been slow to react. Although it is obvious that electronic products do not function in the same way as most traditional print resources, the corollary that electronic publishers will not function in the traditional way of print publishers seems to have come as a surprise.

Nevertheless, it remains an important requirement for library acceptance of DRM that those systems allow for a proper modicum of fair use or fair dealing with protected content if the library is to continue to carry out its traditional role of disseminating knowledge to all who trouble themselves to acquire it.

Purchasing versus Licensing

When a library acquires any new electronic resources, the first key issue to consider is whether the library will be actually purchasing the resource or only obtaining a right or license to use it. Electronic vendors rarely, if ever, offer to sell their electronic products outright today. Rather, they simply provide to libraries something that is far short of the ownership that the collection development process implies—a mere license of the right to use the products, not a copy thereof—and for good measure a license may be revocable under certain conditions. Print materials are even being licensed in some cases, primarily in fields such as law and medicine, where currency of information may be more important than historical or archival significance.

The contrast to a collection development librarian's traditional permanent book acquisition process could not be more stark. Licensing and DRM systems have shifted the focus from reliance on copyright laws to the provisions of the contracts between the rights holder and the user to determine what can be done with a work. Thus, dealing with licensing agreements is an unavoidable task for acquisitions librarians. Moreover, managing and negotiating these licensing agreements presents a daunting task for many libraries as the number of available databases and other electronic resources continues to rapidly increase, and the variety of licensing restrictions and special clauses respectively applicable to them seems to be growing at an even more rapid rate. In addition to the licensing restrictions, these electronic resources may also bring with them DRM systems that serve to enforce (and sometimes effectively extend the scope of) the license agreement. The distinction between purchasing and licensing may appear inconsequential at first blush, but it is critical regarding the fair use rights of the library purchaser, for it determines the library's long-term access to the material, a major collection development consideration.

From the beginning, the drafters of copyright laws have generally agreed that at least some kinds of copying should always be permitted. Over the years there developed the concept of fair use, whereby a purchaser of, for example, a copyrighted book might lawfully copy without fee or restriction a few pages for personal use, copyright notwithstanding. The problem lies in defining what constitutes fair use, which is differently applied in different countries (most countries do not apply the fair use concept as liberally as has traditionally been the case in the United States). As noted above, U.S. copyright law codifies the fair use doctrine in general terms, referring to such permissible purposes or uses as criticism, comment, news reporting, teaching, scholarship, or research. Looking at all these factors, and depending on the circumstances, fair use might cover making not only a single copy but also multiple copies. For example, the statute specifically states that multiple copying for classroom use may fall within the category of fair use copying.

The current U.S. copyright law also recognizes a first sale doctrine, which allows the purchaser of a legally produced copy of a copyrighted work (e.g., a book that has been purchased from the copyright holder, such as a publisher) the right to sell or loan that copy to others. But if the actual legal title to the work itself is still retained by the vendor (i.e., if the work itself is not sold), access to the work is said to be licensed, and the purchaser obtains only a right to the use of the item, rather than the full bundle of rights that a purchaser ordinarily obtains when he buys a book. This means that, since a sale has not occurred, copyright concepts such as fair use and first sale doctrine are simply not directly applicable.

These distinctions are important in the library context. For instance, a licensed right of use does not automatically allow the library to do all the things it typically and traditionally has done with its library materials (such as loan, circulate, or even sell the work to others). In a licensing regime, by contrast, what the library can legally do with the resource being obtained is limited to those activities or uses that are specifically set forth in the contract or license document pursuant to which the library acquires the item. Therefore, the license document itself becomes a much more critical instrument than a typical purchase order, and in the case of libraries the terms of use contained in a license agreement become matters of such importance that they should always be carefully negotiated by the library with the vendor of the item whenever possible.

This distinction is particularly sharply drawn for library purchases of computer software. Many, but not all, purchase agreements for computer software allow the buyer to make a backup copy of the software in case the original is destroyed. If this element is not contained in the purchasing agreement, Section 117 of the Copyright Act actually authorizes such a backup if the software was purchased. But Section 117 does not apply to licensed software. If a library is not a purchaser of software, the library has no Section 117 rights; rather, it has only the rights set out in the licensing agreement, which may not allow for archival or backup copies.

Initially, when many libraries began ordering computer software and CD-ROMs, the so-called shrink-wrap licenses printed in small type on the envelopes containing the software were often simply ignored; many users thought, probably with some justification, that these originally somewhat obscure, unusual, and often almost hidden licenses were so one-sided as to be virtually unenforceable. However, most librarians have begun to realize that these provisions, as they have become more conventional in the commercial context, may indeed be enforceable.

Librarians also must deal with licenses for web-accessed databases and journals, for which they must sign a license agreement with a publisher or distributor before being able to access the resource at all. With this in mind, it is always advisable to inquire about the terms of the applicable licensing agreement before ordering a product. Many publishers are willing to send the library an advance copy of the license agreement; the library can thus review the license to determine whether the intended or expected use is indeed an allowable one. Some publishers, unfortunately, do not even mention the existence of a licensing agreement in their catalogs and brochures, and the contract is simply sent after the order is placed. It thus remains possible for a product to be received and the invoice paid before the library even gets the contract and sees the conditions imposed on its usage of the product—a most unhappy situation.

License Negotiation

The rights the library may have to search, copy, and use the information contained in a licensed resource are, as a matter of contract law, strictly those set forth in the license agreement. Therefore, librarians entering into licensing agreements must face four major challenges:

- Understanding the content of the agreement
- Determining the wording required for their library or institution
- Pinpointing those areas of the agreement that require negotiation
- Identifying who should negotiate and ultimately sign the agreement

When licensing content from an international publisher, it is also important for the library to consider not only how treaties bind those in the country in which the library is located, but also the extent, if any, to which copyright protection may be provided by the laws of the country where the publisher is headquartered.

Acquisitions librarians negotiating licenses typically encounter one of two basic licensing concepts:

- Contracts for online services or access licenses (e.g., LexisNexis), usually manifested by a specific written contract signed by at least the licensee, that is, the library.
- Contracts governing the use of a licensor's software on the licensee's equipment or network (essentially software licenses). Agreement of the parties to the terms of such a contract usually is not evidenced by a signed contract at all but rather by a broken shrink-wrap package or a click-through "OK" initiated by the licensee installing the software, without which click the software cannot be installed.

Online services or access licenses involve significant ongoing obligations not typically or necessarily involved with software licenses, such as the licensor's obligations to provide access or the licensee's continuing obligation to pay for services as received. Software licenses are not always viewed by librarians as being distinct from the ownership of the works involved, but this distinction is important because they are not really the same. With a license, the right to use the information is typically all you get. Complicating matters, license agreements used by different vendors vary widely and are neither standardized nor all that predictable, so it is important to read each license carefully.

Always consider the following points:

- How does the vendor define "site" and "user"? For example, a site could be undesirably limited to a particular computer, building, or campus. A user could be a registered borrower at a public library, a faculty or staff member or a student for an academic library or school media center, an on-site user, anyone who comes into the library, or anyone who accesses the library via the Internet.
- Can off-site users obtain access to the electronic resource?
- If a library has multiple branches or has units or access nodes located on several campuses, does the license cover only the main location or are all of the locations appropriately provided for?
- Can users print, download, or copy from the resource? If so, is there a limit to the number of copies? Some licenses may specify the number of copies or number of pages that may be copied, and, if so, the library will be responsible for communicating these restrictions to its users.
- Is the library allowed to make copies of the electronic resource, or portions thereof, for interlibrary loan purposes?
- Will you have permanent rights to the information that is licensed in case a licensed database is subsequently canceled or removed by the publisher? Do you have the right to archive the material?
- Does the vendor's software contain electronic "self-help" or a "time bomb" or similar provision that, after a certain period of time, allows the vendor unilaterally to shut down the library's use of an application or resource, either remotely or automatically, on a given date or upon the occurrence of a given event?
- Are you purchasing material that is already in the public domain? Oftentimes expensive bundles of electronic resources include public domain material as a large portion of the licensed product.
- Does the license limit your ability to enhance the information, so long as content integrity is maintained, to make the resource more easily usable by the library's patrons (such as by adding annotations or links to other holdings)?
- What happens if there are unauthorized uses of the resource? A license agreement should not hold the licensee liable for unauthorized uses so long as the licensee has implemented reasonable and appropriate measures to notify its users of restrictions. If such uses occur, the licensor

should be required to give the licensee notice of any suspected license violations and allow a reasonable time for the licensee to look into the matter and take corrective actions if appropriate.
- Does the license agreement hold the licensee harmless from any actions based on a claim that use of the resource in accordance with the license infringes any patent, copyright, trademark, or trade secret of any third party?
- How may you terminate the license? The contract should provide termination rights that are appropriate for each party.

Most important, the person reviewing the proposed license for the library should never assume anything. Get it in writing. Always make sure that everything that the library needs is indeed covered specifically in the license.

Unfortunately, the acquisition of electronic products means that someone in the library needs to be prepared to conduct preliminary negotiations with the licensor or vendor. Obviously, the role of negotiator can be taken up by many different people, for example:

- Library director
- Assistant director
- Acquisitions librarian
- Systems librarian
- Counsel for the library, university, or business

Some libraries find the use of a team approach or combination of people helpful and do not designate a single individual to be responsible for all license negotiations. Often a designated individual from the library will work with the vendor to negotiate needed language and then refer the contract to the organization's attorney for final wording and approval. In any event, it is important for everyone involved to learn the legal jargon of licensing and know what the required language may be for the library or institution. The library should also develop and follow baseline standards for what is acceptable for its licensing contracts. The librarian or other person designated for preliminary license negotiations should be prepared to reject offers and terminate negotiations if no reasonable solution is possible. Products that do not offer licensing contracts that can be made satisfactory for a particular library's clientele may simply not be worth the cost of the license. After all, what good is an electronic resource if you cannot effectively use it for your intended purpose?

It is best not to abdicate responsibility to legal counsel for deciding whether to sign a particular license. The attorney will understand the legal ramifications and be able to explain them to you, but the attorney will not necessarily understand the ramifications of the license restrictions from a library user's point of view. Librarians must stay involved in the process to

Tips for a Successful Licensing Agreement

1. Avoid oral agreements. While not required in every situation, written agreements are best. The written license will contain the items and conditions of use of the licensed content. It is the document you, and those who follow you in your position, will consult for interpretational purposes.

2. Understand the requirements on the library. The obligations the license demands of you are important. If you see a problematic clause, but the other party tells you not to worry because it will never be enforced, get that clause removed. Make sure you can live up to the obligations in the agreement.

3. Cover all issues. Do not avoid inserting any relevant issues into a provision of the agreement just because you think they may scare off the other party. It is best to get everything on the table and in the agreement at the beginning to avoid disputes in the future.

4. Avoid legal jargon when you can. Simple nonlegalistic language that you understand is the best approach. You want the wording to be clear to the two parties signing the agreement and to anyone who may need to interpret and apply the agreement later. Define ambiguous or new technical words.

5. Use consistent words and terms. Do not use content in one clause, material in another, and then publication in a third.

6. Be creative, patient, and flexible.

7. Know when to walk away.

ensure that licenses for electronic materials contain only those provisions that the library and its users can live with.

In general, it appears that licensing agreements are becoming a bit more favorable for library users—as librarians become more familiar with and adept at negotiating, and as publishers and vendors become more familiar with typical library needs and more comfortable with removing or modifying restrictions in their agreements to accommodate those needs. At first, either the library market was deemed not to be the major market for particular electronic products, or vendors simply did not understand how to write a license for the library market. These initial problems are fortunately fast becoming obsolete with more and more electronic resource vendors catering to the library market.

All rights and permissions need to be completely described in a document provided by the publisher or vendor for each electronic product. Some publishers require subscribers to officially and formally sign a license.

Other publishers simply provide a document that describes the conditions and terms governing the use of the resource. Where document execution is required, it is necessary to ensure that the individual who signs the contract has the authority to commit the organization to it. Few large organizations will allow a collection development or acquisitions librarian to sign an official contract. Although electronic aggregators cannot sign contracts on your behalf, many will collect them and provide them for your review. They can also frequently assist you if it is necessary to negotiate terms to satisfy the requirements of your institution or governmental agency. It is vitally important for you to read and understand the requirements for each product, even when the agreement is a shrink-wrap or click-through license on a product downloaded from the web.

Best Practices

A number of organizations have put together useful standards for electronic library resource licensing agreements. These should be reviewed for appropriateness for each particular library's situation. These organizations and the standards they have developed include the following:

- Association of Research Libraries: "Licensing Electronic Resources: Strategic and Practical Considerations for Signing Electronic Information Delivery Agreements" (http://arl.cni.org/scomm/licensing/licbooklet.html). Contains major considerations and good approaches to licensing electronic resources.
- Columbia University Libraries: "Electronic Resource Coordinator Draft License Agreement Checklist" (http://www.columbia.edu/cu/libraries/inside/ner/license-checklist.html). Contains a checklist of 17 items that cover some of the most important rights and provisions to look for in a licensing agreement.
- European Bureau of Library, Information and Documentation Associations: "EBLIDA Position Papers and Statements: Intellectual Property Rights" (http://www.eblida.org/). Although the site is focused on European law, there are helpful links and information on licensing in general, including consortia.
- Licensing Models website: "Model Standard Licenses for Use by Publishers, Librarians and Subscription Agents for Electronic Resources" (http://www.licensingmodels.com). Standard licenses designed for the acquisition of electronic journals and other electronic resources. Four separate licenses are provided in various formats for single academic institutions, academic consortia, public libraries, and corporate and other special libraries. Commentary is provided for each of the four licenses.
- New England Law Library Consortium: "NELLCO Decision Criteria Worksheet for Electronic Acquisitions" (http://www.nellco.org/general/

criteria.htm). Sets out a 31-question checklist geared toward law libraries, but the ideas and concepts behind the questions can easily be used
and adapted by other types of libraries. This checklist covers much
more than simply licensing issues.

- University of Texas System: "Software and Database License Agreement Checklist" (http://www.utsystem.edu/OGC/intellectualproperty/
dbckfrm1.htm). Covers eight major areas of concern and guides librarians through a typical analysis of a licensing contract.

- Yale University: "Licensing Digital Information: A Resource for Librarians" (http://www.library.yale.edu/~llicense/index.shtml). Presents a
collection of materials with the purpose of providing librarians with
a better understanding of the issues raised by licensing agreements in
the digital age.

Digital Rights Management

DRM remains a technological area very much in its infancy, with a multitude
of issues that still need to be resolved. As librarians, we tend to focus on the
problems for libraries, but to be fair it should be noted that DRM is currently
a source of confusion and complexity for publishers as well.

What exactly constitutes a DRM system? DRM includes a range of technologies that give rights owners varying degrees of control over how digital content and services may be used. Generally, DRM technologies enable
copyright holders to protect their electronically accessible material from
unauthorized use through software or hardware, and to determine under
what circumstances users can access the digital content. DRM inherently
deals with contracts—a license is a form of a contract. Beyond controlling
simple access to digital materials, it can also control specific operations on
the content, such as the ability to print, copy, or save, and it can also limit the
number of times a particular operation can be performed, such as allowing
a document to be viewed for a maximum of, for example, four times. Most
DRM systems also persistently protect materials, meaning that the content is
never in an unencrypted state, whether during storage, distribution, or use
(see Figure 9.1, p. 157, for a diagram of a sample DRM system). An end user
must have a key, a permit, or a license before accessing the DRM-controlled
material.

DRM is most often associated with the management and protection of
publishers' assets from e-books, e-serials, e-music, electronic databases, and
compressed or digital films or videos. However, it should be remembered
that DRM technologies may also be utilized by companies or organizations
that need to protect their internal documents from unauthorized users.

DRM can be viewed as a new business model that utilizes the almost
unlimited potential of the web, or it can be viewed as a restriction on fair use

and even upon free speech. Some DRM opponents go so far as to state that the acronym really stands for "digital restriction management." Although DRM systems are usually viewed as enforcing or protecting copyrights, DRM can easily go farther—it is just as easy for a DRM system to prevent access to a public domain work as it is to block access to a work protected by copyright. DRM can also be and is often used to compel users to view materials, such as commercials (or an FBI warning) on a DVD that they might wish to avoid. Whether you view DRM as "good" or "evil" depends greatly upon your position as either a user or producer of digital information and on the particular implementation of DRM technologies.

DRM technologies impose controls on content that correspond to contractual or license terms, regardless of whether or not these license terms conform to copyright law provisions regarding fair use. A library can enter into a contract that limits rights formerly guaranteed under copyright law (U.S. Code, Title 17, Section 108(f)(4)). Unlike the situation with traditional print publications, however, there is no going beyond what the vendor sets as the restrictions for use without further negotiations with the licensor. In the past, libraries have relied heavily on the fair use aspects of the copyright laws allowing for liberal use of copyrighted materials for educational use, research, and personal use in order to deliver services to their users. Fair use activities do not require the authorization of the rights holder, so libraries did not need to seek permission for such use. Libraries must ensure that any DRM systems that control the use of licensed materials do not eliminate the public, educational, and library user rights that the copyright laws allow.

Privacy and the protection of data are also issues to be considered with DRM. DRM systems by their very nature allow the tracking of usage by individuals. Within the European Union such tracking is lawful as long as the user is informed and gives informed consent to the tracking. In the United States, many libraries operate under state-mandated privacy laws that may forbid such tracking. At their simplest, DRM systems impose restrictions on what individuals can do with materials that are bought or licensed from a vendor or rights holder. At the next level of control, DRM systems can report back to the vendor or rights holder on the activities of users. Such reporting could be part of a pay-per-view system, or it could report back to the rights holder all attempts to make unauthorized copies or unauthorized use. Often there are third parties who monitor and collect information about the use of the items. This activity is usually not well disclosed, as knowledge of these data-collecting activities requires reading the fine print in privacy statements.

DRM technologies can be used in a variety of business models for distribution of content including paid downloads, subscriptions, pay-per-view (or pay-per-listen), usage metering, peer-to-peer distribution, and selling rights. It is important for librarians to be alert to the proper balance between DRM uses and user rights as the technology is still developing.

Characteristics of DRM Systems

Currently there are a number of DRM architectural approaches that allow copyright holders to control the use of their copyrighted works. These systems may make use of a number of forms of proprietary rendering software such as Adobe Acrobat (PDF) or all or part of the Real Networks Media Suite or the Content Scrambling System for DVDs or many others. There is no one system that predominates in the marketplace at this point as the technology is still evolving, but it is important to note that interoperability between these different technologies remains almost nil, a situation that has serious implications for libraries and individual consumers. Whatever approach is used, DRM systems associate rules to content that effectively impose constraints on the use and distribution of electronic materials. The DRM system thereby serves to enforce the license between a content provider and the consumer.

The basic functions of a DRM system are:

- controlling the access to copyrighted works and possibly other information products;
- restricting the unauthorized copying of those works;
- identifying the relevant copyright holders and possibly the conditions of use; and
- protecting the integrity of the identification information.

In short, DRM includes everything that someone does with content in order to trade or make use of it.

The components of a DRM system can include all or some of the following:

- Secure containers that make the content inaccessible to nonauthorized users
- Rights expression, which describes to whom the content is authorized for use
- A content identification and description system to identify content and to associate descriptive metadata with it
- Identification of people and organizations that are intended to interact with the content
- Algorithms to authenticate people or organizations that desire to interact with the content
- Technologies to persistently associate the identifiers and other information with the content (watermarks, fingerprints, etc.)
- Mechanisms to report events such as the purchase of a piece of content (pay-per-view)
- Payment systems

Some or all of these components work together to provide a trusted environment for the secure handling of digital content between the contracting or licensing parties.

DRM Terms

Authorization is the process of determining whether or not the requested use of information or content is allowed under the licensing agreement.

Clients are the components of the DRM system that reside on the library's side such as the rendering application and the user's identification mechanism.

Encryption is the use of algorithms that restrict access, analysis, and manipulation of digital materials in their native form without proper access authorization.

Licensing phrasing is the process of determining the conditions under which the content providers offer their materials. These conditions may be standardized or defined individually for each client or group of users.

Watermarking involves embedding a signal directly into the content; an example of one variety of DRM systems is provided in Figure 9.1. DRM systems may be more simplified than this one, but most of the potential attributes of a DRM system are represented in the figure. The signal is imperceptible to humans but can be detected by a computer. The signal represents the license associated with the content. In addition to watermarking, copyright holders can also create digital identifiers for copies of their works by "fingerprinting" a digital version. Fingerprinting converts the content of the work into a unique digital identification mark by applying an algorithm to selected features of that work.

Wrapping is the process whereby the license and the encrypted content itself are bundled in an additional mechanism, the result of which is the secure container that prevents unauthorized access throughout the life of the content.

The process of using a document from a DRM-controlled source involves the following steps (see Figure 9.1 and the sidebar DRM Terms):

- User request for a resource from a remote source through a file transfer or through streaming technologies.
- Encryption of files in an individualized form for the user's environment.
- User attempts to take some action (such as making a copy) and the rendering application determines whether the request requires authorization.
- If necessary, the attributes of the user's request are sent to a license server by a DRM client component.
- License server determines the applicable policies or rules based on the submitted request attributes.
- If the use is not already licensed, a financial transaction may occur.
- A license package is assembled and securely transferred to the client.

Figure 9.1. Sample Digital Rights Management Process

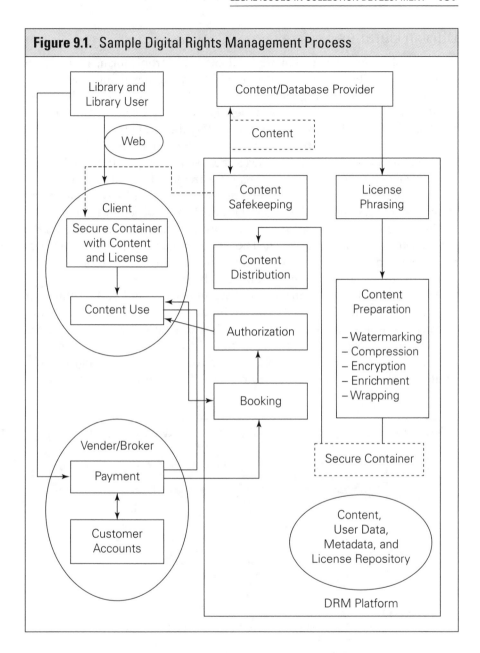

- DRM client authenticates the received policies or rules, decrypts the content, and issues an authorization for viewing or printing or whatever action was requested.
- Only then is content rendered or otherwise provided for use as requested by the end user.

DRM in Libraries

With e-books and journals that are available in electronic form, a number of databases that libraries are now routinely licensing have embedded DRM systems that can be configured to library options based on the licensing fee that the library pays. For example, Figure 9.2 is a screen capture of a FirstSearch result when the article is owned by the local library.

The user can find the article through the FirstSearch database, but once this particular article is selected, the DRM system sends the user back to the local library where it is owned with options for searching the local catalog. In this case the library has licensed the right for users to receive full-text e-mail delivery only in the case where the material is not already owned by the library.

Figure 9.3 is a screen capture of the delivery option for an article that is not owned by the same library. The DRM system determines when searchers are authorized to receive full text and when they are not based on the holdings of the library that has licensed the database services.

All is not lost for librarians in the brave new world of DRMs. While fair use, as provided for in the U.S. copyright laws and, as noted above, traditionally taken advantage of by libraries in carrying out their core role as key disseminators of information, has come increasingly eroded in the digital environment, most librarians believe strongly that traditional fair use rights must be maintained with regard to electronic resources as with print

Figure 9.2. OCLC FirstSearch DRM, Periodical Owned by Local Library

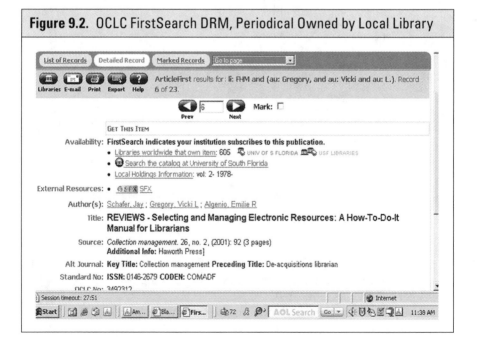

Figure 9.3. Sample InfoTrack DRM Document Delivery Option for Periodical Not Owned by Local Library

<u>Browser Print</u> — *Full Text* —
Reformat for printing (approximately 4 pages) from your browser. To return to InfoTrac, use the *back* function of your browser.

E-Mail Delivery — *Full Text* —

We will send a plain text version to the e-mail address you enter (e.g. *bettyg@library.com*).

E-Mail Address:

Subject
(defaults to title):

Submit E-mail Request

publications, and they are working to ensure the license agreements they sign respect this fundamental right. Meanwhile, however, electronic publishers and other holders of copyright on materials available electronically see a significant distinction. They base the distinction on the potential for essentially free transferability of limitless numbers of perfect electronic copies, unrestricted by the traditional print environment factors of copy quality degradation and the physical time and space restraints that manual copying typically imposed. Striking a balance between these competing interests is difficult, but librarians have to recognize that, increasingly, our purchase of and reliance upon electronic resources is moving us away from traditional, familiar copyright considerations and its fair use and first use concepts into the unfamiliar world of licensing and contract law.

The DRM approach differs from traditional copyright management in that it is proactive rather than reactive, allowing creators and providers of digital content to control access to and use of their products. DRM technologies restrict unauthorized use on the front end rather than only after an infringement, whereas a copyright holder can respond only with a lawsuit. It is this up-front nature of DRM that must concern librarians and users since it involves a determination of fair use ultimately governed by algorithms rather than a particular circumstance or use. For DRM technologies to be successful in the long run, the DRM industry will have to find a way to balance compensation to the rights holders with the rights of end users to access and make fair use of digital information.

Donations: Legal and Tax Issues

Libraries other than special libraries maintained by private businesses or corporations for internal research or archival purposes are often the beneficiaries of gifts of books, documents, papers, and even electronic archives made by individuals and corporations. These gifts, which usually arrive at the library en masse upon a person's death or upon the closing down of a professional practice, can contain relatively rare and out-of-print resources that can be of considerable worth to the library. Public libraries with needs for multiple copies of popular works can benefit as well from such donations in order to replace worn out or lost copies or simply to supplement a meager acquisitions budget. There is always much chaff with the wheat, however, and discussion of how to evaluate these materials for the development of a library's collection belongs elsewhere. The legal issues discussed here are related to provenance and tax deductibility of the value of the items given.

Provenance

First, consider where the items came from. That is to say, how confident are you that the donor is truly the rightful owner of the materials being donated? If they are not the property of the donor, it presents a serious problem, since the library can acquire no rights from a person merely in unlawful possession. The old saw concerning possession being "nine points" of the law has applicability in some circumstances, but not to the question of legality of ownership. For most family libraries proposed for donation, there is no problem—the works given are typically of a type ordinarily obtained at a bookstore or by mail order—unless, of course, the donor is a well-known shoplifter!

But when rare or potentially valuable items are involved, some investigation is always appropriate. Does the donor have adequate proof of where the valuable item came from or what was paid for it? If it is represented as having been found in Grandma's attic after all these years, how likely does that seem in the circumstances? Checking with known holders of the same work, such as state archive departments or libraries that typically hold such items, may be useful in this regard.

Likewise, when a large collection arrives with items numbering in the thousands, check the bona fides of what is being represented to you. Did another library actually close? Is this the person that the closing library actually authorized to dispose of the items, and so on? (These questions should be asked in nongift situations as well.)

The main legal point to keep in mind is that gift acquisitions always have to be viewed with an appropriately skeptical eye—always look the gift horse in the mouth.

Tax Deductions

The U.S. Internal Revenue Code (and the tax codes of most states that impose a personal or corporate income tax) provide for deductions from taxable income for the value of gifts of books, journals, and other similar materials made by individuals, estates, trusts, and corporations to the libraries of qualifying organizations, which are generally educational, governmental, or charitable entities. Similar deductions are allowed to estates respecting estate and other similar death taxes. These deductions are not unlimited in amount and vary depending upon various factors based on the nature or level of income, and so on, of the contributor. These factors are applicable to the individual donor but are not of much concern to the library donor.

The factors that are important from the recipient's point of view are (a) qualification of the recipient institution under the tax codes as an entity gifts to which may be deductible, and (b) duties of the recipient respecting valuation and acknowledgment of receipt of the gift in order that the taxing authorities will give the donor a deduction for the gift.

Concerning recipient qualification, it is important to note that it is not necessary for a library to be, or be part of, a qualifying institution to receive a gift, only for the gift to be potentially tax deductible. Generally speaking, qualifying entities include governmental units, such as cities or counties, tax-exempt corporations operating educational institutions, such as most private universities and schools, and public schools, colleges, and universities, and in each case their subsidiary units or subdivisions. A nongovernmental entity, in order to be eligible for tax-deductible contributions, may have to apply to the Internal Revenue Service for a determination of its status. If so, and if the application is approved, the institution will receive a letter from the IRS confirming its status (often referred to as a 501(c)(3) letter, the name being derived from the applicable section of the Internal Revenue Code for most tax-exempt entities). Potential donors may wish to see a copy of this letter, and it is a good idea to have one in your desk drawer that you can pull out for the occasion.

If the library does not qualify for deductible donations (and to be sure, checking with your institution's legal counsel may be advisable) then it is certainly appropriate to advise potential donors of the fact before a gift is completed. For some, this fact will be irrelevant, that is, when the donor wants to make the gift anyway regardless of deductibility, but in most situations it will be an important consideration.

In the event your institution qualifies, and the proposed gift is one the library wishes to receive, then there are important duties to be performed. Gifts such as books, manuscripts, and papers are referred to in the law as "in-kind" gifts to distinguish them from cash gifts. Large-value in-kind gifts (i.e., books and journals with an appraised value of more than $5,000, or smaller gifts that are part of a series of gifts of books and journals made by a single donor in a single tax year and having an aggregate value of more than $5,000) are required to be treated specially. The majority of gifts in kind made to most libraries are likely to be valued for tax purposes at less than $5,000 and here the rules are simpler, the gifts being normally deductible by the donor at the full fair market value of the items contributed unless they are put to an unrelated use by the donor organization, meaning use in a manner that is "unrelated to the purpose or function constituting the basis of the charitable organization's exemption under section 501" (26 CFR 1.170A-4(b)(3)). Acquiring the gift for the purpose of selling it would be an example of an unrelated use.

No deduction is allowed for federal tax purposes for a contribution of $250 or more unless the gift is contemporaneously acknowledged in writing by the recipient entity. The acknowledgment must generally describe the items received and state whether the organization provided the donor anything in return for the gift and, if so, a good-faith estimate of the value of the benefits provided. Most of the time, book donors will not receive anything other than maybe a de minimis value, but if the amounts are large and, for example, a big party is thrown for the donor, the value of the meal and so on might best be listed (the donor has to subtract whatever this amounts to from the deduction).

For gifts valued over $5,000, the rules get more complicated. Generally a taxpayer is required to get a written appraisal of the property donated supporting at least the deduction taken. The library should avoid making any representations as to such value; the responsibility for obtaining an appraisal is the donor's and the library should not undertake to provide it.

More troublesome are requirements recently imposed by the Internal Revenue Service on recipients such as libraries to report the sale or disposition of any part of a large gift if the sale or disposition occurs within three years of the date of the gift. These reporting requirements are intended to better enforce the rule on unrelated use described above. The government seems to fear that taxpayers may be offloading vast quantities of more or less unusable items onto qualifying organizations that have no use for them, in other words, that the purpose of the charitable deduction is not really being carried out through such gifts.

With the small in-kind donations (less the $5,000) there are few problems. But the larger gifts present significant record-keeping problems that many libraries will not want to have to face (failure to make the required reports can subject the library to a fine of as much as $10,000). Even the largest libraries have had to adjust their gift-receiving policies. The "Gifts" webpage of the University of California Library (http://www.lib.berkeley.Gifts/gifts.html) notes:

> The Library's intention in accepting gifts is that they be added to its holdings if needed. Thus every effort is made to accept as gifts only

items appropriate for addition to Library collections. Owing to the extent of the Library's holdings it is normally the case that many gift volumes will not be added to the Library's collections; yet it is never possible to predict which, nor is Library staff able to maintain records of a detail sufficient to report to donors after the fact which volumes have been retained and which have not. In determining the appropriate amount to claim as a charitable contribution for a gift-in-kind on their federal tax return, donors and their accountants may wish to consult Title 26 of the Code of Federal Regulations, including the following sections: 1.170A-1(c)(1), 1.170A-4(b)(1), 1.170A-4(b)(2), 1.170A-4(b)(3), 1.170A-4(b)(3)(i), 1.170A-4(b)(3)(ii), 1.6050L-1(a)(2)(i).

While such statements, and the lengthy citation of mind-numbingly complex-sounding treasury regulations, undoubtedly have a tendency to discourage large in-kind gifts, adoption of a substantially similar policy by most libraries in respect to large charitable donations is probably indicated.

Diversity Issues

Often when we hear the word *diversity* we think only of racial diversity and, although this is an important issue, diversity as a concept also encompasses gender, sexual orientation, age, and special needs issues. Ignoring these issues can lead to problems with your users and potential legal actions.

An important concern in providing for the needs of a growing multicultural community is the need to adopt a vision of collection development appropriate to the community to be served. Multicultural communities require materials in the language(s) in which the residents are the most comfortable (regardless of the appropriateness of the goal of English competency), biographies representing persons of various racial and ethnic backgrounds, picture books featuring characters that reflect the many different minorities, and resources that encourage young adults to research and take pride in their cultures. Diversity in collection development is also important for promoting public awareness and knowledge of other cultures even when the particular community that the library serves is not all that diverse (Carlton, 1993).

Fundamental philosophical issues also must be considered as libraries reach out to their multicultural communities. There must be a commitment on the part of library administrators and librarians to an expansion of their own cultural awareness, which can often be fostered through additions that result in more diverse staff. For librarians to better serve diverse communities, they must clearly understand who the library serves and the needs of those users. To be most effective, the resulting vision must be known, recognized, and supported by all employees, from top management all the way down to the library pages (Carlton, 1993). In a 1992 article, Quezada emphasized the importance of making all of a library's mainstream activities accessible to often underserved populations, rather than just offering token programs aimed at minority users. Working with a trainer or facilitator who specializes in cultural diversity can assist all library employees in examining their own beliefs and learning to be better aware of and to appreciate the beneficial aspects of other cultures. It should be a library's mission to ensure that library services are available to the entire community, especially those who have been traditionally underserved (Quezada, 1992).

Alternative Literature

Publications that represent a minority viewpoint are often referred to as alternative literature. These sorts of items are generally published by small, independent presses. Care should be taken in reviewing items from these presses, as they are sometimes managed by groups with an extreme right, left, or even radical political persuasion. The publications of these presses may not, however, be ignored even though librarians may judge them to be biased and not presenting a balanced position. They may be the only publications available to present these views in a positive light, and thus may be the only way to collect materials representative of all sides of an issue.

Gender and Sexual Orientation Issues

Gender and sexual orientation issues are at the source of many present-day tensions between libraries and their users.

One example is the dilemma of gay men's book clubs in Wisconsin:

> Because of the absence of dialogue, a tense relationship appears to exist between Wisconsin's gay men's book discussion groups and their local public libraries. Public library directors express interest in accommodating these groups if approached but face budget restrictions and local communities that may oppose these gatherings: gay men's book clubs prefer meeting in private homes and other openly gay-friendly environments largely because of conservatism of cultural institutions in their collective memories. (Pruitt, 2010: 121)

While a library may say that all are welcome, they may have to prove that in some way before diverse groups will begin to feel welcome in their institution.

Americans with Disabilities Act Issues

One in five Americans has some condition that qualifies as a disability under the Americans with Disabilities Act. But the guidelines and standards that apply to libraries to meet the needs of the disabled are often unclear and difficult to achieve. While the majority of these guidelines affect primarily the service activities of the library, a number apply to the management of the collection as well. It is on those that we concentrate in this section.

Legal Issues

The United States, along with 81 other nations, has signed the United Nations Convention on the Rights of Persons with Disabilities. The purpose of this convention is "to promote, protect and ensure the full and equal enjoyment of all human rights and fundamental freedoms by all persons with disabilities, and to promote respect for their inherent dignity" (United Nations, 2008: screen 1). Consistent with this convention, the United States adopted the Americans with Disabilities Act during the presidency and at the urging of George H. W. Bush. While this act's obvious manifestations have been many, such as curb cuts, elevator access to all floors of public buildings, building code changes to accommodate wheelchairs, a proliferation of ramps, wider doors, and so on, its effects on library collections have been more subtle, but no less real.

Collection Development for Special Needs

The services needed by the visually impaired must be taken into account in libraries:

> Visually impaired people have the same information needs as sighted people. Just as sighted people might read a newspaper, listen to a CD or download electronic information from the Internet, visually impaired people also want access to relevant information in their chosen accessible format. Developing an efficient library service for print-disabled people is extremely important, because there are significantly fewer books available commercially in accessible formats compared to what is published in print for the general public. The need to build collections in alternative formats and make them available for readers who are unable to browse shelves makes it necessary to develop special services. (Kavanagh and Skold, 2005: 1)

Handman (2002) describes building video collections for the hearing impaired and the visually impaired in multitype libraries. Part III of his book deals specifically with their concerns and other special user needs. He also has chapters dealing with cultural diversity that are important basic resources.

The variety of hardware and software needed to fully serve the blind and physically handicapped can create a financial strain for most libraries.

Through a national network of cooperating libraries, the National Library Service for the Blind and Physically Handicapped (NLS) provides a free library program of Braille and audio materials circulated to eligible borrowers in the United States by postage-free mail. NLS is a part of the Library of Congress. Most libraries need to avail themselves of these NLS services and assistance.

The NLS website has a copy of their collection building plan, which is a good place to begin to learn about services to special needs users. Their policy states the goals of NLS:

> The NLS mission includes two goals: to develop and maintain an inventory of Braille and recorded materials that will meet the reading preferences and information needs of a highly diverse clientele; and to develop coordinated library service for all persons eligible for this service. (http://www.loc.gov/nls/aboutcolls.html)

NLS serves users directly and also assists and coordinates services with a network of libraries with users having access to a regional or subregional library.

The collection development policy delineates the kinds of materials that NLS is required to provide.

> NLS patrons should have access to the same types of books and information available to the general public through public libraries.
>
> The recreation and information needs of the aged, the young, professional people, and other specific groups should be reflected proportionally in the collections in relation to the overall readership served.
>
> The collections should offer standard classic and informational titles, along with works of popular and recreational interest.
>
> Selection of any given book is not to be interpreted as an endorsement of the views expressed therein. Books selected are reproduced in their entirety and remain available even if they are offensive or unacceptable to some readers. NLS supports intellectual freedom and subscribes to the American Library Association's Library Bill of Rights and Freedom to Read Statement.

Their collection development policy is much like the ones studied in Chapter 3 but with a special focus on the kinds of materials that the blind and physically handicapped need along with the equipment to use those resources. It should serve as a baseline for any library.

Vocabulary

Americans with Disabilities Act	alternative literature
assisted technologies	copyright
Creative Commons license	digital rights management
diversity	fair use
first sale doctrine	intellectual property
licensed resources	provenance
public domain	visually impaired

Activities

Organize into groups of three to four students to consider the following scenarios.

1. You purchase a top-selling book at a local bookstore. After reading it, you give it to another student in your class. After she reads it, she arranges to sell it via the web. Have either of you broken any intellectual property laws? Why or why not?

2. Your principal comes to the media center and requests that you (the media specialist) duplicate a DVD that he has borrowed from the library because he thinks it would be useful in the sixth-grade social studies classes. It was originally shown on PBS, so he tells you it is okay to copy it for educational use. If you follow his instructions, has either of you broken the copyright law? If yes, the media specialist, the principal, or both?

3. You are a land-grant university collection development librarian. A widow shows up with her late husband's law library in the back of her minivan and hands you some receipts indicating that, over the years, he paid well over $50,000 for the volumes. Some are old but in quite good condition. The sets appear to be current and complete with no missing volumes. Your library's university has been considering establishment of a law school for some time but the state legislature has been reluctant to provide funds, noting the existence of another state-supported law school and the heavy library requirements the American Bar Association imposes for law school accreditation. She asks whether you agree with her that the books have likely only increased in value since their purchase and that, as a condition of her gift, the library name its entire law book collection for her husband. Should you accept the gift? What other information might you need?

4. A mother with a two-year-old child walks into your library and encounters a children's book display that includes titles such as *Heather Has*

Two Mommies and *Daddy's Roommate*. The mother immediately becomes irate and demands that the display be taken down as she does not want her child exposed to gay literature. Assume that your supervisor is not around. How do you handle the situation?

Discussion Questions

1. Discuss ways that an academic library, a public library, or a school media center may provide some services to special needs users.
2. Discuss referral procedures for services that a special needs user cannot get from your library.
3. Discuss the use and importance of a collection development policy when dealing with donations to the library.

References

Carlton, Debbie Yumiko. 1993. *Public Libraries and Cultural Diversity. ERIC Digest.* ED358871.

Handman, Gary P. 2002. *Video Collection Development in Multi-type Libraries: A Handbook.* Westport, CT: Greenwood Press.

Kavanagh, Rosemary, and Beatrice Christensen Skold, eds. 2005. *Libraries for the Blind in the Information Age: Guidelines for Development.* IFLA Professional Reports, No. 86. The Hague: International Federation of Library Associations and Institutions.

Pruitt, John. 2010. "Gay Men's Book Club versus Wisconsin's Public Libraries: Political Perceptions in the Absence of Dialogue." *Library Quarterly* 80 (April): 121–141.

Quezada, Shelley, ed. 1992. "Mainstreaming Library Services to Multicultural Populations: The Evolving Tapestry." *Wilson Library Bulletin* 66 (February): 28–44; 120–121.

Schlosser, Melanie. 2006. "Fair Use in the Digital Environment: A Research Guide." *Reference and User Services Quarterly* 46 (Fall): 11–17.

Sony Corp. of America vs. Universal City Studios, 464 U.S. 417 (1984).

United Nations. 2008. "Convention on the Rights of Persons with Disabilities." http://www.un.org/disabilities/defaultasp?navid=12&pid=150.

U.S. Census Bureau. 2005. "School Enrollments—Social and Economic Characteristics of Students, October 2003." Current Population Reports P20-554. http://www.census.gov/prod/2005pubs/p20-554.pdf.

Selected Readings

Agosta, Denise E. 2007. "Building a Multicultural School Library: Issues and Challenges." *Teacher Librarian* 34, no. 3: 27–31.

Albright, Megan. 2006. "The Public Library's Responsibilities to LGBT Communities: Recognizing, Representing, and Serving." *Public Libraries* 45, no. 5: 52–56.

Alexander, Linda B., and Sarah D. Miselis. 2007. "Barriers to GLBTQ Collection Development and Strategies for Overcoming Them." *Young Adult Library Services* 5, no. 3: 43–49.

Algenio, Emilie, and Alexis Thompson-Young. 2005. "Licensing E-books: The Good, the Bad, and the Ugly." *Journal of Library Administration* 42, nos. 3/4: 113–128.

Alire, Camila A., and Jacqueline Ayala. 2007. *Serving Latino Communities.* 2nd ed. New York: Neal-Schuman.

Angst, Thomas. 2001. "American Libraries and Agencies of Culture." *American Studies* 42, no. 3: 5–22.

Armstrong, Tracey. 2005. "Copyright Clearance Center: Providing Compliance Solutions for Content Users." *Journal of Library Administration* 42, nos. 3/4: 55–64.

Bloomquist, Shannon. 2005. "Autism Resources for Public Libraries: Issues, Challenges, and Recommended Resources." *Indiana Libraries* 24, no. 3: 23–31. https://scholarworks.iupui.edu/handle/1805/1404.

Bluh, Pamela, and Cindy Hepfer, eds. 2006. *Managing Electronic Resources: Contemporary Problems and Issues.* Chicago: Association for Library Collections and Technical Services.

Bosch, Stephen. 2005. "Using Model Licenses on Library Collections." *Journal of Library Administration* 42, nos. 3/4: 65–81.

Burke, Susan K. 2008. "Removal of Gay-Themed Materials from Public Libraries: Public Opinion Trends." *Public Library Quarterly* 27, no. 3: 247–264.

Chou, Min, and Oliver Zhou. 2005. "The Impact of Licenses on Library Collections." *Acquisitions Librarian* 17, nos. 33/34: 7–23.

Christou, Corilee, and Gail Dykstra. 2002. "Through a 'Content Looking Glass'—Another Way of Looking at Library Licensing of Electronic Content." *Against the Grain* 14 (November): 18–22.

Cuban, Sondra. 2007. *Serving New Immigrant Communities in the Library.* Westport, CT: Greenwood Press.

Darby, Mary Ann, and Miki Pryne. 2002. *Hearing All the Voices: Multicultural Books for Adolescence.* Lanham, MD: Scarecrow Press.

Durrant, Fiona. 2006. *Negotiating Licenses for Digital Resources.* London: Facet.

East, Kathy, and Rebecca L. Thomas. 2007. *Across Areas: A Guide to Multicultural Literature for Children.* Westport, CT: Libraries Unlimited.

Eschenfelder, Kristin R. 2008. "Every Library's Nightmare? Digital Rights Management, Use Restrictions, and Licensed Scholarly Digital Resources." *College and Research Libraries* 69 (May): 205–223.

Fons, Theodore A., and Timothy D. Jewell. 2007. "Envisioning the Future of ERM Systems." *Serials Review* 52, nos. 1/2: 151–166.

Gillespie, Tarleton. 2007. *Wired Shut: Copyright and the Shape of Digital Culture.* Cambridge, MA: MIT Press.

Gilton, Donna L. 2007. *Multicultural and Ethnic Children's Literature in the United States.* Lanham, MD: Scarecrow Press.

Gould, Thomas H.P., Tomas A. Lipinski, and Elizabeth A. Buchanan. 2005. "Copyright Policies and the Deciphering of Fair Use in the Creation of Reserves at University Libraries." *Journal of Academic Librarianship* 31 (May): 182–197.

Harris, Lesley Ellen. 2002. *Licensing Digital Content: A Practical Guide for Librarians.* Chicago: ALA.

Hill, Nanci Milone. 2007. "Out and About: Serving the GLBT Population @ Your Library." *Public Libraries* 46, no. 4: 18–24.

Hoffmann, Gretchen McCord. 2005. *Copyright in Cyberspace 2.* New York: Neal-Schuman.

Jaeger, Paul T. 2008. "User-Centered Policy Evaluations of Section 508 of the Rehabilitation Act: Evaluating E-government Websites for Accessibility." *Journal of Disability Policy Studies* 19, no. 1: 24–33.

Kramer, Elsa F. 2007. "Digital Rights Management: Pitfalls and Possibilities for People with Disabilities." *Journal of Electronic Publishing* 10 (Winter). E-journal. Accessed November 3, 2009. http://www.journalofelectronic-publishing.org/.

Kranich, Nancy. 2000. "A Question of Balance: The Role of Libraries in Providing Alternatives to Mainstream Media." *Collection Building* 19, no. 3: 85–90.

Pike, George H. 2007. "First Sale Doctrine Put to the Test." *Information Today* 24 (October): 17, 19.

Robertson, Deborah A. 2005. *Cultural Programming for Libraries: Linking Libraries, Communities and Culture.* Chicago: American Library Association.

Simpson, Stacy H. 2006. "Why Have a Comprehensive and Representative Collection? GLBT Material Selection and Services in the Public Library." *Progressive Librarian* no. 27 (Summer): 44–51.

Stemper, Jim, and Susan Barribeau. 2006. "Perpetual Access to Electronic Journals: A Survey of One Academic Research Library's Licenses." *Library Resources and Technical Services* 50 (March): 91–109.

Vandenbark, R. Todd. 2010. "Tending a Wild Garden: Library Web Design for Persons with Disabilities." *Information Technology and Libraries* 29 (March): 23–29.

Van Tassel, Joan. 2006. *Digital Rights Management: Protecting and Monetizing Content.* Amsterdam: Focal Press.

10

Professional Ethics and Intellectual Freedom

Overview

In this chapter we look at ethical issues that concern collection development and management librarians and examine intellectual freedom issues specifically as they relate to the collection. Professional values are important as they affect our decision making and priorities in our jobs. These concepts are studied in many different courses in library and information science education, but here we are primarily concerned with how they relate to library collections. Professional ethics guide our actions as professional librarians.

Intellectual freedom is one of the cornerstones of our professional values and guides many of the decisions that we make as professionals.

Professional Ethics

The first thing that we must consider is just exactly what we mean by "ethics." Wilkinson and Lewis (2003) state that ethics, morality, and values all involve human behavior but with different interpretations and are sometimes confused. Zipkowitz (1996: 2) defines ethics as "the moral principles of right and wrong, good and bad, to which we as a profession have subscribed as a covenant between us as professionals and our clients, peers and society." Although values in particular play heavily into library work of all types, this section focuses on ethics as it relates to collection development and acquisitions librarians. In the second section, we deal with intellectual freedom, one of the core values of librarianship.

Professional ethics provide a guideline for everyday library activities. Anytime your job relates to money and access issues, you are likely to run into situations where professional ethics come into play. Administrators may also put pressure on librarians not to weed outdated materials because the administrator wants to keep up the number of titles in the collection for accreditation reasons, or perhaps for membership in a particular library organization, such as the Association of Research Libraries or other groups. In library and information science education, ethics is often part of each course rather than a separate class. In collection development and acquisitions, behavior with vendors is often the main ethical concern. Almost all of the library and information studies professional organizations have adopted codes of ethics as they relate to their specific area of the discipline.

Codes of Professional Ethics

> Ethical behavior is the result of an internal or personal code and an external context provided by institutional and professional principles. A personal code of ethics may develop out of civic and religious convictions. People do what makes them feel good about themselves and avoid what makes them feel bad. They are also influenced by the frame of reference for behavior developed by the groups of which they are members. In other words, behavior can be a consequence of how one feels others around him or her perceive this behavior. People understand and react to what happens according to the particular frame of reference they are using for ethical behavior. (Johnson, 2009: 52–53)

Many library and information science professional associations have approved and published codes of ethics for their groups, although a variety of names are used for the same concept. The sidebar on p. 173 contains the professional guidelines for the American Society for Information Science & Technology (ASIS&T), which serve as the organization's ethical standard. They pertain to behavior with clients or employees, the profession, and society.

The ASIS&T guidelines cover many aspects of the profession as a whole, but the Association for Collections and Technical Services (ALCTS), a division of the American Library Association, has approved a statement of principles for acquisitions librarians that are quite pertinent for this book. Because of the very nature of acquisitions, interactions with a vendor can become problematic if the librarian accepts too many dinners at conferences and begins to feel some obligation to buy the vendor's products. Acquisitions librarians are often able to choose vendors on their own, which leaves them open to persuasion by vendors. For a beginning acquisitions librarian it is very important to remember to accept nothing that makes you feel obligated to a vendor. If you can go out for dinner or lunch with a vendor and still say no to the product if it is not right for the library, go ahead, as you may learn something of value for later. But if you are the type of individual who will feel guilty saying no to a friend, stay away from those kinds of situations. Some libraries insist that

ASIS&T Professional Guidelines

Dedicated to the Memory of Diana Woodward

ASIS&T recognizes the plurality of uses and users of information technologies, services, systems and products as well as the diversity of goals or objectives, sometimes conflicting, among producers, vendors, mediators, and users of information systems.

ASIS&T urges its members to be ever aware of the social, economic, cultural, and political impacts of their actions or inaction.

ASIS&T members have obligations to employers, clients, and system users, to the profession, and to society, to use judgement and discretion in making choices, providing equitable service, and in defending the rights of open inquiry.

Responsibilities to Employers/Clients/System Users

- To act faithfully for their employers or clients in professional matters.

- To uphold each user's, provider's, or employer's right to privacy and confidentiality and to respect whatever proprietary rights belong to them, by limiting access to, providing proper security for and ensuring proper disposal of data about clients, patrons or users.

- To treat all persons fairly.

Responsibility to the Profession

To truthfully represent themselves and the information systems which they utilize or which they represent, by

- not knowingly making false statements or providing erroneous or misleading information

- informing their employers, clients or sponsors of any circumstances that create a conflict of interest

- not using their position beyond their authorized limits or by not using their credentials to misrepresent themselves

- following and promoting standards of conduct in accord with the best current practices

- undertaking their research conscientiously, in gathering, tabulating or interpreting data; in following proper approval procedures for subjects; and in producing or disseminating their research results

- pursuing ongoing professional development and encouraging and assisting colleagues and others to do the same

- adhering to principles of due process and equality of opportunity.

(continued)

ASIS&T Professional Guidelines (continued)

Responsibility to Society

To improve the information systems with which they work or which they represent, to the best of their means and abilities by

- providing the most reliable and accurate information and acknowledging the credibility of the sources as known or unknown
- resisting all forms of censorship, inappropriate selection and acquisitions policies, and biases in information selection, provision and dissemination
- making known any biases, errors and inaccuracies found to exist and striving to correct those which can be remedied.

To promote open and equal access to information, within the scope permitted by their organizations or work, and to resist procedures that promote unlawful discriminatory practices in access to and provision of information, by

- seeking to extend public awareness and appreciation of information availability and provision as well as the role of information professionals in providing such information
- freely reporting, publishing or disseminating information subject to legal and proprietary restraints of producers, vendors and employers, and the best interests of their employers or clients.

Information professionals shall engage in principled conduct whether on their own behalf or at the request of employers, colleagues, clients, agencies or the profession.

Adopted May 30, 1992

© American Society for Information Science & Technology 1992. Used by permission.

---

their librarians accept nothing from a vendor to be sure that nothing unethical may occur. The statement by the ALCTS specifically establishes ethical behaviors for acquisitions librarians (see sidebar, p. 175).

Although it is the responsibility of librarians to negotiate the best deals and discounts for their library, it is important to avoid misleading the vendor on the potential dollar amounts of your purchases to get a larger discount or to avoid other sharp practice tactics. Vendors have to make a profit, so misleading them into situations where they are unable to do so is ethically wrong.

Bushing (1993: 48) lists four standards for ethical behavior: "honesty, respect for people, professional integrity, and good business practices." In a concise form, they represent much of what is included in the ALCTS statement on page 175.

Statement on Principles and Standards of Acquisitions Practice

In all acquisitions transactions, a librarian:

1. gives first consideration to the objectives and policies of his or her institution;

2. strives to obtain the maximum ultimate value of each dollar of expenditure;

3. grants all competing vendors equal consideration insofar as the established policies of his or her library permit, and regards each transaction on its own merits;

4. subscribes to and works for honesty, truth, and fairness in buying and selling, and denounces all forms and manifestations of bribery;

5. declines personal gifts and gratuities;

6. uses only by consent original ideas and designs devised by one vendor for competitive purchasing purposes;

7. accords a prompt and courteous reception insofar as conditions permit to all who call on legitimate business missions;

8. fosters and promotes fair, ethical, and legal trade practices;

9. avoids sharp practice;

10. strives consistently for knowledge of the publishing and bookselling industry;

11. strives to establish practical and efficient methods for the conduct of his/her office;

12. counsels and assists fellow acquisitions librarians in the performance of their duties, whenever occasion permits.

Developed by the ALCTS Acquisitions Section Ethics Task Force; endorsed by the ALCTS Acquisitions Section and adopted by the ALCTS Board of Directors, Midwinter Meeting, February 7, 1994.

A more recent factor that has influenced the development and use of ethical guidelines for acquisitions librarians involves the licensing agreements that have become so prevalent. These contracts often contain clauses that could affect ethical concerns such as patron privacy and confidentiality. The legal and ethical issues have become entangled and increasingly complex. Acquisitions librarians have to be aware of both kinds of potential pitfalls (Wilkinson and Lewis, 2003: 235).

The American Library Association has a code of ethics for librarians (see sidebar, p. 176), and the ALCTS developed a supplement to the ALA Code of Ethics that deals particularly with collection development and acquisitions (see sidebar, p. 177).

Code of Ethics of the American Library Association

As members of the American Library Association, we recognize the importance of codifying and making known to the profession and to the general public the ethical principles that guide the work of librarians, other professionals providing information services, library trustees and library staffs.

Ethical dilemmas occur when values are in conflict. The American Library Association Code of Ethics states the values to which we are committed, and embodies the ethical responsibilities of the profession in this changing information environment.

We significantly influence or control the selection, organization, preservation, and dissemination of information. In a political system grounded in an informed citizenry, we are members of a profession explicitly committed to intellectual freedom and the freedom of access to information. We have a special obligation to ensure the free flow of information and ideas to present and future generations.

The principles of this Code are expressed in broad statements to guide ethical decision-making. These statements provide a framework; they cannot and do not dictate conduct to cover particular situations.

I. We provide the highest level of service to all library users through appropriate and usefully organized resources; equitable service policies; equitable access; and accurate, unbiased, and courteous responses to all requests.

II. We uphold the principles of intellectual freedom and resist all efforts to censor library resources.

III. We protect each library user's right to privacy and confidentiality with respect to information sought or received and resources consulted, borrowed, acquired, or transmitted.

IV. We respect intellectual property rights and advocate balance between the interests of information users and rights holders.

V. We treat co-workers and other colleagues with respect, fairness, and good faith, and advocate conditions of employment that safeguard the rights and welfare of all employees of our institutions.

VI. We do not advance private interests at the expense of library users, colleagues, or our employing institutions.

VII. We distinguish between our personal convictions and professional duties and do not allow our personal beliefs to interfere with fair representation of the aims of our institutions or the provision of access to their information resources.

VIII. We strive for excellence in the profession by maintaining and enhancing our own knowledge and skills, by encouraging the professional development of coworkers, and by fostering the aspirations of potential members of the profession.

Adopted January 22, 2008, by the ALA Council.

**Guidelines for ALCTS Members to Supplement the
American Library Association Code of Ethics, 1994**

The following guidelines are to assist ALCTS members in the interpretation and application of the ALA Code of Ethics as it applies to issues of concern to ALCTS.

Within the context of the institution's missions and programs and the needs of the user populations served by the library an ALCTS member:

1. strives to develop a collection of materials within collection policies and priorities;

2. strives to provide broad and unbiased access to information;

3. strives to preserve and conserve the materials in the library in accordance with established priorities and programs;

4. develops resource sharing programs to extend and enhance the information sources available to library users;

5. promotes the development and application of standards and professional guidelines;

6. establishes a secure and safe environment for staff and users;

7. fosters and promotes fair, ethical and legal trade and business practices;

8. maintains equitable treatment and confidentiality in competitive relations and manuscript and grant reviews;

9. supports and abides by any contractual agreements made by the library or its home institution in regard to the provision of or access to information resources, acquisition of services, and financial arrangements.

Developed by the ALCTS Task Force on Professional Ethics; adopted by the ALCTS Board of Directors, Midwinter Meeting, February 7, 1994.

Having a code of ethics is one of the hallmarks of a profession. It is important to periodically review the code of ethics most closely tied to the work that you do. These codes are an excellent reminder of the practices that we should all be following as professional librarians.

A specific ethical concern of librarianship is intellectual freedom and issues of censorship.

Intellectual Freedom and Censorship

Here we look at intellectual freedom issues as a fundamental value of librarianship affecting collection development and management. For our purposes we focus on the collection, although the subject of intellectual freedom encompasses much more.

Robert Hauptman (1988: 66) defines censorship as "the active suppression of books, journals, newspapers, theater pieces, lectures, discussions, radio and television programs, films, art works, etc.—either partially or in the entirety—that are deemed objectionable on moral, political, military, or other grounds."

Branin (1997: 148–149) provides a short history of intellectual freedom and the library profession:

> Our library profession's stand on intellectual freedom has not been consistent over the years, and the interpretation of intellectual freedom concepts has always been difficult and controversial. In fact, until the 1930s in this country, many librarians believed that censorship was one of their professional duties. For example, in 1908, the American Library Association (ALA) President Arthur Bostwick made the following remark in his inaugural address at the ALA Annual Conference: "'Some are born great; some achieve greatness, some have greatness thrust upon them.' It is in this way that the librarian has been a censor of literature. . . . Books that distinctly commend what is wrong, that teach how to sin and tell how pleasant sin is, sometimes with and sometimes without the added sauce of impropriety, are increasingly popular, tempting the author to imitate them, and publisher to produce, and the bookseller to exploit. Thank Heaven they do not tempt the librarian."

By the late 1930s, the ALA position was beginning to change. Attempted censorship of John Steinbeck's *The Grapes of Wrath* eventually resulted in ALA adopting the Library Bill of Rights in 1948 (see sidebar, p. 179). It took almost ten years to be officially approved, but it has become one of the most cherished tenets of librarianship.

Types of Libraries and Efforts to Censor

Attempts at censorship can happen in any type of library. We typically think only of schools and public libraries when we talk about censorship, but, if you search the literature, you find that no type of library is immune to challenges or self-censorship by librarians. When dealing with children's materials, censorship has always been particularly controversial. In 1967, the word *age* was added to the fifth statement in the Library Bill of Rights: "A person's right to use a library should not be denied or abridged because of origin, age, background, or views." The ALA position is that librarians do not censor what a child can read; only his or her parents can do that.

Scales (2009) discusses various scenarios where school media specialists need to defend library media center selections and the rights of students to have access to such materials.

Library Bill of Rights

The American Library Association affirms that all libraries are forums for information and ideas, and that the following basic policies should guide their services.

I.   Books and other library resources should be provided for the interest, information, and enlightenment of all people of the community the library serves. Materials should not be excluded because of the origin, background, or views of those contributing to their creation.

II. Libraries should provide materials and information presenting all points of view on current and historical issues. Materials should not be proscribed or removed because of partisan or doctrinal disapproval.

III. Libraries should challenge censorship in the fulfillment of their responsibility to provide information and enlightenment.

IV. Libraries should cooperate with all persons and groups concerned with resisting abridgment of free expression and free access to ideas.

V.   A person's right to use a library should not be denied or abridged because of origin, age, background, or views.

VI. Libraries that make exhibit spaces and meeting rooms available to the public they serve should make such facilities available on an equitable basis, regardless of the beliefs or affiliations of individuals or groups requesting their use.

Adopted June 19, 1939, by the ALA Council; amended October 14, 1944; June 18, 1948; February 2, 1961; June 27, 1967; January 23, 1980; inclusion of "age" reaffirmed January 23, 1996.

Jones (2009) should be reviewed for an excellent portrayal of the issues in intellectual freedom and other ethical situations in an academic library. Often students ask why a statement of intellectual freedom and a challenge procedure are necessary in an academic library. Their first impression is that in a higher education institution, of course, everyone believes in and practices intellectual freedom. Jones does an excellent job of presenting the real situation to her readers.

The FBI's Library Awareness Program (LAP) is an example of attempted intervention in academic libraries. The FBI tried to enlist librarians to check the library records of people under investigation, claiming that they were not investigating controversial authors, but only the people who wanted to read them. Although this may appear to be a privacy and confidentiality issue only, it may also involve self-censorship. If the FBI had been able to continue this program, library selectors may have become wary of buying works by controversial authors and works on terrorism or other issues that might interest the FBI. Librarians were also asked to track photocopying and database usage (Robins, 1993: 376–378). The FBI told the National Commission on Library and Information Science that the Soviets considered librarians to be excellent spy material, partly because librarians could deposit disinformation in their libraries (Robins, 1993: 393).

After the events of September 11, 2001, the federal government took millions of documents off the shelves of the National Archives and removed many documents, maps, photographs, and other similar resources from government websites (Bass and Herschaft, 2007). U.S. Government Depository libraries were told to remove certain documents from their shelves for the same reason. Depository libraries received a letter dated October 12, 2002, that told them to destroy all copies of the CD-ROM *Source Area Characteristics of Large Public Surface-Water Supplies in the Coterminous United States: An Information Resource for Source-Water Assessment, 1999* (Asher, 2010). This situation caused a great deal of discussion among librarians on the balance between censorship and security.

Public libraries are frequently involved in challenges and attempted censorship of all kinds of materials. While children's materials are frequently challenged, adult literature is also attacked.

A somewhat humorous, but nevertheless misguided, action by a public librarian was reported as a news item in the December 1971 issue of *School Library Journal* (quoted in Marcovitz and Zimmer, 2006: 51–52):

> Maurice Sendak might faint but a staff member of Caldwell Parish Library [Louisiana], knowing that the patrons of the community might object to the illustrations in *In the Night Kitchen*, solved the problem by diapering the little boy with white tempura paint. Other librarians might wish to do the same.

Self-censorship by librarians can occur in the selection process, but this is an example of library material mutilation that amounts to censorship.

The ALA Office of Intellectual Freedom provides printed materials such as the *Intellectual Freedom Manual* and also personal guidance to librarians facing a censorship challenge. No librarian should navigate this situation alone as ALA and often state library associations have offices or committees dedicated to intellectual freedom. These offices have been known to enter lawsuits where intellectual freedom is at issue.

Vocabulary

censorship	ethics	intellectual freedom
professional values	sharp practice	

Discussion Questions

1. Discuss the differences among the terms *ethics, morality,* and *values* as they relate to librarianship and specifically to collection development and acquisitions.
2. Discuss the differences between public and private schools as they relate to intellectual freedom issues.
3. Discuss the concerns of censorship and self-censorship when selecting library materials.
4. What ethical concerns should you consider when a publisher asks for an endorsement of a product, for example, a set of reference books or a database, that will be included in the advertisements for that product?
5. Your vendor representative comes to your library periodically to review your orders and make you aware of new products that may be of interest to your library users. This time he asks you out to lunch on his tab to continue the discussion. What factors should you consider before answering one way or the other?

Activity

Choose a work from the ALA List of Banned Books. Divide the class into two or more teams. Each team takes one side of a censorship challenge. Spend about 30 minutes preparing your case. Then each side presents their arguments for or against withdrawing the book from the library collection. If you have at least four teams, the members of the other two teams can serve as judge and jury. Discuss which team made the most compelling argument for their side of the issue.

References

American Library Association. 1994. *ALA Code of Ethics Supplement (ALCTS): Guidelines for ALCTS Members to Supplement the American Library Association Code of Ethics, 1964.* Chicago: American Library Association. http://www.ala.org/ala/mgrps/divs/alcts/resources/alaethics.cfm.

———. 1995/2008. *American Library Association Code of Ethics.* Chicago: American Library Association. http://www.ala.org/ala/aboutala/offices/oif/statementspols/codeofethics/codeethics.cfm.

———. 1996. *Library Bill of Rights.* Chicago: American Library Association. http://staging.ala.org/ala/aboutala/offices/oif/statementspols/statementsif/librarybillrights.cfm.

Asher, Gena. 2010. "Government Documents Removal: Censorship or Security." Accessed April 28. http://www.slis.indiana.edu/news/story.php?story_id=411.

Association for Library Collections and Technical Services. 1994. *Statement on Principles and Standards of Acquisitions Practice.* Chicago: American Library Association. http://www.pla.org/ala/mgrps/divs/alcts/ resources/collect/acq/acqethics.cfm.

Bass, Frank, and Randy Herschaft. 2007. "1 Million Archived Pages Removed Post- 9/11." *USA Today* (March 13). http://www.usatoday. com/news/washington/2007-03-13-archives_N.htm.

Branin, Joseph J. 1997. "Collection Management and Intellectual Freedom." In *Collection Management for the 1990s,* edited by Joseph J. Branin, 148–195. Chicago: American Library Association.

Bushing, Mary C. 1993. "Acquisition Ethics: The Evolution of Models for Hard Times." *Library Acquisitions: Theory and Practice* 17: 47–52.

Hauptman, Robert. 1988. *Ethical Challenges in Librarianship.* Phoenix: Oryx.

Johnson, Peggy. 2009. *Fundamentals of Collection Development and Management.* 2nd ed. Chicago: American Library Association.

Jones, Barbara M. 2009. *Protecting Intellectual Freedom in Your Academic Library.* Chicago: American Library Association.

Marcovitz, Hal, and Kyle Zimmer. 2006. *Maurice Sendak.* New York: Chelsea House.

Robins, Natalie. 1993. *Alien Ink: The FBI's War on Freedom of Expression.* New York: William Morrow.

Scales, Pat R. 2009. *Protecting Intellectual Freedom in Your School Library: Scenarios from the Front Lines.* Chicago: American Library Association.

Wilkinson, Frances C., and Linda K. Lewis. 2003. *The Complete Guide to Acquisitions Management.* Westport, CT: Libraries Unlimited.

Zipkowitz, Fay. 1996. *Professional Ethics in Librarianship: A Real Life Casebook.* Jefferson, NC: McFarland.

Selected Readings

American Library Association. 2010. *The Intellectual Freedom Manual.* 8th ed. Chicago: American Library Association.

Association for Library Services to Children. 2000. *Intellectual Freedom for Children: The Censor Is Coming.* Chicago: American Library Association.

Chmara, Theresa. 2009. *Privacy and Confidentiality Issues: A Guide for Libraries and Their Lawyers.* Chicago: American Library Association.

Dole, Wanda V., Jitka M. Hurych, and Wallace C. Koehler. 2000. "Values for Librarians in the Information Age: An Expanded Examination." *Library Management* 21: 285–297.

Doyle, Tony. 2002. "Selection versus Censorship in Libraries." *Collection Management* 27, no. 1: 15–25.

Gibson, Jeffrey. 2007. "Championing Intellectual Freedom: A School Administrator's Guide." *Knowledge Quest* 36, no. 2: 46–48.

Gorman, Michael. 2000. *Our Enduring Values*. Chicago: American Library Association.

Intner, Sheila S. 2004. "Dollars and Sense: Censorship versus Selection, One More Time." *Technicalities* 24, no. 3: 1, 7.

LaRue, James. 2007. *New Inquisition: Understanding and Managing Intellectual Freedom Challenges*. Westport, CT: Libraries Unlimited.

Martin, Ann M. 2007. "Preparing for a Challenge." *Knowledge Quest* 36, no. 2: 54–56.

11

Preservation

Overview

Preservation was traditionally seen as the job of just the few large research libraries maintaining archival collections, and within those institutions only the business of a few select specialist staff. But it is an important aspect of collection development in any library. That which you collect is not very useful if it is not preserved. Today more and more librarians are waking up to the fact that even quite small libraries may and often do possess unique materials deserving long-term preservation, even if the items only pertain to people or events in their local area. The growth of electronic materials in libraries is also affecting how librarians must view their preservation activities. In this chapter, we take a look at some of the important issues of preservation in all types of libraries.

Preservation may be described as involving all those library activities aimed at preventing, retarding, or stopping the deterioration of materials, so that the intellectual content may be saved for future users. Preservation has also been succinctly called an act of "responsible custody" (Barr, 1946: 218). For many years this has meant physical safekeeping of the books and papers that are so vulnerable to the ravages of moisture, time, and, yes, human hands. Preservation issues therefore quite appropriately rise to the top of many librarians' thinking, and perhaps even more strongly when electronic journals, in particular, are considered. In the rush to convert to electronic products and media, the traditional role of every library in preserving and archiving information for its particular community of users should not be forgotten. Libraries' users have generally depended on their librarians to perform not only the pure collection development functions of selecting, purchasing, organizing, and making available currently needed resources, but also, as an inherent corollary to these actions, the saving and preserving of information media that may have lasting value.

In the past, libraries were mainly concerned with taking steps to preserve the physical artifact (or a photocopied or microfilmed facsimile of the artifact) that contained the information, rather than preserving the information itself. Traditional library preservation strategies have therefore long been established for physical objects, but these strategies do not always transfer neatly to the preservation of a digital object.

Preservation of digital materials is an increasingly important issue for research, development, and discussion, with the general perception being that preservation of digital objects is more problematic than that of print or other formats. As more and more materials are available only in digital format with no hard copy to be preserved, digital preservation becomes an imperative for librarians if future users of such materials are to be able to access them.

Preservation of Books and Other Physical Objects

A major physical medium problem in most of today's research collections is brittle books, that is, books whose pages tear if folded only once or twice or that simply fall apart when removed from the shelves. Brittle pages result from the use of acidic paper. Such paper became popular after about 1840, when much of the papermaking industry moved from the use of linen and cotton rags to wood pulp. To make the new pulp product more attractive, acid was introduced, mainly as a part of the whitening process. The effect, if initially satisfying, is nevertheless insidious because it often may remain hidden for some years. In addition, the toxic glues, dyes, and other materials used in the binding process can contribute to the deterioration of printed materials.

Before 1900, techniques used to repair printed materials drew on traditional, time-consuming, and careful bookbinding practices. With the explosion in publishing during the 20th century, more and more materials needed repair sooner than expected; but with the high cost of traditional proper repair, corners were cut with increasing frequency—sloppy half-efforts involving consumer cellophane tape, grocery-store glues, and pastes.

> Using Scotch brand cellophane tape, household glues and pastes, and flimsy, acidic pamphlet binders accelerated deterioration. Benign neglect has been more effective in preserving materials. Librarians have become more conscious of the consequences of poor techniques and materials. Commercial suppliers now offer a variety of archivally sound and reversible materials for cleaning, repairing, and storing materials. (Johnson, 2009: 165)

Librarians need to take a cue from the initial lines of the Hippocratic oath—first, do no harm.

Traditionally, the preservation of books and other physical objects is generally an issue of material conservation. Some of the most sophisticated techniques in book conservation require specialized training and lab facilities, arcane and complex atmospheric regulation equipment, and so on, but many effective actions can be performed in most libraries. Techniques to repair book hinges, for example, require little more than glue and a knitting needle. Care needs to be exercised, of course: sometimes a little transparent tape carefully applied appears to meet the immediate need, but the long-term effect can be disastrous. More significantly, nearly all libraries still rebind materials, which is an important form of preservation and conservation.

Controlling temperature and humidity are also important in the preservation of physical objects. High temperatures and humidity can lead to mold infestations that can easily spread throughout the collection. In very specialized collections of materials not printed on acid-free paper, deacidification processes might be performed in-house or outsourced to a company that specializes in them.

In a library with good environmental and moisture controls, special collections may be built on the concept of preserving materials. Restricted access allows librarians to better control who uses materials and the conditions under which they are used. Libraries with truly rare or unique materials may require gloves and monitor who uses materials and where they use them.

From a straightforward collection development standpoint, considerations can be taken into account during the acquisitions process that can help ensure that library materials enjoy longer life without the need to resort to extraordinary and expensive measures later. For instance, many items are now printed on acid-free paper, which greatly prolongs the life of printed materials. To spot these, look for a small infinity sign on the title page or verso of the title page; these are guaranteed by the publisher to be acid-free. While some items are available in cheaper formats, the additional cost in respect to a specific work, if any, is usually negligible, and often particular items may be available only in an acid-free paper format anyway. If two works on the same subject are otherwise equally appropriate for acquisition, the paper may be a considered a decisive factor. Additionally, it is simply expedient to ensure that, of items available in multiple formats, those acquired have the best possible bindings and covers, commensurate with considerations of cost, availability, and budgetary constraints.

In addition to the types of preservation and conservation measures usually practiced, conservation in research libraries has become a matter of special concentration and concern.

The field of research library conservation emerged and has evolved significantly during the past fifty years. Professional organizations and training programs have been established; new treatment techniques have been developed and promoted through conferences, workshops, and publications; and increasingly, special and general collections practitioners have collaborated on treatment solutions. Despite the significant challenges faced by research libraries in the twenty-first century as substantial resources are allocated to electronic information discovery and delivery opportunities, research libraries continue to collect print collections. (Baker and Dube, 2010: 21)

A huge flood in Florence, Italy, in 1966 was something of a watershed in the preservation arena, as efforts to save and repair the priceless written treasures of that most famous of European Renaissance cities spurred significant study of the effectiveness of book and paper conservation methods, not only by those directly affected but by librarians and archivists everywhere. The Florence experience thus marked the real beginning of cooperation and collaboration on conservation issues among research libraries, which has borne significant fruit. The details of these new methods and protocols are beyond the scope of this textbook, but for those interested can form an important area for further study.

Although conserving library materials in special collections has become integral to preservation efforts in research libraries, modern books are also in need of conservation. Unfortunately, one of the most felicitous developments in the democratic dispersion of knowledge that has occurred in the last 50 years, the move to open shelving in most libraries, where the reader may come and browse without the need to request the services of an intermediary with access to the library's stacks, has resulted in a lack of supervision, with the upshot that newer, popular materials can sometimes be quickly rendered in worse condition than the older, rare materials to which access is restricted. The problem is broader than simply greater usage. Modern production methods now generally used in book publishing, resulting from increasing mechanization, have rendered many new books inherently more fragile than some older materials (Baker and Dube, 2010: 22).

In a 1963 symposium, Banks discussed how to care for large segments of a collection that demonstrated a number of problems, resulting in a new approach and the need for special skills. He coined the term *collections conservator*, which still seems quite apropos today. The role of a collections conservator is to institute and utilize conservation procedures in collections that do not require the item-by-item special treatment that may often be needed in a typical special collection (Baker and Dube, 2010: 23).

Programs of study that examine all aspects of archives, special collections, preservation, and conservation are becoming increasingly common in library and information science departments. For further information, the student may wish to review the selected readings for this chapter.

Preservation Microfilming

Before the electronic digitization of book pages came along, preservation by the photographic microfilming of materials that were rare, deteriorating, or easily subject to deterioration, such as newspapers, appeared by the early 1970s to be the answer to most libraries' preservation needs, especially following the development of the more random-access microfiche storage method for photographed works. However, some materials proved too deteriorated to withstand the photographing process. Nicholson Baker (2001), in his book *Double Fold*, called the country's attention to the unexpected consequences of preservation microfilming in an extremely negative manner. He described the worst consequences of the microfilming process used in connection with the U.S. Newspaper Project, where some badly deteriorated or otherwise damaged newspapers were discarded after being microfilmed. These items were already damaged and were not further harmed during the microfilming but were apparently discarded on the presumption that the microfilm would be the equivalent of or better than the old damaged original. This practice was stopped, but not before many people began rejecting local microfilming due to this criticism.

Disaster Plans

Although the responsibility for a total disaster plan usually rests with the library administration, the collection development head and staff should take an active role in drawing up those parts of the plan that deal directly with the collection as a whole. This is especially true now that most collections involve combinations of print, audiovisual, and electronic resources. Natural disasters such as tornadoes, earthquakes, floods, and hurricanes can hit with little or no warning, such as the highly publicized flood that did major damage at the University of Hawaii's library in 2004. Plans have to be in place to be implemented immediately once all people are safe and the building is declared safe to enter, so that as much of the collection as possible can be saved or rehabilitated.

A number of key items are important in any disaster plan. First, unpleasant as it may be, there must be a detailing of what is to be saved first, with collection development staff serving in the role of triage decision makers. Another important item for the plan is simply a list of the names, phone numbers, and Internet addresses of vendors that can help in resupplying destroyed but high-priority items, providing the library with refrigerated trailers for damaged print materials, and so on. Materials needed quickly for disaster recovery should be both on-site in a disaster kit, closet, or other area known to staff, and backed up or duplicated off-site. A simple but highly useful and practical template for developing an emergency response plan is available on the web (Brown, 2007).

For electronic materials, advance creation of backups and their off-site storage in case the library is damaged too badly to enter for a long period are relatively easy, but to be useful they must be kept current. While daily backups may be too much to ask, at least multiple backups should be provided for. Unfortunately, unless systems and backups are constantly checked, sometimes backups simply refuse to load. As much as possible, backups should be tested periodically to make sure that they are not corrupted and that personnel know how to use the system.

Preservation of Digital Objects

It was traditionally assumed that, if a publication were printed on long-life, acid-free paper and if reasonable environmental conditions for its storage were maintained, access to the information could continue for an essentially indefinite period, or at least for quite a long time. This work was often well done—the oldest printed Gutenberg Bibles in existence remain readable today, if not exactly easily usable in the sense of unrestricted access to the original. It is only relatively recently in library history, however, that the format of materials has become problematic for the preservation for future use of the information contained in those formats.

> The recognition of digitization as a preservation strategy is a relatively new and still-controversial concept within the cultural heritage community, which has generally viewed digitization activities as a form of copying for easier and broader access. The Association of Research Libraries officially adopted digitization as an acceptable preservation strategy in 2004, by recognizing the sheer impossibility of redoing digitization work as technology evolves and acquiescing to the notion that technology capabilities and standards are sufficiently mature for the task at hand. (Conway, 2010: 64)

Good enough, but a potential problem must be kept in mind. Although libraries have always needed to deselect or weed their collections of unneeded, out-of-date, duplicate, or otherwise no longer useful books and serials, this process has almost always been accomplished (barring natural disasters, fires, or other accidents) through a conscious and careful decision on the part of librarians. However, electronic products open up the unhappy specter of the unconscious and quite unintentional discarding, in effect, of the information itself through the obsolescence of the resource medium. For instance, if you purchase a serial on CD-ROM today, how certain can you be that you will in fact be able to access the material appearing in its issues in the year 2020, or for that matter even two years from now? If you purchase web access to that serial, what happens if you drop the subscription next year, or if the company that provides access is bought out by another vendor that subsequently changes its access policies in ways incompatible with your systems or policies, or provides continued access only at significantly increased cost? If you decide to preserve a website, do you also have to preserve all the links made from that page if it is to be truly useful? If so, where do you stop? Electronic storage and digitization are wonderful things in many ways, but they require a constant vigilance that hard copy materials do not. The Dead Sea Scrolls, if incomplete and requiring a significant degree of transliteration, remain readable today as they were thousands of years ago. But there are computer discs and tapes from 30 years ago that languish for lack of equipment to read them and even for programmers alive today who recall the early computer languages in which they were written. These are not issues only for research libraries; they are matters of concern for every library that does not want to find that its backup archive requires the equivalent of an eight-track tape player.

Not only electronic serials or e-books need to be preserved. Data CDs and DVDs are important parts of the collection of many libraries. It is recommended that the physical CD and DVD discs be archived at temperatures less than 68 degrees Fahrenheit and at a relative humidity between 20 percent and 50 percent. When handled they need to be held by the outer edge or center hole with care not to scratch the disc (Byers, 2003: vi). But who really does this? The ubiquity of copying software makes cavalier handling of these items perhaps less problematic, but again the need is for something to be done before disaster strikes. Disaster includes damage to backup CDs and DVDs even when the main collection is unaffected.

The various types of digital media to be archived and preserved for both current and future use include the following:

- Digitally reformatted works that are scanned or digitized versions of physical items.
- Digital documents, and so on, that do not have an analog or print counterpart (born digital).
- Individual resources such as texts, still images, audio recordings, and so on that are from a single individual source.
- Collective resources such as websites, blogs, wikis, e-journals, and so on.
- Data sets that consist of numerous individual pieces of scientific, computer, and other cultural data that make up a comprehensive set of materials.
- Communication records such as e-mails, instant messages, Tweets, Facebook postings, and other similar online activities that comprise an individual's or group's record of communication.
- Metadata that assist in long-term storage and retrieval by being included with the different digital media resources. Metadata record the different features such as format, version, and what devices or software is needed to access the saved information.

Possibly digital preservation's most interesting recent development is the shift from large, project-based imaging initiatives to the digitization of more everyday items. Earlier print preservation efforts evolved similarly. Initially these projects centered upon the recognized great collections, but eventually developed into efforts to preserve deteriorating materials of all types as they were found. This trend to digitize all deteriorating materials is not widespread, but, given that libraries such as the University of Michigan have begun to develop such projects, it is a virtual certainty that the approach will become more widespread in the future.

Some note should be made of the phenomenon of the ease of electronic self-publishing, usually associated only with "vanity" materials produced by individually affluent authors. These have always constituted a tiny percentage of print materials, but recently self-publishers have become mass producers of great chunks of information on the web. These born digital materials are highly ephemeral, however, and thus a problem for preservationists.

Let's look at a few of the problems involved.

Is Digitized Information Preserved (or Preservable)?

Digital preservation involves both born digital and digitized documents. Born digital documents were initially created using some form of digital technology. Digital preservation of such materials is necessary to the maintenance of their authenticity, reliability, and accessibility. Although sometimes the layperson may think of digital information as being potentially preserved for eternity, it is becoming clear that at the present this is certainly not the case. Electronic formats keep changing and show no signs of settling down to a standard "King's English" that promises to endure. So unless the information contained in older formats is constantly being transferred to newer media, it can quickly become lost. For example, try locating today a 5¼-inch floppy drive (the predominant storage format for most microcomputers a mere 20 years ago) in order to read documents stored on that type of disc. Not an easy process already. But for those, especially business and library early adopters, who have data on the even older 8-inch disc format dominant in the 1970s, accessing and moving the information contained on them to a current format remains, if doable, both expensive and labor intensive. As 3½-inch disc drives disappeared from new computers to be replaced by CD-RW and flash card drives about ten years ago, and other smaller media and memory sticks and cards have come along, it seems certain that any portable data storage will inevitably become inaccessible. Even as august a body as the National Archives finds itself constantly searching for, or even attempting to build from scratch, some older piece of technology or equipment so that they can transfer information from an obsolete format to a new one. It has become clear that the preservation of digital information requires both the financial wherewithal and a firm commitment to migrating data from one format to another to ensure that the data can continue to be read.

These same concerns also apply to print documents that have been selected for digitization. Once in digital format, these documents join the merry-go-round of materials needing to be kept up to date. But even when information is kept in a readable format, you must also consider the physical durability of that format. At present the average life span of magnetic tape appears to be considerably less than that of most books, even those printed on acidic paper. Magnetic disc formats, while apparently somewhat better, have yet to meet the test of time, even assuming adequate protection from magnets, motors, and electric detection equipment; for optical disc formats, such as CD-ROMs and DVDs, the life expectancies are apparently considerably longer, but there is no consensus on just how long. There appear to be variations depending on the type of disc—estimates vary all the way from 10 to 100 years—but the life expectancies are still paltry when compared to those of most printed materials.

In addition to hardware format challenges, the library must also be concerned about the software used to generate the documents. In 1989 the latest in word-processing software included such now extinct, or nearly so, programs as WordStar and XyWrite. Can we be positive that ten years from now we will have the software to read or convert a document produced using one of today's standard word-processing programs? It is clear that when we move away from standard ASCII text to formatted, word-processed documents, we necessarily become very dependent on the proper software to read the document, suggesting perhaps the need for a standard for electronic archives.

Today, to preserve information, many archives have undertaken to convert their materials to a format that they hope will remain independent of software or platform. Such formats today are usually pure ASCII texts, which are easy to save, but which lack the benefits of fancy fonts, boldfaced and italicized text, justification, and so on. Although this approach seems the best, it is an expensive one without any guarantees. After all, what future does ASCII have?

Another important consideration is that, unlike the case of print materials, where good fortune often plays a crucial part in long-term preservation, there is no salvation in just doing nothing; electronic materials will be preserved and usable in the future only if positive action is taken now. In the past, many printed sources were saved by serendipity, that is, they just happened to survive on someone's bookshelf or in some library's storage area.

Some libraries are beginning to create what are called "dim archives" of print copies of journals that they are primarily acquiring in electronic form. The idea is that materials in a dim archive are stored remotely for retrieval when needed and used only when the electronic version is no longer available. These materials are not fully processed nor arranged for public access. A few libraries have created "dark archives" in which materials are stored for use as backups but only in a worst-case scenario.

Another important issue is the sheer ephemeral nature of digital information. It may change or simply disappear before it can be captured and preserved. Print archives contain the papers of individuals and authors that allow historians or literary scholars to trace the development of a work through its many drafts. In the electronic age, those drafts are likely not saved but simply overwritten by the latest version of the text.

The digitization strategy called LOCKSS (Lots of Copies Keep Stuff Safe), which was developed at Stanford University, is a model for creating multiple, geographically distant archives of digital materials. It is an open source, peer-to-peer, decentralized digital preservation infrastructure. LOCKSS is becoming increasingly accepted by publishers and librarians. Whether it addresses all relevant issues may vary from library to library, and whether it becomes a truly standard approach remains to be seen (see http://lockss.stanford.edu).

Other long-term storage options include the MetaArchive Cooperative, which is an archiving structure that is dedicated to preservation and retrieval activities. A major consideration for this and other maturing archiving solutions is that depositories must establish trust that these open archival information systems can and will keep up with the developments in technology. One of the advantages of the MetaArchive Cooperative is that it holds documents that are not openly shareable but are still vital for preservation. Oral histories, digitized photographs, manuscripts, and other intellectual property are stored within this system even though they are not currently shareable due to copyright limitations.

Similarly, CLOSED LOCKSS (CLOCKSS) is the dark archiving component of LOCKSS. It allows scholarly journals and other publications, documents, and so on to be preserved for posterity. Like the examples above, materials in CLOCKSS are not available for sharing, but are being kept in the digital archive for posterity.

Collection development librarians simply cannot ignore the electronic information preservation problem. Generally, libraries are seen as collecting items of lasting importance rather than ephemeral. To meet this expectation, libraries must be able to access permanent archives of information that are available only in electronic form. In searching for a solution, librarians are justifiably reluctant to depend on commercial vendors, and they must therefore make the necessary commitment to move with the technology so as not to be left with something like the equivalent of a reel-to-reel audiotape archive.

How does collection development deal with this problem? A March 1998 statement of the International Coalition of Library Consortia (ICLC) argues that libraries, if they are to meet their typical preservation and collection mandates, must be able to purchase or license information perpetually, not just temporarily, to retain control over the preservation of the information contained in the media. This control necessarily includes the right to make backup copies. The problem is exacerbated when information is accessed only remotely, and the ICLC also argues that a provider should not be used unless there is some form of guarantee that the information will be perpetually available.

Who Should Archive an Electronic Resource?

There are several possible answers to the question of who should archive electronic materials.

Publisher or Vendor/Aggregator

Although many publishers currently attempt to archive their electronic publications, most of them make no commitment regarding the permanence of their archives. When it is no longer commercially profitable to do so, it appears unlikely that publishers will continue to make and maintain archives of their electronic materials. Librarians also worry that a publisher may go out of business or be sold to another company that decides that it is not in its financial interests to continue the original archival arrangements. To make matters worse, even fewer publishers have indicated a commitment to moving their materials to current formats as needed for their preservation. Collection development librarians in academic and research libraries should, and typically do, strive to purchase materials with an eye to permanent retention, making preservation and archival issues extremely important to them; the publisher's safeguards likely will not be sufficient for a library's needs.

Some good approaches do exist. One example of a vendor approach to preservation is OCLC's FirstSearch Electronic Collections Online, which offers to subscribers perpetual access to its electronic resources. Another is JSTOR, which was established in 1995 as an independent, not-for-profit organization to provide academic libraries with back runs of important journals in electronic form. JSTOR has straightforward licenses with publishers and subscribing institutions. By emphasizing back runs, JSTOR strives to avoid competing with publishers, whose principal revenues come from current subscriptions.

The Library Itself

Traditionally, libraries have always done their own archiving, whether through binding journal issues or microfilming. It is conceivable that, given the permission of the publisher, libraries could archive many of their electronic materials as well. However, the library must then make the same commitment to keeping materials in a current and usable format. If done in every library, these activities would certainly be expensively duplicative. Librarians would doubtless feel safest or most comfortable with this solution, but it is probably not a cost-effective approach to a general problem and it frankly does not seem to be the method chosen by most libraries at this time. The one exception appears to be materials produced locally, which many libraries do archive on the basis that they will likely be the sole source for these items in the future. As noted above, a few libraries have begun creating dim or dark archives of their journals, so that in a worst-case scenario, they will have access to a print copy of the journal if the electronic one is no longer accessible.

Cooperative Arrangements

As libraries have done with shared online cataloging for years, a cooperative arrangement can be worked out to preserve electronic resources, which seems to be a highly desirable approach. One idea is that publishers could provide for a nonprofit organization that would archive and convey materials as needed and make particular titles and volumes available to libraries that held, or once held, a subscription. A number of efforts are under way along these lines. For example, the Committee on Institutional Cooperation's Electronic Journal Collection is an effort by the major academic libraries in the United States both to archive and to offer access to freely available electronic journals. An additional example of a consortial approach by academic libraries is JSTOR, which archives electronic journals for a fee.

The Google Books Library Project is a good example of a cooperative arrangement to preserve books by digitizing them. The problems with that project are not technical issues, but rather ones of intellectual property (see Chapter 9 for intellectual property concerns). There are also a number of quality issues, as you might expect with people digitizing materials all day long (see Duguid, 2007).

Who Should Be Concerned with Preservation Issues?

When reviewing the library literature dealing with electronic resources, it is obvious that a good many libraries have determined, whether consciously or by default, that preservation of electronic-format materials may not get much attention. Apparently preservation issues are not on their checklists of points to consider when purchasing or licensing an electronic resource. In some cases, it has been baldly stated that preservation issues were not of concern to a particular library when selecting materials. But some libraries are obviously very concerned with such issues, even if they do not have answers for all the preservation issues that are necessarily raised.

We submit that this is an area where no library can consider itself an island. Some type of cooperation is necessary if vendors and publishers are to make significant contributions to ensuring continued access to electronic materials. If the library community is not concerned, then the vendors and publishers obviously will not commit significant corporate dollars to keep their materials available in perpetuity. Also, libraries may need to follow the lead of those few cooperative efforts that have begun working actively toward the preservation of electronic resources. Currently these efforts are mostly in the area of electronic serials but can be expected to widen in the near future.

But some may say this issue is only for research libraries. Although research libraries are naturally most likely to be able and motivated to commit resources to cooperative preservation efforts, it is really a matter of concern for all libraries. Many smaller libraries currently rely on interlibrary loan for many specialized materials from academic or research libraries. What if the library that you have always depended on does not have hardcopy access to the material or, by the terms of a licensing agreement, cannot even loan you the material, much less print or copy any of it for your use? Preservation concerns involving electronic resources are properly the concern of all libraries, and only by indicating that concern when you purchase or license materials can you help to ensure that these materials will continue to be accessible.

Institutional Repositories for Access and Preservation

In today's world, ever-increasing quantities of resources are available in digital format, not all of which are easily published in print format; for instance, multimedia elements may not be conducive to publication in a book or journal. Extensive data sets may be associated with journal articles that are not reproducible in a print format. For this information to be available for people to obtain and use, it has to be located somewhere, and institutional repositories are increasingly the answer to the question of access and preservation of these materials. Institutional repositories serve as digital warehouses for materials written by faculty of a particular institution or authors in a particular geographic area or corporation, and so on. The institutional repository holds digital materials, while the dim archive is a repository of print materials.

A given institutional repository does not necessarily have to be exclusively for the use of members of that institution or for materials from only one institution. Consortial repositories exist for a number of independent institutions that collaborate and pool their resources. In these cases, the various member libraries or other organizations can all input and access all the materials.

Although a repository can preserve, and make accessible, materials produced in an institution or consortium, at the same time an individual repository forms a part of an international system of distributed, interoperable repositories available through the web. Thus, the repositories provide a foundation for a new model of publishing centered on the author rather than on the publisher.

For librarians who are interested in setting up an institutional repository, open source software is currently available. The source code for DSpace (http://libraries.mit.edu/dspace-mit/technology/download.html) is available for downloading as well as documentation and FAQs. At the Massachusetts Institute of Technology (MIT) the institutional repository is subdivided into collections by departments or individuals. Smaller libraries need not construct such an elaborate repository, but the software allows a range of options to customize a digital repository that is right for your institution.

DSpace is also designed to support a federation of depositories of institutions who adopt this system. The DSpace project at MIT has envisioned multiple solutions to the issues surrounding access control, digital rights management, versioning, retrieval, faculty receptivity, community feedback, and flexible publishing capabilities. DSpace has also been designed to encourage author participation through ease of use and to integrate with third-party software, allowing it to be coupled with other components.

Conclusion

Preservation concerns regarding electronic resources are far from being adequately resolved. For the foreseeable future, concerns regarding continued hardware and software availability of the present generation of electronic materials will remain. Access to licensed material involves both these issues and the legal right of future access to material that was previously licensed. Collection development librarians thus must do all they can to ensure that the licenses that their libraries sign today are not for limited access for a particular time period but allow continued access in the future. Without this, collection efforts can easily go for naught. If there is no protection from losing access to material when vendors merge with larger companies or go out of business entirely, the library will have wasted its funds and its patrons will not be well served.

Preservation efforts are improving in both digital and print repository contexts. Particularly within a consortium of libraries, the creation of dim archives of print materials is especially appealing for journals that are available in both print and electronic copies. Licensing access to electronic journals with the provision of one print copy to the consortium is more likely to ensure that there will be continuing access to the title.

To be secure in the knowledge of continued access in the future, cooperative arrangements between vendors and libraries are probably required. It would be extremely naive to assume that for-profit publishers will continue to maintain a resource when it is no longer profitable simply because future users might need access to it. Cooperative arrangements in the nonprofit sector are probably required to maintain perpetual access. Such arrangements, of course, will require the cooperation of vendors and publishers to allow libraries or special nonprofit organizations, such as JSTOR, to preserve access to materials.

The movement toward the creation of institutional repositories may actively involve collection development librarians in the preservation and access of local materials that are linked to similar resources in repositories around the globe.

> The financial challenges of the processes involved in preserving electronic records into perpetuity are significant. . . . It is necessary to develop financial management tools that will support the decision-making processes in which archives and special collections engage when preserving electronic records. . . . Applying business concepts such as cost-benefit analysis, decision-making models, and cost models, in combination with archival precepts and collection management principles, to the challenges of preserving electronic records will assist large institutions such as archives and special collections in making decisions that will support their mission statement and act in the best interests of their users, both present and future. (Sanett, 2002: 388)

Vocabulary

CLOCKSS	conservation	disaster plan
dark archive	deacidification	dim archive
disaster plan	DSpace	institutional repository
JSTOR	LOCKSS	preservation

Activity

1. Divide the class into four groups based on type of library (school media center, public, academic, or special). Each student should have brought to the class at least one book or other analog media, whether in old, new, damaged, or mint condition. (Or the instructor may wish to supply sample materials of each type.) Each group should critique their materials based on the type of library and answer the following questions:
   - Is the material worth preserving?
     - If not, weed.

- Can it be repaired and returned to the collection? Is rebinding appropriate?
  - If the answer to either of the above is yes, take the appropriate steps to repair the material. If the answer is no, continue to the next bullet.
- Is it appropriate to add the material to a special collection either in the library or through a cooperative arrangement?
- If the material is worth saving, but not in adequate condition for the special collection shelves, is digitizing or microfilming the material appropriate? Discuss the factors that should be considered before undertaking a conversion of the material.
- Taking the most interesting or challenging of your materials, prepare a brief report concerning your decisions that will be shared with the entire class.

2. Next do a similar procedure for electronic items found on a website of your choosing. What is worth preserving for the future? What can be safely deleted after a given period of time? How do you best ensure its survival?

Discussion Questions

1. Is digitization the answer to preserving printed materials? Discuss the advantages and disadvantages.
2. Discuss the considerations (practical and legal) that must be taken into account before beginning a digitization project.

References

Baker, Nicholson. 2001. *Double Fold: Libraries and the Assault on Paper*. New York: Random House.

Baker, Whitney, and Liz Dube. 2010. "Identifying Standard Practices in Research Library Book Conservation." *Library Resources and Technical Services* 54 (January): 21–33.

Barr, Pelham. 1946. "Book Conservation and University Library Administration." *College and Research Libraries* 7 (July): 214–219.

Brown, Karen. 2007. "Worksheet for Outlining a Disaster Plan." Northeast Document Conservation Center. http://www.nedcc.org/resources/leaflets/3Emergency_Management/04DisasterPlanWorksheet.php.

Byers, Fred R. 2003. *Care and Handling of CDs and DVDs: A Guide for Librarians and Archivists*. Washington, DC: Council on Library and Information Resources and the National Institute of Standards and Technology.

Conway, Paul. 2010. "Preservation in the Age of Google: Digitization, Digital Preservation and Dilemmas." *Library Quarterly* 80 (January): 61–79.

Duguid, Paul. 2007. "Inheritance and Loss? A Brief Survey of Google Books." *First Monday* 12, no. 8. http://firstmonday.org/htbin/cgiwrap/bin/ojs/index.php/fm/issue/view/251.

Johnson, Peggy. 2009. *Fundamentals of Collection Development and Management.* 2nd ed. Chicago: American Library Association.

Sanett, Shelby. 2002. "Toward Developing a Framework of Cost Elements for Preserving Authentic Electronic Records into Perpetuity." *College and Research Libraries* 63 (September): 388–404.

Selected Readings

Bolger, Laurie. 2003. "Disaster Planning." *Information Outlook* 7 (July): 27–30.

Leetaru, Kalev. 2008. "Mass Digitization: The Deeper Story of Google Books and the Open Content Alliance." *First Monday* 13 (October). http://www.firstmonday.org.

Library of Congress. 2010. "National Digital Information Infrastructure and Preservation." Library of Congress. http://www.digitalpreservation.gov.

Merrill-Oldham, Jan, and Nancy Carlson Schrock. 2000. "The Conservation of General Collections." In *Preservation Issues and Planning,* edited by Paul N. Banks and Roberta Pilette. Chicago: American Library Association.

Ray, Emily. 2006. "The Prague Library Floods of 2002: Crisis and Experimentation." *Libraries and the Cultural Record* 41 (Summer): 381–391.

Stemper, Jim, and Susan Barribeau. 2006. "Perpetual Access to Electronic Journals: A Survey of One Academic Research Library's Licenses." *Library Resources and Technical Services* 50, no. 2: 91–109.

Thomas, Sarah. 2002. "From Double Fold to Double Bind." *Journal of Academic Librarianship* 28 (May): 104–108.

Turpening, Patricia K. 2002. "Survey of Preservation Efforts in Law Libraries." *Law Library Journal* 94, no. 3: 363–393.

Whitaker, Beth M., and Lynne M. Thomas. 2009. *Special Collections 2.0: New Technologies for Rare Books, Manuscripts, and Archival Collections.* Santa Barbara, CA: Libraries Unlimited.

12

The Future of Collection Development and Management

Overview

The time of this writing (Fall 2010) might be called an awkward one for collection development librarians, seemingly between two stools in requiring deep and thorough familiarity with the full range of both print and electronic resources. By this point in your study, though, it is fairly certain that you have developed many of your own ideas about collection development and how it is evolving. In this final chapter we examine several views of the future of library collection development. Consider them as you would any other prognostication—with more than a few grains of salt. But be assured of one thing: the field will continue to change as library resources evolve and change.

In the preface to the first edition of her book in 2004, Peggy Johnson states:

> Collection development and management are the meat and potatoes of libraries. If you don't have a collection, you don't have a library. In the earliest libraries, people concentrated on building collections and locating materials to add, though the need for preservation has been with us for the duration of libraries. Medieval monks often spent their entire lives copying manuscripts to preserve them—and creating questions about the mutability of content similar to those that trouble us today. (p. ix)

In the second edition, she adds, "The roles of collections librarians are expanding in new and exciting ways. In many libraries of all types, collection development and management are part of a suite of challenging responsibilities" (Johnson, 2009: vii).

In just a few short years, the responsibilities of collection development librarians indeed changed a great deal in most libraries. Electronic resources are no longer novel, but rather a standard part of the process of acquiring materials for library users. Electronic databases, e-books, and e-serials are no longer considered flashy or fluff, but, to use Johnson's metaphor, a significant part of the meat and potatoes of many collections.

Now let's look at some other takes on the future of collection development and the duties of collection development librarians.

Views on the Future of Collection Development

At ALA Midwinter 2010, in a discussion group of the Association for Library Collections and Technical Services, a group of librarians, mostly from academic libraries, discussed their present and future roles in the collection development process. They noted that Cassell (2008: 89) lists the major collection development roles as follows:

- working with vendors on customizing approval plans;
- developing, monitoring, and adjusting monograph approval plan profiles;
- monitoring e-book packages and selecting e-books;
- monitoring electronic resource packages;
- selection of all formats of materials not arriving through approval plans;
- developing the most cost-effective ways to handle interlibrary loan requests such as buying the books requested;
- more emphasis on assessing the collections;
- more outreach publicizing collections; and
- developing guidelines for selection of materials in all formats such as always buying material in electronic form if available.

All agreed that these roles continue to be significant, but that there is an ebb and flow of function going on, indicating that assessment is now or may soon be the key role, in contrast to a traditional acquisitions function.

Derek Law (2009), in an article about the future of information and information professionals, lists a number of tools and themes that should form the foundation for the roles of the library and the librarian:

- "Building e-research collections and contributing to a virtual research environment of digitally created material": This is already happening in a lot of research libraries, but the trend will trickle down to other types of libraries over time. All libraries have some unique materials that they can contribute to a virtual research environment. These materials might include small, local newspapers, local publications such as pamphlets and records, local histories, and so on. As time passes, digital creation and retrieval of the materials may become a much larger function of the collection development librarian than purchasing material for the library collection.

- "Recognizing the importance of quality assurance, trust metrics and relevance ranking": As researchers depend upon virtual materials for their research, they need to be assured of the quality and integrity of digital resources.
- "Managing institutional digitally created assets and making the content available": Instead of one large digital library, it is far more likely that the digital content of the future will be decentralized, making each library the custodian of its own materials, and thus needing to be able to manage materials locally and make them available on the web.
- "Adding value to content": One of the best ways of adding value to content is providing the necessary metadata for effective and efficient retrieval of the information stored in digital repositories.
- "Providing training in information fluency": Training users in information fluency appears to be a role that librarians will have for the foreseeable future. Librarians can make all the material in the world available, but to be effective, they must also train their users to retrieve and even more importantly evaluate the materials found.
- "Offering policy and standards advice": A necessary degree of standardization is important to the future retrieval of electronic materials. Without standards and policies, relevant materials will not be located (quoted material from Law, 2009: 18).

Most of Law's themes have at least an indirect bearing on the future role of collection development librarians. The most telling difference from the past concerns more active involvement in the actual creation and maintenance of locally produced digital materials. The other has to do with quality assurance, much along the lines of the assessment process discussed at the recent ALA midwinter conference mentioned above. When libraries purchase material from a reputable publisher, there is an element of assurance that the material is accurate and thoroughly researched; this quality has traditionally been more than implied, with good vendors almost always providing materials subject to approval, and so on. Librarians in the future will likely not have the luxury of depending on review by an established publisher for many digital materials produced locally, or anywhere else for that matter. Librarians will need better ways of guiding users to the best quality materials. Consistent with that will be librarians' growing role as teachers, training users in information literacy and fluency. Young people will know how to use the hardware, often much better than their elders certainly, but they will need to develop the discernment skills needed to separate the proverbial wheat from the chaff, and the correct general rule from the merely anecdotal incident.

The Albertsons Library at Boise State University has of late hired many new librarians to replace retiring or resigning librarians (Kozel-Gains and Stoddardt, 2009). These newer librarians, typically with less than three years' academic library experience, are generally involved in meeting the opportunities and challenges of subject liaison responsibilities using innovative web-based tools, such as faculty-directed blogs, personalized faculty research pages, and a wiki-based liaison manual. A review of these efforts confirms that new technologies are only as good as the face-to-face communication and follow-up that accompany their implementation (Kozel-Gains and Stoddard, 2009).

> Without doubt, technology is changing the way libraries and information centers do business. Some writers . . . suggest that the "virtual library" means the demise of collection development. However, those who understand the concept know that the issue of selection and collection building will remain an important function in whatever environment technology brings. (Evans and Saponaro, 2005: 16)

Conclusion

As stated earlier, collection development is presently split, nearly down the middle, between print and electronic resources. I personally believe that it will be a long time (indeed, never) before hard copy print vanishes as a popular medium for the transmission of knowledge and information, but it clearly is becoming a less and less significant part of the acquisitions process at many libraries. As with all areas of library work, continuing education, involvement with professional associations, and reading the newly published library literature will be important to maintain your professional skills if you intend to become a good collection development librarian.

To me, collection development has always been and will surely remain the most exciting area of library work. The responsibilities of the job and the formats of materials are changing, but collecting and providing access to the materials that users want and need, while always a challenge, will nevertheless remain the most rewarding goal we as librarians can accomplish.

Discussion Questions

1. How do you see this digital age in which we live affecting the role of the collection development librarian? How will the other responsibilities of collection management figure into that role?

2. Speculate on the more distant future.
   - By 2030, do you think that collection development or management will be the major duties of a collections librarian? By then, will we even need collection development librarians?
   - In academic libraries, will collections librarians be more involved with faculty in the creation and making available of research or collecting research as we do now?

References

Cassell, Kay Ann. 2008. "Focus on Collection Development: A Report on ALA Midwinter 2008." *Collection Building* 27, no. 2: 89.

Evans, Edward G., and Margaret Zarnosky Saponaro. 2005. *Developing Library and Information Center Collections.* 5th ed. Westport, CT: Libraries Unlimited.

Johnson, Peggy. 2004. *Fundamentals of Collection Development and Management.* Chicago: American Library Association.

———. 2009. *Fundamentals of Collection Development and Management.* 2nd ed. Chicago: American Library Association.

Kozel-Gains, Melissa A., and Richard A. Stoddart. 2009. "Experiments and Experiences in Liaison Activities: Lessons from New Librarians in Integrating Technology, Face-to-Face, and Follow-Up." *Collection Management* 34 (April–June): 130–142.

Law, Derek. 2009. "Waiting for the (Digital) Barbarians." *Information Outlook* 13 (December): 15–18.

Selected Readings

Atkinson, Ross. 2006. "Six Key Challenges for the Future of Collection Development." *Library Resources and Technical Services* 50 (October): 244–251.

Powers, Audrey. 2007. "Reconfiguring Collection Development for the Future." *Charleston Conference Proceedings*: 24–33. Accessed March 12, 2009. http://works.bepress.com/audrey_powers/23.

Walters, Taylor O. 2007. "Reinventing the Library: How Repositories Are Causing Librarians to Rethink Their Professional Roles." *Portal: Libraries and the Academy* 7 (April): 213–225.

Bibliography of Selected Readings

Acquisitions

Abel, Richard. "The Origins of the Library Approval Plan." *Publishing Research Quarterly* 11 (Spring 1995): 46–56.

Alabaster, Carol. *Developing an Outstanding Core Collection: A Guide for Libraries.* Chicago: American Library Association, 2002.

Amsley, Dawn. "Out-of-Print, Out of Mind? A Case Study of the Decision to Outsource Out-of-Print Acquisitions." *Library Collections, Acquisitions and Technical Services* 29, no. 4 (2005): 433–442.

Atkinson, Ross. "Acquisitions Librarian as Change Agent in the Transition to the Electronic Library." *Library Resources and Technical Services* 39 (January 1992): 7–20.

Born, Kathleen. "Strategies for Selecting Vendors and Evaluating Their Performance—From the Vendor's Perspective." *Journal of Library Administration* 16, no. 3 (1992): 111–116.

Brush, Denise. "Circulation Analysis of an Engineering Monograph Approval Plan." *Collection Building* 26, no. 2 (2007): 59–62.

Bussey, Holly. "More Bang for Your Buck." *Information Outlook* 11 (June 2007): 35–43.

Campbell, Jerry D. "Getting Comfortable with Change: A New Budget Model for Libraries in Transition." *Library Trends* 42 (Winter 1994): 448–459.

Carrigan, Dennis P. "Improving Return on Investment: A Proposal for Allocating the Book Budget." *Journal of Academic Librarianship* 18 (November 1992): 292–297.

Dali, Keren, and Juris Dilevko. "Beyond Approval Plans: Methods of Selection and Acquisition of Books in Slavic and East European Languages in North American Libraries." *Library Collections, Acquisitions and Technical Services* 29, no. 3 (2005): 238–269.

Debachere, M. C. "Problems in Obtaining Grey Literature." *IFLA Journal* 21 (May 1995): 94–98.

Diedrichs, C. P. "Rethinking and Transforming Acquisitions: The Acquisitions Librarian's Perspective." *Library Resources and Technical Services* 42, no. 2 (1998): 113–125.

Eaglen, Audrey. *Buying Books: A How-to-Do-It Manual for Librarians.* New York: Neal-Schuman, 2000.

Farrell, Katherine Treptow, and Janet E. Lute. "Document-Management Technology and Acquisitions Workflow: A Case Study in Invoice Processing." *Information Technology and Libraries* 24 (September 2005): 117–122.

Fenner, Audrey. "The Approval Plan: Selection Aid, Selection Substitute." *Acquisitions Librarian* 16, nos. 31/32 (2004): 227–240.

Fisher, William. "Access or Acquisition: The Impact and Implications of Electronic Publishing." *Library Acquisitions: Practice and Theory* 16 (1992): 155–160.

Fowler, David, and Janet Arcand. "Monographic Acquisitions Time and Cost Studies: The Next Generation." *Library Resources and Technical Services* 47 (July 2003): 109–124.

Furr, Patricia. "Electronic Acquisitions: How E-commerce May Change the Way That Your Library Buys Books." *Mississippi Libraries* 70, no. 2 (Summer 2006): 26–27.

Giambi, Dina M. "Library Approval Vendor Selection: What's Best Practice." *Library Acquisitions: Theory and Practice* 22 (1998): 225–226.

Gozzi, Cynthia. "Acquisitions Management Information: Do Administrators Really Care?" *Library Administration and Management* 9 (Spring 1995): 85–87.

Harri, Wilbert. "Implementing Electronic Data Exchange in the Library Acquisitions Environment." *Library Acquisitions: Practice and Theory* 18 (Spring 1994): 115–117.

Heller, Anne. "Online Ordering: Making Its Mark." *Library Journal* 124 (September 1, 1999): 153–158.

Hellriegel, Patricia, and Kaat Van Wonterghem. "Package Deals Unwrapped . . . or the Librarians Wrapped Up? 'Forced Acquisitions' in the Digital Library." *Interlending and Document Supply* 35, no. 2 (2007): 66–73.

Hiott, Judith, and Carla Beasley. "Electronic Collection Management: Completing the Cycle—Experiences at Two Libraries." *Acquisitions Librarian* 17, nos. 33/34 (2005): 159–178.

Holley, Robert P., and Kalyani Ankem. "The Effect of the Internet on the Out-of-Print Book Market: Implications for Libraries." *Library Collections, Acquisitions and Technical Services* 29, no. 2 (2005): 118–139.

Kent, P. "How to Evaluate Serial Suppliers." *Library Acquisitions: Practice and Theory* 18 (Spring 1994): 83–87.

Kulp, C., and K. Rupp-Serrano. "Organizational Approaches to Electronic Resource Acquisition: Decision-Making Models in Libraries." *Collection Management* 30, no. 4 (2005): 3–19.

Lam, Helen. "Library Acquisitions Management: Methods to Enhance Vendor Assessment and Library Performance." *Library Administration and Management* 18 (Summer 2004): 146–154.

Lugg, Rick, and Ruth Fischer. "Acquisitions' Next Step." *Library Journal* 130, no. 12 (July 2005): 30–32.

Melcher, Daniel, with Margaret Saul. *Melcher on Acquisition*. Chicago: American Library Association, 1971.

Mueller, Susan. "Approval Plans and Faculty Selection: Are They Compatible?" *Library Collections, Acquisitions and Technical Services* 29, no. 1 (2005): 61–70.

Murphy, Sarah Anne. "The Effects of Portfolio Purchasing on Scientific Subject Collections." *College and Research Libraries* 69 (July 2008): 332–340.

Nardini, Robert F. "Approval Plans: Politics and Performance." *College and Research Libraries* 54 (September 1993): 417–425.

O'Neill, Ann L. "How the Richard Abel Co., Inc., Changed the Way We Work." *Library Acquisitions: Practice and Theory* 17, no. 1 (1993): 41–46.

Orkiszewski, Paul. "A Comparative Study of Amazon.com as a Library Book and Media Vendor." *Library Resources and Technical Services* 49 (Summer 2005): 204–209.

Quinn, Brian. "The Impact of Aggregator Packages on Collection Management." *Collection Management* 25, no. 3 (2001): 53–74.

Schaffner, Bradley L. "Electronic Resources: A Wolf in Sheep's Clothing?" *College and Research Libraries* 62 (June 2001): 239–249.

Schmidt, Karen A., ed. *Understanding the Business of Library Acquisitions*. 2nd ed. Chicago: American Library Association, 1999.

Stephenson, Carol, and Helen Sagi. "Paperless and Streamlined Book Ordering." *Feliciter* 54, no. 3 (2008): 100–101.

Warzala, Martin. "The Evolution of Approval Services." *Library Trends* 43 (Winter 1994): 514–523.

Whitaker, Martha. "The Challenge of Acquisitions in the Digital Age." *Portal: Libraries and the Academy* 8 (October 2008): 439–445.

Wilkinson, Frances C., and Linda K. Lewis. *The Complete Guide to Acquisitions Management*. Westport, CT: Libraries Unlimited, 2003.

Budgeting and Finance

Allen, Frank R. "Materials Budgets in the Electronic Age: A Survey of Academic Libraries." *College and Research Libraries* 57 (March 1996): 133–143.

Anderson, Douglas. "Allocation of Costs for Electronic Products in Academic Library Consortia." *College and Research Libraries* 67 (March 2006): 123–135.

Bailey, Timothy P., Jeannette Barnes Lessels, and Rickey D. Best. "Using Universal Borrowing Data in the Library Book Fund Allocation Process." *Library Collections, Acquisitions, and Technical Services* 29, no. 1 (2005): 90–98.

Canepi, Kitti. "Fund Allocation Formula Analysis: Determining Elements for Best Practice in Libraries." *Library Collections, Acquisitions, and Technical Services* 31, no. 1 (2007): 12–24.

Clendenning, Lynda Fuller, J. Kay Martin, and Gail McKenzie. "Secrets for Managing Materials Budget Allocations: A Brief Guide for Collections Managers." *Library Collections, Acquisitions, and Technical Services* 29, no. 1 (2005): 99–108.

Dunn, John A., Jr., and Murray S. Martin. "The Whole Cost of Libraries." *Library Trends* 42 (Winter 1994): 564–578.

Gerhard, Kristin H. "Pricing Models for Electronic Journals and Other Electronic Academic Materials: The State of the Art." *Journal of Library Administration* 42, nos. 3/4 (2005): 1–25.

Gregory, Vicki L. "Development of Academic Library Budgets in Selected States with an Emphasis on the Utilization of Formulas." *Journal of Library Administration* 12, no. 1 (1990): 23–45.

Hahn, Karla L. "Tiered Pricing: Implications for Library Collections." *Portal: Libraries and the Academy* 5, no. 2 (2005): 151–163.

Martin, Murray S. *Collection Development and Finance: A Guide to Strategic Library-Materials Budgeting.* Chicago: American Library Association, 1995.

Martin, Murray S., and Milton T. Wolf. *Budgeting for Information Access: Managing the Resource Budget for Absolute Access.* Chicago: American Library Association, 1998.

Schmidt, Karen, Wendy Allen Shelburne, and David Steven Vess. "Approaches to Selection, Access, and Collection Development in the Web World." *Library Resources and Technical Services* 52 (July 2008): 184–191.

Smith, A. Arro, and Stephanie Langenkamp. "Indexed Collection Budget Allocations: A Tool for Quantitative Collection Development Based on Circulation." *Public Libraries* 46, no. 5 (2007): 50–54.

Walters, William H. "A Regression-Based Approach to Library Fund Allocation." *Library Resources and Technical Services* 51 (October 2007): 263–278.

Weston, Claudia V. "Breaking with the Past: Formula Allocation at Portland State University." *Serials Librarian* 45, no. 4 (2004): 43–53.

Wu, Eric FuLong, and Katherine M. Shelfer. "Materials Budget Allocation: A Formula Fitness Review." *Library Collections, Acquisitions, and Technical Services* 31, nos. 3/4 (2007): 171–183.

Censorship and Intellectual Freedom

American Library Association, Office for Intellectual Freedom. *Intellectual Freedom Manual*. 6th ed. Chicago: American Library Association, 2002.

Association for Library Services to Children. *Intellectual Freedom for Children: The Censor Is Coming*. Chicago: American Library Association, 2000.

Bukoff, Ronald N. "Censorship and the American College Library." *College and Research Libraries* 56, no. 5 (1995): 395–407.

Bushman, J. "Librarians, Self-censorship, and Information Technologies." *College and Research Libraries* 55 (May 1994): 221–228.

Dresang, Eliza T. "Intellectual Freedom and Libraries: Complexity and Change in the Twenty-First-Century Digital Environment." *Library Quarterly* 76 (April 2006): 169–192.

Farrell, Sandie. "Sex: See Also 'Hornet's Nest.'" *School Library Journal* 43 (June 1997): 51.

Fine, Sara. "How the Mind of a Censor Works: The Psychology of Censorship." *School Library Journal* 42 (January 1996): 23–27.

Gibson, Jeffrey. "Championing Intellectual Freedom: A School Administrator's Guide." *Knowledge Quest* 36, no. 2 (2007): 46–48.

Hopkins, D. M. "A Conceptual Model of Factors Influencing the Outcome of Challenges to Library Materials in Secondary School Settings." *Library Quarterly* 63 (January 1993): 40–72.

Intner, Sheila S. "Dollars and Sense: Censorship versus Selection, One More Time." *Technicalities* 24, no. 3 (2004): 1, 7.

Jones, Barbara M. *Protecting Intellectual Freedom in Your Academic Library*. Chicago: American Library Association, 2009.

LaRue, James. *New Inquisition: Understanding and Managing Intellectual Freedom Challenges*. Westport, CT: Libraries Unlimited, 2007.

Martin, Ann M. "Preparing for a Challenge." *Knowledge Quest* 36, no. 2 (2007): 54–56.

Mason, Marilyn Gell. "Sex, Kids, and the Public Library." *American Libraries* 28 (June/July 1997): 104–106.

Peck, Richard. "From Strawberry Statements to Censorship." *School Library Journal* 43 (January 1997): 28–29.

Peck, Robert S., and Ann K. Symons. "Kids Have First Amendment Rights, Too." *American Libraries* 28 (September 1997): 64–65.

Podrygula, S. "Censorship in an Academic Library." *College and Research Library News* 55 (February 1994): 76–78.

Reichman, Henry. *Censorship and Selection: Issues and Answers for Schools*. Rev. ed. Chicago: American Library Association, 1993.

Robins, Natalie. *Alien Ink: The FBI's War on Freedom of Expression*. New York: William Morrow, 1993.

Scales, Pat R. *Protecting Intellectual Freedom in Your School Library: Scenarios from the Front Lines*. Chicago: American Library Association, 2009.

Collection Development: Practices and Policies

Abel, Richard. "The Return of the Native." *American Libraries* 29 (January 1998): 76–78.

Armstrong, William W. "The Creation of a German Language Children's Literature Collection." *Collection Building* 22, no. 2 (2003): 60–67.

Atkins, Stephens. "Mining Automated Systems for Collection Management." *Library Administration and Management* 10 (Winter 1996): 16–19.

Axtmann, Margaret Maes. "The Best of Times, the Worst of Times: Collection Development in the 21st Century." *AALL Spectrum* 6 (November 2001): 6–7.

Billings, Harold. "Library Collections and Distance Information: New Models of Collection Development for the 21st Century." *Journal of Library Administration* 24, nos. 1/2 (1996): 3–17.

Branin, Joseph, Frances Groen, and Suzanne Thorin. "The Changing Nature of Collection Management in Research Libraries." *Library Resources and Technical Services* 44 (January 2000): 23–32.

Brown, Vandella. "African-American Fiction: A Slamming Genre." *American Libraries* 28 (November 1997): 48–50.

Bruggeman, Lora. "'Zap! Whoosh! Kerplow!' Build High-Quality Graphic Novel Collections with Impact." *School Library Journal* 43 (January 1997): 22–27.

Buckland, Michael. "What Will Collection Developers Do?" *Information Technology and Libraries* 14 (September 1995): 155–159.

Campbell, Sharon. "Guidelines for Writing Children's Internet Policies." *American Libraries* 29 (January 1998): 91–92.

Chu, F. T. "Librarian-Faculty Relations in Collection Development." *Journal of Academic Librarianship* 23 (January 1997): 15–20.

Coleman, Jim. "The RLG Conspectus: A History of Its Development and Influence and a Prognosis for Its Future." *Acquisitions Librarian* 4, no. 7 (1992): 25–43.

DeFelice, Barbara, and Constance Rinaldo. "Crossing Subject Boundaries: Collection Management of Environmental Studies in a Multi-library System." *Library Resources and Technical Services* 38 (October 1994): 333–341.

Demas, Samuel, Peter McDonald, and Gregory Lawrence. "The Internet and Collection Development: Mainstreaming Selection of Internet Resources." *Library Resources and Technical Services* 39 (July 1995): 275–290.

Dick, Jeff T. "Bracing for Blu-ray." *Library Journal* 134 (November 2009): 33–35.

Dittemore, Margaret R. "Changing Patterns of Faculty Participation in Collection Development." *Collection Management* 16 (1992): 79–89.

Erickson, Rodney. "Choice for Cooperative Collection Development." *Library Acquisitions: Practice and Theory* 16, no. 1 (1992): 43–49.

Futas, Elizabeth. *Collection Development Policies and Procedures.* 3rd ed. Phoenix: Oryx Press, 1995.

Gardner, Richard K. *Library Collections: Their Origins, Selection, and Development.* New York: McGraw-Hill, 1981.

Gherman, Paul M. "Collecting at the Edge—Transforming Scholarship." *Journal of Library Administration* 42, no. 2 (2005): 23–34.

Hardesty, Larry, and Collette Mak. "Searching for the Holy Grail: A Core Collection for Undergraduate Libraries." *Journal of Academic Libraries* 19 (January 1994): 362–371.

Hazen, Dan C. "Collection Development Policies in the Information Age." *College and Research Libraries* 56 (January 1995): 29–31.

Hoffman, Frank W., and Richard J. Wood. *Library Collection Development Policies: Academic, Public, and Special Libraries.* Lanham, MD: Scarecrow Press, 2005.

Hoppe, D. "Paradise Lost? A Brief History of Alternative Media in Public Libraries." *Wilson Library Bulletin* 68 (March 1994): 26–30.

Hughes, Margaret J. "Video Selection for the Public Library: Special Needs." *Acquisitions Librarian* no. 11 (1994): 3–17.

Johnson, Peggy. *Fundamentals of Collection Development and Management.* Chicago: American Library Association, 2004.

———. "Writing Collection Development Policies: Getting Started." *Technicalities* 14 (October 1994): 2–5.

———. "Writing Collection Development Policy Statements: Format, Context, Style." *Technicalities* 14 (August 1994): 4–7.

Kachel, Debra E. "Looking Inward before Looking Outward: Preparing the School Library Media Center for Cooperative Collection Development." *School Library Media Quarterly* 23 (Winter 1995): 101–113.

Kane, Laura Townsend. "Access vs. Ownership: Do We Have to Make a Choice?" *College and Research Libraries* 58 (January 1997): 59–67.

Kelly, Julia Ann. "Collecting and Accessing 'Free' Internet Resources." *Journal of Library Administration* 20, no. 4 (1996): 99–110.

Koehn, Shona L., and Suliman Hawamdeh. "The Acquisition and Management of Electronic Resources: Can We Justify the Cost?" *Library Quarterly* 80 (April 2010): 161–174.

Kreamer, Jean Thibodeaux. "Video and Libraries: Present Status and Future Trends." *Acquisitions Librarian* no. 11 (1994): 19–28.

Laing, Kathleen. "Audiovisual Materials and Secondary Schools." *Acquisitions Librarian* no. 11 (1994): 97–110.

Law, Derek. "Waiting for the (Digital) Barbarians." *Information Outlook* 13 (December 2009): 15–18.

Leach, Ronald G., and Judith E. Tribble. "Electronic Document Delivery: New Options for Libraries." *Journal of Academic Librarianship* 18 (January 1993): 359–364.

Lee, Hur-Li. "What Is a Collection?" *Journal of the American Society for Information Science* 51 (October 2000): 1106–1113.

Levine-Clark, Michael, and Margaret M. Jobe. "Collecting Law and Medical Titles for General Academic Collections: What Use Statistics Can Tell Us." *Collection Building* 28, no. 4 (2009): 140–145.

Lougee, Wendy P. "Beyond Access: New Concepts, New Tensions for Collection Development in a Digital Environment." *Collection Building* 14, no. 3 (1995): 19–25.

Manoff, Marlene. "Academic Libraries and the Culture Wars: The Politics of Collection Development." *Collection Management* 16 (1992): 1–17.

Medina, Sue O. "The Evolution of Cooperative Collection Development in Alabama Academic Libraries." *College and Research Libraries* 53 (January 1992): 7–19.

Moore, Mary Y. "Washington State's Cooperative Collection Development Project." *Journal of Interlibrary Loan and Information Supply* 2, no. 3 (1992): 33–38.

Murphy, Joyce Fellows. "Spoken Word Cassettes." *Acquisitions Librarian* no. 11 (1994): 49–64.

Neville, Robert, James Williamson III, and Carol C. Hunt. "Faculty-Library Teamwork in Book Ordering." *College and Research Libraries* 59 (November 1998): 524–533.

Newcomer, Nara L. "Back to Basics: International Collection Development on a Shoestring." *Collection Building* 28, no. 4 (2009): 164–169.

Oder, Norman. "AV Rising: Demand, Budgets, and Circulation Are ALL Up." *Library Journal* 123 (November 15, 1998): 30–33.

———. "Outsourcing Model—or Mistake? The Collection Development Controversy in Hawaii." *Library Journal* 122 (March 15, 1997): 28–31.

Piontek, Sherry, and Kristen Garlock. "Creating a World Wide Web Resource Collection." *Collection Building* 14, no. 3 (1995): 12–18.

Porter, G. Margaret. "Making the Interdisciplinary Multicultural: Collection Building for the New Millennium." In *Continuity and Transformation: The Promise of Confluence*, edited by Richard AmRhein, 417–422. Chicago: ACRL, 1995.

Quinn, Brian. "Some Implications of the Canon Debate for Collection Development." *Collection Building* 14, no. 1 (1994): 1–10.

Schneider, Karen G. "The McLibrary Syndrome." *American Libraries* 29 (January 1998): 66–67.

Scott, Sandara. "Cooperative Collection Development: A Resource Sharing Activity for Small Libraries." *Colorado Libraries* 18, no. 2 (1992): 27–28.

Sweetland, James H. "Adult Fiction in Medium-Sized U.S. Public Libraries: A Survey." *Library Resources and Technical Services* 38 (April 1994): 149–160.

Taylor, Rhonda Harris, and Nancy Larson Bluemel. "Pop-up Books: An Introductory Guide." *Collection Building* 22, no. 1 (2003): 21–32.

Taylor, Robert S. "Value-Added Processes in the Information Cycle." *Journal of the American Society for Information Science* 33 (September 1982): 341–346.

Triche, C. "Video and Libraries: Video in the School." *Wilson Library Bulletin* 67 (June 1993): 39–40.

Tucker, James Cory, and Matt Torrence. "Collection Development for New Librarians: Advice from the Trenches." *Library Collections, Acquisitions and Technical Services* 28, no. 4 (2004): 397–409.

Van Orden, Phyllis J. *Selecting Books for the Elementary School Library Media Center.* New York: Neal-Schuman, 2000.

Veatch, James R. "Insourcing the Web." *American Libraries* 30 (January 1999): 64–67.

Webb, John. "Managing Licensed Networked Electronic Resources in a University Library." *Information Technology and Libraries* 17 (December 1998): 198–206.

Collection Evaluation

Adams, Brian, and Bob Noel. "Circulation Statistics in the Evaluation of Collection Development." *Collection Building* 27, no. 2 (2008): 71–73.

Agee, Jim. "Collection Evaluation: A Foundation for Collection Development." *Collection Building* 24, no. 3 (2005): 92–95.

Alessi, Dana L. "Me and My Shadow: Vendors as the Third Hand in Collection Evaluation." *Journal of Library Administration* 17, no. 2 (1992): 47–57.

Bobal, Alison M., Margaret Mellinger, and Bonnie E. Avery. "Collection Assessment and New Academic Programs." *Collection Management* 33, no. 4 (2008): 288–301.

Bolton, Brooke A. "Women's Studies Collections: A Checklist Evaluation." *Journal of Academic Librarianship* 35 (May 2009): 221–226.

Butkovich, Nancy J. "Use Studies: A Selective Review." *Library Resources and Technical Services* 40 (October 1996): 359–368.

Chung, Hye-Kyung. "Evaluating Academic Journals Using Impact Factor and Local Citation Score." *Journal of Academic Librarianship* 33 (May 2007): 393–402.

Culbertson, Michael, and Michelle Wilde. "Collection Analysis to Enhance Funding for Research Materials." *Collection Building* 28, no. 1 (2009): 9–17.

Delaney-Lehman, Maureen J. "Assessing the Library Collection for Diversity." *Collection Management* 20, nos. 3/4 (1996): 29–37.

Dilevko, Juris, and Esther Atkinson. "Evaluating Academic Journals without Impact Factors for Collection Management Decisions." *College and Research Libraries* 63 (November 2002): 562–577.

Dilevko, Juris, and Keren Dali. "Improving Collection Development and Reference Services for Interdisciplinary Fields through Analysis of

Citation Patterns: An Example Using Tourism Studies." *College and Research Libraries* 65 (May 2004): 216–241.

Ferguson, Anthony W. "Collection Assessment and Acquisitions Budgets." *Journal of Library Administration* 17, no. 2 (1992): 59–70.

Franklin, Brinley, and Terry Plum. "Assessing the Value and Impact of Digital Content." *Journal of Library Administration* 48, no. 1 (2008): 41–57.

Fundy, Gerri, and Alesia McManus. "Using a Decision Grid Process to Build Consensus in Electronic Resources Cancellation Decisions." *Journal of Academic Librarianship* 31 (November 2005): 533–538.

Haycock, Laurel A. "Citation Analysis of Education Dissertations for Collection Development." *Library Resources and Technical Services* 48 (April 2004): 102–106.

Kachel, Debra E. "Looking Inward before Looking Outward: Preparing the School Library Media Center for Cooperative Collection Development." *School Library Media Quarterly* 23 (Winter 1995): 101–113.

Leiding, Reba. "Using Citation Checking of Undergraduate Honors Thesis Bibliographies to Evaluate Library Collections." *College and Research Libraries* 66 (September 2005): 417–429.

McAbee, Sonja L., and William L. Hubbard. "The Current Reality of National Book Publishing Output and Its Effect on Collection Assessment." *Collection Management* 28, no. 4 (2003): 67–78.

McClure, Jennifer Z. "Collection Assessment through WorldCat." *Collection Management* 34 (April–June 2009): 79–93.

Mosher, Paul. "Quality and Library Collections: New Directions in Research and Practice in Collection Evaluation." *Advances in Librarianship* 13 (1984): 214.

Nisonger, Thomas E. "Use of the Checklist Method for Content Evaluation of Full-Text Databases." *Library Resources and Technical Services* 52 (January 2008): 4–17.

Pancheshnikov, Yelena. "A Comparison of Literature Citations in Faculty Publications and Student Theses as Indicators of Collection Use and a Background for Collection Management at a University Library." *Journal of Academic Librarianship* 33 (November 2007): 674–683.

Perrault, Anna H. "National Collecting Trends: Collection Analysis Methodology and Findings. *Library and Information Science Research* 21, no. 1 (1999): 47–67.

Samson, Sue, Sebastian Derry, and Holly Eggleston. "Networked Resources, Assessment and Collection Development." *Journal of Academic Librarianship* 30 (November 2004): 476–481.

Schaffner, Ann C., Marianne Burke, and Jutta Reed-Scott. "Automated Collection Analysis: The Boston Library Consortium Experience." *Advances in Library Resource Sharing* 3 (1992): 35–49.

St. Clair, Gloriana. "Assessment: How and Why." In *Virtually Yours: Models for Managing Electronic Resources and Services*, edited by Peggy Johnson and Bonnie MacEwan, 58–70. Chicago: American Library Association, 1999.

Vallmitjana, Nuria, and L. G. Sebate. "Citation Analysis of Ph.D. Dissertations References as a Tool for Collection Management in an Academic Chemistry Library." *College and Research Libraries* 69 (January 2008): 72–81.

Wisneski, Richard. "Collection Development Assessment for New Collection Development Librarians." *Collection Management* 33, nos. 1/2 (2008): 143–159.

Copyright and Licensing

Algenio, Emilie, and Alexis Thompson-Young. "Licensing E-books: The Good, the Bad, and the Ugly." *Journal of Library Administration* 42, nos. 3/4 (2005): 113–128.

Armstrong, Tracey. "Copyright Clearance Center: Providing Compliance Solutions for Content Users." *Journal of Library Administration* 42, nos. 3/4 (2005): 55–64.

Bosch, Stephen. "Using Model Licenses on Library Collections." *Journal of Library Administration* 42, nos. 3/4 (2005): 65–81.

Branscomb, Anne Wells. *Who Owns Information: From Privacy to Public Access.* New York: Basic Books, 1994.

Chou, Min, and Oliver Zhou. "The Impact of Licenses on Library Collections." *Acquisitions Librarian* 17, nos. 33/34 (2005): 7–23.

Christou, Corilee, and Gail Dykstra. "Through a 'Content Looking Glass'— Another Way of Looking at Library Licensing of Electronic Content." *Against the Grain* 14 (November 2002): 18–22.

Crews, Kenneth D. "Licensing for Information Resources: Creative Contracts and the Library Mission." In *Virtually Yours: Models for Managing Electronic Resources and Services*, edited by Peggy Johnson and Bonnie MacEwan, 98–110. Chicago: American Library Association, 1999.

Doering, William, and Galadriel Chilton. "A Locally Created ERM: How and Why We Did It." *Computers in Libraries* 28 (September 2008): 6–48.

Durrant, Fiona. *Negotiating Licenses for Digital Resources.* London: Facet, 2006.

Eschenfelder, Kristin R. "Every Library's Nightmare? Digital Rights Management, Use Restrictions, and Licensed Scholarly Digital Resources." *College and Research Libraries* 69 (May 2008): 205–223.

Fons, Theodore, A., and Timothy D. Jewell. "Envisioning the Future of ERM Systems." *Serials Review* 52, nos. 1/2 (2007): 151–166.

Gasaway, Laura N. "Copyright in the Electronic Era." *Serials Librarian* 24, nos. 3/4 (1994): 153–162.

Gasaway, Laura, and Sarah K. Wiant. *Libraries and Copyright: A Guide to Copyright Law in the 1990s.* Washington, DC: Special Libraries Association, 1994.

Gillespie, Tarleton. *Wired Shut: Copyright and the Shape of Digital Culture.* Cambridge, MA: MIT Press, 2007.

Gould, Thomas H. P., Tomas A. Lipinski, and Elizabeth A. Buchanan. "Copyright Policies and the Deciphering of Fair Use in the Creation of Reserves at University Libraries." *Journal of Academic Librarianship* 31 (May 2005): 182–197.

Gregory, Vicki L. "Delivery of Information via the World Wide Web: A Look at Copyright and Intellectual Property Issues." Paper delivered at the ACRL National Conference in Nashville, April 1997. http://www.ala. org/acrl/paperhtm/e40.html.

Gregory, Vicki L., and William Stanley Gregory. "Copyright on the Internet: What's an Author to Do?" In *Electronic Publishing: Applications and Implications,* edited by Elizabeth Logan and Myke Gluck, 131–141. Medford, NJ: Information Today, 1997.

Harris, Lesley Ellen. *Licensing Digital Content: A Practical Guide for Librarians.* Chicago: American Library Association, 2002.

Hoffmann, Gretchen McCord. *Copyright in Cyberspace 2.* New York: Neal-Schuman, 2005.

Kramer, Elsa F. "Digital Rights Management: Pitfalls and Possibilities for People with Disabilities." *Journal of Electronic Publishing* 10 (Winter 2007). E-journal. Accessed November 3, 2009. http://www. journalofelectronicpublishing.org/.

Lehman, Bruce. "Royalties, Fair Use and Copyright in the Electronic Age." *Educom Review* 30 (November/December 1995): 30–35.

McGinnis, Suzan D. "Selling Our Collective Souls: How License Agreements Are Controlling Collection Management." *Journal of Library Administration* 31, no. 2 (2000): 63–70.

Okerson, Ann. "The Current National Copyright Debate: Its Relationship to the Work of Collection Managers." *Journal of Library Administration* 20, no. 4 (1996): 71–84.

Pike, George H. "First Sale Doctrine Put to the Test." *Information Today* 24 (October 2007): 17, 19.

Potter, William Gray. "Scholarly Publishing, Copyright, and the Future of Resource Sharing." *Journal of Library Administration* 21, nos. 1/2 (1995): 49–66.

Robinson, S. "Copyright or Wrong: The Public Performance Dilemma." *Wilson Library Bulletin* 66 (April 1992): 76–77.

Rupp-Serrano, Karen, ed. *Licensing in Libraries: Practical and Ethical Aspects.* Binghamton, NY: Haworth, 2005.

Samuelson, Pamela. "Copyright's Fair Use Doctrine and Digital Data." *Publishing Research Quarterly* 11 (Spring 1995): 27–39.

Schlosser, Melanie. "Fair Use in the Digital Environment: A Research Guide." *Reference and User Services Quarterly* 46 (Fall 2006): 11–17.

Schockmel, Richard B. "The Premise of Copyright, Assaults on Fair Use, and Royalty Use Fees." *Journal of Academic Librarianship* 22 (January 1996): 15–25.

Stemper, Jim, and Susan Barribeau. "Perpetual Access to Electronic Journals: A Survey of One Academic Research Library's Licenses." *Library Resources and Technical Services* 50 (Spring 2006): 91–109.

Strong, William S. *The Copyright Book: A Practical Guide.* Cambridge, MA: MIT Press, 1992.

Sutherlan, L. "Copyright and Licensing in the Electronic Environment." *Serials Librarian* 23, nos. 3/4 (1993): 143–147.

Valauskas, Edward J. "Copyright: Know Your Electronic Rights!" *Library Journal* 117, no. 13 (1992): 40–43.

Van Tassel, Joan. *Digital Rights Management: Protecting and Monetizing Content.* Amsterdam: Focal Press, 2006.

Webb, John. "Managing Licensed Networked Electronic Resources in a University Library." *Information Technology and Libraries* 17 (December 1998): 198–206.

Diversity and ADA Issues

Agosta, Denise E. "Building a Multicultural School Library: Issues and Challenges." *Teacher Librarian* 34, no. 3 (2007): 27–31.

Albright, Megan. "The Public Library's Responsibilities to LGBT Communities: Recognizing, Representing, and Serving." *Public Libraries* 45, no. 5 (2006): 52–56.

Alexander, Linda B., and Sarah D. Miselis. "Barriers to GLBTQ Collection Development and Strategies for Overcoming Them." *Young Adult Library Services* 5, no. 3 (2007): 43–49.

Alire, Camila A., and Jacqueline Ayala. *Serving Latino Communities.* 2nd ed. New York: Neal-Schuman, 2007.

Angst, Thomas. "American Libraries and Agencies of Culture." *American Studies* 42, no. 3 (2001): 5–22.

Bloomquist, Shannon. "Autism Resources for Public Libraries: Issues, Challenges, and Recommended Resources." *Indiana Libraries* 24, no. 3 (2005): 23–31. Accessed April 7, 2010. https://scholarworks.iupui.edu/handle/1805/1404.

Burke, Susan K. "Removal of Gay-Themed Materials from Public Libraries: Public Opinion Trends." *Public Library Quarterly* 27, no. 3 (2008): 247–264.

Carlton, Debbie Yumiko. *Public Libraries and Cultural Diversity.* ERIC Digest. ED358871, May 1993.

Cuban, Sondra. *Serving New Immigrant Communities in the Library.* Westport, CT: Greenwood Press, 2007.

Darby, Mary Ann, and Miki Pryne. *Hearing All the Voices: Multicultural Books for Adolescents*. Lanham, MD: Scarecrow Press, 2002.

East, Kathy, and Rebecca L. Thomas. *Across Areas: A Guide to Multicultural Literature for Children*. Westport, CT: Libraries Unlimited, 2007.

Gilton, Donna L. *Multicultural and Ethnic Children's Literature in the United States*. Lanham, MD: Scarecrow Press, 2007.

Handman, Gary P. *Video Collection Development in Multi-type Libraries: A Handbook*. Westport, CT: Greenwood Press, 2002.

Hill, Nanci Milone. "Out and About: Serving the GLBT Population @ Your Library." *Public Libraries* 46, no. 4 (2007): 18–24.

Kavanagh, Rosemary, and Beatrice Christensen Skold, eds. *Libraries for the Blind in the Information Age: Guidelines for Development*. IFLA Professional Reports, No. 86. The Hague: International Federation of Library Associations and Institutions, 2005.

Kranich, Nancy. "A Question of Balance: The Role of Libraries in Providing Alternatives to Mainstream Media." *Collection Building* 19, no. 3 (2000): 85–90.

Pruitt, John. "Gay Men's Book Club Versus Wisconsin's Public Libraries: Political Perceptions in the Absence of Dialogue." *Library Quarterly* 80 (April 2010): 121–141.

Quezada, Shelley, ed. "Mainstreaming Library Services to Multicultural Populations: The Evolving Tapestry." *Wilson Library Bulletin* 66 (February 1992): 28–44, 120–121.

Robertson, Deborah A. *Cultural Programming for Libraries: Linking Libraries, Communities and Culture*. Chicago: American Library Association, 2005.

Simpson, Stacy H. "Why Have a Comprehensive and Representative Collection? GLBT Material Selection and Services in the Public Library." *Progressive Librarian* no. 27 (Summer 2006): 44–51.

Vandenbark, R. Todd. "Tending a Wild Garden: Library Web Design for Persons with Disabilities." *Information Technology and Libraries* 29 (March 2010): 23–29.

Weissinger, Thomas. "The Core Journal Concept in Black Studies." *Journal of Academic Librarianship* 36 (March 2010): 119–124.

Ethics and LIS Values

Bushing, Mary C. "Acquisition Ethics: The Evolution of Models for Hard Times." *Library Acquisitions: Theory and Practice* 17 (1993): 47–52.

Chmara, Theresa. *Privacy and Confidentiality Issues: A Guide for Libraries and Their Lawyers*. Chicago: American Library Association, 2009.

Dole, Wanda V., Jitka M. Hurych, and Wallace C. Koehler. "Values for Librarians in the Information Age: An Expanded Examination." *Library Management* 21 (2000): 285–297.

Gorman, Michael. *Our Enduring Values.* Chicago: American Library Association, 2000.

Hauptman, Robert. *Ethical Challenges in Librarianship.* Phoenix: Oryx, 1988.

Severson, Richard W. *The Principles of Information Ethics.* Armonk, NY: M.E. Sharpe, 1997.

Zipkowitz, Fay. *Professional Ethics in Librarianship: A Real Life Casebook.* Jefferson, NC: McFarland, 1996.

Gifts and Exchange Programs

Ballestro, John, and Philip C. Howze. "When a Gift Is Not a Gift: Collection Assessment Using Cost-Benefit Analysis." *Collection Management* 30, no. 3 (2005): 49–66.

Bostic, Mary. "Gifts to Libraries: Coping Effectively." *Collection Management* 14, nos. 3/4 (1991): 175–184.

Cassell, Kay Ann. *Gifts for the Collection: Guidelines for the Library.* The Hague: International Federation of Library Associations and Institutions, 2008.

Chadwell, Faye A. "Good Gifts Stewardship." *Collection Management* 35 (April–June 2010): 59–68.

Hill, Dale S. "Selling Withdrawn and Gift Books on eBay: Does It Make Sense?" *Journal of Interlibrary Loan, Document Delivery and Information Supply* 14, no. 2 (2003): 37–40.

Kertesz, Christopher J. "The Unwanted Gift: When Saying 'No Thanks' Isn't Enough." *American Libraries* 32 (March 2001): 34–36.

Leonhardt, Thomas W. "The Gift and Exchange Function in ARL Libraries: Now and Tomorrow." *Library Acquisitions: Practice and Theory* 21 (1997): 141–149.

———. "A Survey of Gifts and Exchange Activities in 85 Non-ARL Libraries." *Acquisitions Librarian* 22 (1999): 51–58.

Morrisey, Locke J. "Ethical Issues in Collection Development." *Journal of Library Administration* 47, nos. 3/4 (2008): 163–171.

Roberts, Elizabeth Ann. *Crash Course in Library Gift Programs: The Reluctant Curator's Guide to Caring for Archives, Books, and Artifacts in a Library Setting.* Westport, CT: Libraries Unlimited, 2008.

Marketing and Outreach

Angelis, Jane, and Joan M. Wood. "A New Look at Community Connections: Public Relations for Public Libraries." *Illinois Libraries* 81 (Winter 1999): 23–24.

Burkhardt, Andy. "Social Media: A Guide for College and University Libraries." *College and Research Library News* 71 (January 2010): 10–12.

Doucett, Elizabeth. *Creating Your Library Brand: Communicating Your Relevance and Value to Your Patrons.* Chicago: American Library Association, 2008.

Empey, Heather, and Nancy E. Black. "Marketing the Academic Library: Building on the '@Your Library' Framework." *College and Undergraduate Libraries* 12, no. 1 (2006): 19–33.

Fagan, Jody Condit. "Marketing the Virtual Library." *Computers in Libraries* 29 (July/August 2009): 25–30.

Flowers, Helen F. *Public Relations for School Library Media Programs: 500 Ways to Influence People and Win Friends for Your School Library Media Center.* New York: Neal-Schuman, 1998.

Fry, Amy. "Lessons of Good Customer Service." *Library Journal* 134 (September 1, 2009): 33–34.

Kohl, Susan. *Getting Attention: Leading Edge Lessons for Publicity and Marketing.* Boston: Butterworth-Heinemann, 2000.

Malenfant, Kara J. "Leading Change in the System of Scholarly Communication: A Case Study of Engaging Liaison Librarians for Outreach to Faculty. *College and Research Libraries* 71 (January 2010): 63–76.

Matthews, Brian, and Jon Bodnar. *Promoting the Library.* SPEC Kit 306. Washington, DC: Association of Research Libraries, September 2008.

Singh, Rajesh. "Does Your Library Have an Attitude Problem towards 'Marketing'? Revealing Inter-relationships between Marketing Attitudes and Behavior." *Journal of Academic Librarianship* 35 (January 2009): 25–32.

Steinmacher, Michael. "Underlying Principles of Library Public Relations." *Kentucky Libraries* 64 (Winter 2000): 12–15.

Steman, Thomas, and Susan Motin. "History Day: Another Outreach Opportunity for Academic Libraries." *College and Research Libraries News* 71 (January 2010): 26–29.

Needs Assessment

Biblarz, Dora, Stephen Bosch, and Chris Sugnet, eds. *Guide to Library User Needs Assessment for Integrated Information Resource Management and Collection Development.* Lanham, MD: Scarecrow Press, 2001.

Bishop, Kay. *The Collection Program in Schools: Concepts, Practices, and Information Sources.* 4th ed. Westport, CT: Libraries Unlimited, 2007.

Blake, Julie C., and Susan P. Schleper. "From Data to Decisions: Using Surveys and Statistics to Make Collection Management Decisions." *Library Collections, Acquisitions, and Technical Services* 28 (2004): 460–464.

Bost, Wendi, and Jamie Conklin. "Creating a One-Stop Shop: Using the Catalog to Market Collections and Services." *Florida Libraries* 49 (Fall 2006): 5–7.

Duff, Wendy M., and Catherine A. Johnson. "A Virtual Expression of Need: An Analysis of E-mail Reference Questions." *American Archivist* 64 (Spring/Summer 2001): 43–60.

Evans, Edward G. "Needs Analysis and Collection Development Policies for Culturally Diverse Populations." *Collection Building* 11, no. 4 (1992): 16–27.

Farmer, Lesley S. J. "Collection Development in Partnership with Youth: Uncovering Best Practices." *Collection Management* 26, no. 2 (2001): 67–78.

Gregory, Vicki L. *Selecting and Managing Electronic Resources.* Rev. ed. New York: Neal-Schuman, 2007.

Grover, Robert. "A Proposed Model for Diagnosing Information Needs." *School Library Media Quarterly* 21 (Winter 1993): 95–100.

Hahn, K. L., and L. A. Faulkner. "Evaluative Usage-Based Metrics for the Selection of E-journals." *College and Research Libraries* 63 (September 2002): 215–227.

Ismail, Lizah. "What They Are Telling Us: Library Use and Needs of Traditional and Non-traditional Students in a Graduate Social Work Program." *Journal of Academic Librarianship* 35 (November 2009): 555–564.

Karp, Rashelle S., ed. *Powerful Public Relations: A How-to Guide for Libraries.* Chicago: American Library Association, 2002.

Koontz, Christie, and Dean Jue. "Unlock Your Demographics." *Library Journal* 129 (March 1, 2004): 32–33.

Logan Heights Branch Library [San Diego, CA]. "Community Library Needs Assessment Components." Accessed March 31, 2009. http://www.sandiego.gov/public-library/pdf/logan_needs.pdf.

Matthews, Brian. *Marketing Today's Academic Library: A Bold New Approach to Communicating with Students.* Chicago: American Library Association, 2009.

Thorsen, Jeanne. "Community Studies: Raising the Roof and Other Recommendations." *Acquisitions Librarian* no. 20 (1998): 5–13.

University of Arizona. "Needs Assessment Tutorial." Accessed January 26, 2008. http://digital.library.arizona.edu/nadm/tutorial/.

Van House, Nancy A. "User Needs Assessment and Evaluation for the UC Berkeley Electronic Environmental Library Project: A Preliminary Report." Accessed March 31, 2009. http://www.csdl.tamu.edu/DL95/papers/vanhouse/vanhouse.html.

Westbrook, Lynn, and Steven A. Tucker. "Understanding Faculty Information Needs." *Reference and User Studies Quarterly* 42 (Winter 2002): 144–148.

New Technologies

ABC News. "Internet Phenomenon Provides Unique Insights into Peoples' Thoughts." People of the Year; Bloggers. December 30, 2004. http://abcnews.go.com/WNT/person ofweek/story?id=372266&page=1.

Abram, Stephen. "Web 2.0—Huh?! Library 2.0, Librarian 2.0." *Information Outlook* (December 1, 2005): 44–46.

Aharony, Noa. "Web 2.0 Use by Librarians." *Library and Information Science Research* 31 (January 2009): 29–37.

Anderson, Chris. *The "Long Tail": Why the Future of Business Is Selling Less of More.* New York: Hyperion, 2006.

Breeding, Marshall. "Web 2.0? Let's Get to Web 1.0 First." *Computers in Libraries* (May 1, 2006): 30–33.

Buczynski, James A. "Looking for Collection 2.0." *Journal of Electronic Resources Librarianship* 20, no. 2 (2008): 90–100.

Burkhanna, Kenneth J., Jamie Seeholzer, and Joseph Salem Jr. "No Natives Here: A Focus Group Study of Student Perceptions of Web 2.0 and the Academic Library." *Journal of Academic Librarianship* 35 (November 2009): 523–532.

Casey, Michael E., and Laura C. Savastinuk. *Library 2.0: A Guide to Participatory Library Service.* Medford, NJ: Information Today, 2007.

Courtney, Nancy, ed. *Library 2.0 and Beyond: Innovative Technologies and Tomorrow's User.* Westport, CT: Libraries Unlimited, 2007.

Farkas, Meredith G. *Social Software in Libraries: Building Collaboration, Communication, and Community Online.* Medford, NJ: Information Today, 2007.

Friedman, Thomas L. *The World Is Flat: A Brief History of the Twenty-First Century.* Updated and expanded ed. New York: Farrar, Straus and Giroux, 2006.

Kozel-Gains, Melissa A., and Richard A. Stoddart. "Experiments and Experiences in Liaison Activities: Lessons from New Librarians in Integrating Technology, Face-to-Face, and Follow-Up." *Collection Management* 34 (April–June 2009): 130–142.

Lessig, Lawrence. *The Future of Ideas: The Fate of the Commons in a Connected World.* New York: Random House, 2001.

Lin, Andrew. *The Wikipedia Revolution: How a Bunch of Nobodies Created the World's Greatest Encyclopedia.* New York: Hyperion, 2009.

Miller, Paul. "Web 2.0: Building the New Library." *Ariadne* 45 (October 30, 2005). http://www.ariadne.ac.uk/issue45/miller/intro.html.

Mossberger, Karen, Caroline J. Tolbert, and Ramona S. McNeal. *Digital Citizenship: The Internet, Society, and Participation.* Cambridge, MA: MIT Press, 2008.

O'Sullivan, Dan. *Wikipedia: A New Community of Practice?* Farnham, England: Ashgate, 2009.

Rheingold, Howard. *Smart Mobs: The Next Social Revolution.* Cambridge, MA: Basic Books, 2002.

Scoble, Robert, and Shel Israel. *Naked Conversations: How Blogs Are Changing the Way Businesses Talk with Customers.* Hoboken, NJ: John Wiley, 2006.

Tapscott, Don. *Grown Up Digital: How the Net Generation Is Changing Your World.* New York: McGraw Hill, 2009.

Tapscott, Don, and Anthony D. Williams. *Wikinomics: How Mass Collaboration Changes Everything.* New York: Penguin, 2006.

Tucker, James Cory, Jeremy Bullian, and Matthew C. Torrance. "Collaborate or Die! Collection Development in Today's Academic Library." *Reference Librarian* nos. 83/84 (2003): 219–236.

Preservation

Baker, Whitney, and Liz Dube. "Identifying Standard Practices in Research Library Book Conservation." *Library Resources and Technical Services* 54 (January 2010): 21–33.

Byers, Fred R. *Care and Handling of CDs and DVDs: A Guide for Librarians and Archivists.* Washington, DC: Council on Library and Information Resources and the National Institute of Standards and Technology, 2003.

Child, Margaret S. "Preservation Issues for Collection Development Staff." *Wilson Library Bulletin* 67 (1992): 20–21, 106.

Clements, David W. G. "Problems of Cooperative Microfilming." *Collection Management* 15 (1992): 503–507.

Conway, Paul. "Preservation in the Age of Google: Digitization, Digital Preservation and Dilemmas." *Library Quarterly* 80 (January 2010): 61–79.

———. "Selecting Microfilm for Digital Preservation: A Case Study from Project Open Book." *Library Resources and Technical Services* 40 (January 1996): 67–77.

Cunha, George M. "Disaster Planning and a Guide to Recovery Resources." *Library Technology Reports* 28 (September/October 1992): 533–623.

Duguid, Paul. "Inheritance and Loss? A Brief Survey of Google Books." *First Monday* 12, no. 8 (2007). http://firstmonday.org/htbin/cgiwrap/bin/ojs/index.php/fm/issue/view/251.

Ferguson, Anthony W. "Preservation Decision-Making Basics: A University Library Collection Developer's Perspective." *Acquisitions Librarian* 2 (1989): 239–246.

Fitzsimmons, Joseph J. "A Realistic Look at the Future of Preservation." *Microform Review* 21 (1992): 13–15.

Forster, Judith. *Disaster Planning and Recovery: A How-to-Do-It Manual for Librarians and Archivists.* New York: Neal-Schuman, 1992.

Friedlander, Amy. "Digital Preservation Looks Forward." *Information Outlook* 6 (September 2002): 12–18.

Gertz, Janet. "Selection for Preservation: A Digital Solution for Illustrated Texts." *Library Resources and Technical Services* 40 (January 1996): 78–83.

Lavender, Kenneth, and Scott Stockton. *Book Repair.* New York: Neal-Schuman, 1992.

Library of Congress. "National Digital Information Infrastructure and Preservation." Accessed January 29, 2010. http://www.digitalpreservation.gov.

Merrill-Oldham, Jan, and Nancy Carlson Schrock. "The Conservation of General Collections." In *Preservation Issues and Planning*, edited by Paul N. Banks and Roberta Pilette. Chicago: American Library Association, 2000.

Oakley, Robert L. "Copyright and Preservation: An Overview." *The Bookmark* 50 (Winter 1992): 121–124.

Ray, Emily. "The Prague Library Floods of 2002: Crisis and Experimentation." *Libraries and the Cultural Record* 41 (Summer 2006): 381–391.

Sedinger, Thomas. "Preservation and Conservation in the School Library." *Book Report* 10 (January/February 1992): 34.

Stemper, Jim, and Susan Barribeau. "Perpetual Access to Electronic Journals: A Survey of One Academic Research Library's Licenses." *Library Resources and Technical Services* 50, no. 2 (2006): 91–109.

Thomas, Sarah. "From Double Fold to Double Bind." *Journal of Academic Librarianship* 28 (May 2002): 104–108.

Turpening, Patricia K. "Survey of Preservation Efforts in Law Libraries." *Law Library Journal* 94, no. 3 (2002): 363–393.

Resource Sharing and Cooperative Collection Development

Allen, Barbara McFadden. "Consortia and Collections: Achieving a Balance between Local Action and Collaborative Interest." *Journal of Library Administration* 28, no. 4 (1999): 85–90.

Atkinson, Ross. "Uses and Abuses of Cooperation in a Digital Age." *Collection Management* 28, nos. 1/2 (2003): 1–20.

Burgett, James, John Haar, and Linda L. Phillips. *Collaborative Collection Development: A Practical Guide for Your Library.* Chicago: American Library Association, 2004.

Chan, Gayle, and Anthony W. Ferguson. "Digital Library Consortia in the 21st Century: The Hong Kong JULAC Case." *Collection Management* 27, nos. 3/4 (2002): 13–27.

Connell, Ruth R. "Eight May Be Too Many: Getting a Toe-Hold on Cooperative Collection Building." *Collection Management* 33, nos. 1/2 (2008): 17–28.

Croft, Janet Brennan. "Interlibrary Loan and Licensing: Tools for Proactive Contract Management." *Journal of Library Administration* 42, nos. 3/4 (2005): 41–53.

Curl, Margo Warner. "Cooperative Collection Development in Consortium of College Libraries: The CONSORT Experience." *Against the Grain* 14 (December 2002–January 2003): 52–54.

Curl, Margo Warner, and Michael Zeoli. "Developing a Consortial Shared Approved Plan for Monographs." *Collection Building* 23, no. 3 (2004): 122–128.

Dannelly, Gay N. "Remote Access through Consortial Agreements and Other Collection Initiatives: OhioLink and the CIC." *Against the Grain* 8 (November 1996): 24–26, 38.

Dowler, Lawrence. "The Research University's Dilemma: Resource Sharing and Research in a Transinstitutional Environment." *Journal of Library Administration* 21, nos. 1/2 (1995): 5–26.

Eaton, Nancy L. "Resource Sharing: The Public University Library's Imperative." *Journal of Library Administration* 21, nos. 1/2 (1995): 27–38.

Eccles, Karen. "Consortia Build Negotiating Strength." *Information Outlook* 10 (December 2006): 31–37.

Ferguson, Anthony W. "Document Delivery in the Electronic Age: Collecting and Service Implications." *Journal of Library Administration* 20, no. 4 (1996): 85–98.

Gammon, Julie A., and Michael Zeoli. "Practical Cooperative Collecting for Consortia: Books-Not-Bought in Ohio." *Collection Management* 28, nos. 1/2 (2003): 77–105.

Grycz, Czeslaw Jan. "Resource Sharing in the Systematic Context of Scholarly Communication." *Library Trends* 45 (Winter 1997): 499–517.

Hazen, Dan. "Better Mousetraps in Turbulent Times? The Global Resources Network as a Vehicle for Library Cooperation." *Journal of Library Administration* 42, no. 2 (2005): 35–55.

Hoffert, Barbara. "The United Way: Will Public Libraries Follow Academics as They Take Collaborative Collection Development One Step Further?" *Library Journal* 131 (May 1, 2006): 38–41.

Irwin, Ken. "Comparing Circulation Rates of Monographs and Anthologies of Literary Criticism: Implications for Cooperative Collection Development." *Collection Management* 33, nos. 1/2 (2008): 69–81.

Juergens, Bonnie, and Tim Prather. "The Resource Sharing Component of Access." *Journal of Library Administration* 20, no. 1 (1994): 77–93.

Kachel, Debra E. "Look Inward before Looking Outward: Preparing the School Library Media Center for Cooperative Collection Development." *School Library Media Quarterly* 23 (Winter 1995): 101–113.

Kinner, Laura, and Alice Crosetto. "Balancing Act for the Future: How the Academic Library Engages in Collection Development at the Local and Consortial Levels." *Journal of Library Administration* 49 (May/June 2009): 419–437.

Lanier, Don, and Kathryn Carpenter. "Enhanced Services and Resource Sharing in Support of New Academic Programs." *Journal of Academic Librarianship* 20 (March 1994): 15–18.

Lenzini, Rebecca T. "Delivery of Documents and More: A View of Trends Affecting Libraries and Publishers." *Journal of Library Administration* 20, no. 4 (1996): 49–70.

Lynch, Clifford A. "Building the Infrastructure of Resource Sharing: Union Catalogs, Distributed Search, and Cross-Database Linkage." *Library Trends* 45 (Winter 1997): 448–461.

Lyndon, Frederick C. "Remote Access Issues: Pros and Cons." *Journal of Library Administration* 20, no. 1 (1994): 19–36.

———. "Will Electronic Information Finally Result in Real Resource Sharing?" *Journal of Library Administration* 24, nos. 1/2 (1996): 47–72.

Mosher, Paul H. "Real Access as the Paradigm of the Nineties." *Journal of Library Administration* 21, nos. 1/2 (1995): 39–48.

Perrault, Anna. "The Printed Book: Still in Need of CCD." *Collection Management* 24, nos. 1/2 (2000): 119–136.

Perrault, Anna H. "The Role of WorldCat in Resource Sharing." *Collection Management* 28, nos. 1/2 (2003): 63–75.

Sandler, Mark. "Collection Development in the (Age) Day of Google." *Library Resources and Technical Services* 40 (October 2006): 239–243.

Sanville, Tom. "Do Economic Factors Really Matter in the Assessment and Retention of Electronic Resources Licensed at the Library Consortium Level?" *Collection Management* 33, nos. 1/2 (2008): 1–16.

Shaughessy, Thomas W. "Resource Sharing and the End of Innocence." *Journal of Library Administration* 20, no. 1 (1994): 3–17.

Shreeves, Edward. "Is There a Future for Cooperative Collection Development in the Digital Age?" *Library Trends* 45 (Winter 1997): 373–390.

Thomas, Sarah E. "Think Globally, Act Locally: Electronic Resources and Collection Development." *Journal of Library Administration* 36, no. 3 (2002): 93–107.

Tucker, James Cory, Jeremy Bullian, and Matthew C. Torrance. "Collaborate or Die! Collection Development in Today's Academic Library." *Reference Librarian* nos. 83/84 (2003): 219–236.

Woolls, Blanche. "Public Library-School Library Cooperation: A View from the Past with a Prediction for the Future." *Journal of Youth Services in Libraries* 14 (Spring 2001): 8–10.

Selection

Aldrich, Alan W. "Judging Books by Their Covers: Managing the Tensions between Paperback and Clothbound Purchases in Academic Libraries." *College and Research Libraries* 70 (January 2009): 57–70.

Austenfeld, Annie Marie. "Building the College Library Collection to Support Curriculum Growth." *Collection Building* 34 (July–September 2009): 209–227.

Bielke-Rodenbiker, Jean. "Review Sources for Mysteries." *Collection Management* 29, nos. 3/4 (2004): 53–71.

Chen, Shu-Hsien Lai. "Diversity in School Library Media Center Resources." In *Educational Media and Technology Yearbook*, edited by Mary Ann Fitzgerald, Michael Orey, and Robert Maribe Branch, Vol. 27, 216–225. Englewood Cliffs, CO: Libraries Unlimited, 2002.

Coombs, Karen. "Digital Promise and Peril." *Netconnect* (Summer 2007): 24.

Crawford, Gregory A., and Matthew Harris. "Best-Sellers in Academic Libraries." *College and Research Libraries* 62 (May 2001): 216–225.

Dilevko, Juris, and Lisa Gottlieb. "The Politics of Standard Selection Guides: The Case of *Public Library Catalog*." *Library Quarterly* 73 (July 2003): 289–337.

Donatich, John. "Why Books Still Matter." *Journal of Scholarly Publishing* 40 (July 2009): 329–342.

Downey, Elizabeth M. "Graphic Novels in Curriculum and Instruction Collections." *Reference and User Services Quarterly* 49 (December 2009): 181–188.

Fenner, Audrey, ed. *Selecting Materials for Library Collections*. Binghamton, NY: Haworth Information Press, 2004. Copublished as *Acquisitions Librarian* nos. 31/32 (2004).

Gherman, Paul M. "Collecting at the Edge—Transforming Scholarship." *Journal of Library Administration* 42, no. 2 (2005): 23–34.

Greene, Robert J., and Charles D. Spornick. "Favorable and Unfavorable Book Reviews: A Quantitative Study." *Journal of Academic Librarianship* 21 (November 1995): 449–453.

Gregory, Cynthia L. "'But I Want a Real Book': An Investigation of Undergraduates' Usage and Attitudes toward Electronic Books." *Reference and User Services Quarterly* 47 (Spring 2008): 266–273.

Hiebert, Jean T. "Beyond Mark and Park: Classification Mapping as a Collection Development Tool for Psychiatry/Psychology." *Collection Management* 34 (July–September 2009): 182–193.

Hoffert, Barbara. "Every Reader a Reviewer." *Library Journal* 135 (September 1, 2010): 22–25.

———. "Immigrant Nation: How Public Libraries Select Materials for a Growing Population Whose First Language Is Not English." *Library Journal* 133, no. 14 (September 1, 2008): 34–36.

———. "Who's Selecting Now?" *Library Journal* 132 (September 1, 2007): 40–43.

Jobe, Margaret M., and Michael Levine-Clark. "Use and Non-use of *Choice*-Reviewed Titles in Undergraduate Libraries." *Journal of Academic Librarianship* 34 (July 2008): 295–304.

Johnson, Liz, and Linda A. Brown. "Book Reviews by the Numbers." *Collection Management* 33, nos. 1/2 (2008): 83–113.

Johnson, Peggy. "Selecting Electronic Resources: Developing a Local Decision-Making Matrix." *Cataloging and Classification Quarterly* 22, nos. 3/4 (1996): 9–24.

Kovacs, Diane. *Building Electronic Library Collections: The Essential Guide to Selection Criteria.* New York: Neal-Schuman, 2000.

Levine-Clark, Michael, and Margaret M. Jobe. "Do Reviews Matter? An Analysis of Usage and Holdings of *Choice*-Reviewed Titles within a Consortium." *Journal of Academic Librarianship* 33 (December 2007): 639–646.

Mulcahy, Kevin P. "Science Fiction Collections in ARL Academic Libraries." *College and Research Libraries* 67 (January 2006): 15–34.

Neal, Kathryn M. "Cultivating Diversity: The Donor Collection." *Collection Management* 27, no. 2 (2002): 33–42.

O'English, Lorena, J. Gregory, and Elizabeth Blakesley Lindsay. "Graphic Novels in Academic Libraries: From *Maus* to Manga and Beyond." *Journal of Academic Librarianship* 32 (March 2006): 173–182.

Pool, Gail. *Faint Praise: The Plight of Book Reviewing in America.* Columbia, MO: University of Missouri Press, 2007.

Pratt, Gregory F., Patrick Flannery, and Cassandra L. D. Perkins. "Guidelines for Internet Resources Selection." *College and Research Libraries News* 57 (March 1996): 134–145.

Rabine, Julie, and Linda A. Brown. "The Selection Connection: Creating an Internet Web Page for Collection Development." *Library Resources and Technical Services* 44 (January 2000): 44–49.

Randall, William M. "What Can the Foreigner Find to Read in the Public Library?" *Library Quarterly* 1 (1931): 79–88.

Rathe, Bette, and Lisa Blankenship. "Recreational Reading Collections in Academic Libraries." *Collection Management* 30, no. 2 (2005): 73–85.

Safley, Ellen. "Demand for E-books in an Academic Library." *Journal of Library Administration* 45, nos. 3/4 (2006): 445–457.

Schmidt, Karen, Wendy Allen Shelburne, and David Steven Vess. "Approaches to Selection, Access, and Collection Development in the Web World." *Library Resources and Technical Services* 52 (July 2008): 184–191.

Smith, Henrietta M. *The Coretta Scott King Awards Book: 1970–1999.* 3rd ed. Chicago: American Library Association, 2004.

Strothmann, Molly, and Connie Van Fleet. "Books That Inspire, Books That Offend." *Reference and User Services Quarterly* 49 (Winter 2009): 163–179.

Sullivan, Kathleen. "Beyond Cookie-Cutter Selection." *Library Journal* 129 (June 15, 2004): 44–46.

Van Orden, Phyllis J. *Selecting Books for the Elementary School Library Media Center.* New York: Neal-Schuman, 2000.

Wagner, Cassie. "Graphic Novel Collections in Academic ARL Libraries." *College and Research Libraries* 71 (January 2010): 42–48.

Williams, Virginia Kay, and Damen V. Peterson. "Graphic Novels in Libraries: Supporting Teacher Education and Librarianship Programs." *Library Resources and Technical Services* 53 (July 2009): 166–173.

Serials

Alsmeyer, David. "Building the Digital Library at BT Labs." *Library Acquisitions: Practice and Theory* 21, no. 3 (1997): 381–385.

Bailey, Charles W., Jr. "The Coalition for Networked Information's Acquisitions-on-Demand Model: An Exploration and Critique." *Serials Review* 18 (Spring/Summer 1992): 78–81.

———. "Network-Based Electronic Serials." *Information Technology and Libraries* 11 (March 1992): 29–35.

———. "Open Access and Libraries." *Collection Management* 32, nos. 3/4 (2007): 351–383.

Barnes, John H. "One Giant Step, One Small Step: Continuing the Migration to Electronic Journals." *Library Trends* 45 (Winter 1997): 404–415.

Black, Steve. "Impact of Full Text on Print Journal Use at a Liberal Arts College." *Library Resources and Technical Services* 49, no. 1 (2005): 19–26.

Borrelli, Steve, Betty Galbraith, and Eileen E. Brady. "The Impact of Electronic Journals on Use of Print in Geology." *College and Research Libraries* 70 (January 2009): 26–33.

Brooke, F. Dixon, Jr. "Subscription or Information Agency Services in the Electronic Era." *Serials Librarian* 29, nos. 3/4 (1996): 57–65.

Butler, Brett. "Electronic Editions of Serials: The Virtual Library Model." *Serials Review* 18 (Spring/Summer 1992): 102–106.

Carignan, Yvonne. "Who Wants Yesterday's Papers?" *Collection Management* 31, nos. 1/2 (2005): 75–84.

Chiou-Sen, Dora Chen. *Serials Management: A Practical Guide.* Chicago: American Library Association, 1995.

Drake, Miriam A. "Institutional Repositories: Hidden Treasures." *Searcher* 12 (May 2004): 41–45.

———. "Scholarly Communication in Turmoil." *Information Today* 24 (February 2007): 1–19.

Feyereisen, Pierre, and Anne Spoiden. "Can Local Citation Analysis of Master's and Doctoral Theses Help Decision-Making about the Management of the Collection of Periodicals? A Case Study in Psychology and Education Sciences." *Journal of Academic Librarianship* 35 (November 2009): 514–522.

Ganesh, Tirupalavanam G. "Ejournals in Education: Just Generating Excitement or Living Up to the Promise? *Education Libraries* 26 (Summer 2003): 5–15.

Guedon, Jean-Claude. "Mixing and Matching the Green and Gold Roads to Open Access—Take 2." *Serials Review* 34, no. 1 (2008): 41–51.

Hamaker, Charles A. "Re-designing Serials Collections." *Journal of Library Administration* 20, no. 1 (1994): 37–47.

Hawkins, Les. "Network Accessed Scholarly Serials." *Serials Librarian* 29, nos. 3/4 (1996): 19–31.

Jascó, Peter. "Open Access Ready Reference Suites." *Online Information Review* 10, no. 6 (2006): 737–743.

Johnson, Richard K. "Open Access: Unlocking the Value of Scientific Research." *Journal of Library Administration* 42, no. 2 (2004): 107–124.

Ketcham-Van Orsdel, Lee, and Kathleen Born. "E-journals Come of Age: Periodical Price Survey 1998." *Library Journal* 123 (April 15, 1998): 40–45.

Kopak, Rick. "Open Access and the Open Journal Systems: Making Sense All Over." *School Libraries Worldwide* 14, no. 2 (2008): 45–54.

Mancini, Alice Duhon. "Evaluating Commercial Document Suppliers: Improving Access to Current Journal Literature." *College and Research Libraries* 57 (March 1996): 123–131.

McCulloch, Emma. "Taking Stock of Open Access: Progress and Issues." *Library Review* 55, no. 6 (2006): 337–343.

Moghaddam, Golnessa Galyani. "Scholarly Electronic Journal Publishing: A Study Comparing Commercial and Nonprofit/University Publishers." *Serials Review* 51, nos. 3/4 (2007): 165–183.

Murphy, Sarah Anne. "The Effects of Portfolio Purchasing on Scientific Subject Collections." *College and Research Libraries* 69 (July 2008): 332–340.

Nisonger, Thomas E. *Management of Serials in Libraries.* Englewood, CO: Libraries Unlimited, 1998.

Plutchak, T. Scott. "What's a Serial When You're Running on Internet Time?" *Serials Librarian* 52, nos. 1/2 (2007): 79–90.

Prabha, Chandra. "Shifting from Print to Electronic Journals in ARL University Libraries." *Serials Review* 33, no. 1 (2007): 4–13.

Schwartz, Charles A. "Restructuring Serials Management to Generate New Resources and Services—with Commentaries on Restructurings at Three Institutions." *College and Research Libraries* 59 (March 1998): 115–128.

Stern, D. "Open Access or Differential Pricing for Journals: The Road Best Traveled." *Online* 29 (March 2005): 30–35.

Tenopir, Carol. "Should We Cancel Print?" *Library Journal* 124 (September 1, 1999): 138, 142.

Van Orsdel, Lee C., and Kathleen Born. "Periodicals Pricing Survey 2008: Embracing Openness." *Library Journal* 133 (April 15, 2008): 53–58.

Willinsky, John. "The Nine Flavors of Open Access Scholarly Publishing." *Journal of Postgraduate Medicine* 49, no. 3 (2003): 263–267.

Yiotis, Kristin. "The Open Access Initiative: A New Paradigm for Scholarly Communication." *Information Technology and Libraries* 24 (Summer 2005): 157–162.

Weeding

Banks, Julie. "Weeding Book Collections in the Age of the Internet." *Collection Building* 21, no. 3 (2002): 113–119.

Bertland, Linda H. "Circulation Analysis as a Tool for Collection Development." *School Library Media Quarterly* 19 (Winter 1991): 90–97.

Bracke, Marianne Stowell, and Jim Martin. "Developing Criteria for the Withdrawal of Print Content Available Online." *Collection Building* 24, no. 2 (2005): 61–64.

Farber, Evan Ira. "Books NOT for College Libraries." *Library Journal* 122 (August 1997): 44–45.

Lancaster, F. W. "Obsolescence, Weeding, and the Utilization of Space." *Wilson Library Bulletin* 62 (May 1988): 47–49.

Larson, Jeannette. "CREW: A Weeding Manual for Modern Libraries." Austin: Texas Public Library and Archives Commission, 2008. http://www.tsl.state.tx.us/ld/pubs/crew.

Line, Maurice. "Changes in the Use of Literature with Time—Obsolescence Revisited." *Library Trends* 41 (Spring 1993): 665–683.

Manley, Will. "The Manley Arts: If I Called This Column 'Weeding' You Wouldn't Read It." *Booklist* (March 1, 1996): 1108.

———. "S.F.P.L. Blues." *American Libraries* 27 (December 1996): 96.

Metz, Paul, and Caryl Gray. "Public Relations and Library Weeding." *Journal of Academic Librarianship* 31 (May 2005): 273–279.

Nikkel, Terry, and Liane Beltway. "When Worlds Collide: Dismantling the Science Fiction and Fantasy Collection at the University of New Brunswick, Saint John." *Collection Management* 34 (July–September 2009): 194–208.

Roy, Loriene. "Weeding." In *Encyclopedia of Library and Information Science* 54, supplement 17: 352–398. New York: Marcel Dekker, 1994.

Singer, Carol A. "Weeding Gone Wild: Planning and Implementing a Review of the Reference Collection." *Reference and User Services Quarterly* 47 (Spring 2008): 256–263.

Slote, Stanley J. *Weeding Library Collections: Library Weeding Methods.* 4th ed. Englewood, CO: Libraries Unlimited, 1997.

Smith, Rochelle, and Nancy J. Young. "Giving Pleasure Its Due: Collection Promotion and Readers' Advisory in Academic Libraries." *Journal of Academic Librarianship* 34 (November 2008): 520–526.

Wallace, Danny P. "The Young and the Ageless: Obsolescence in Public Library Collections." *Public Libraries* 29 (March/April 1990): 102–105.

Young, Diane J. "Get to Effective Weeding." *Library Journal* 134 (November 15, 2009): 36.

Index